Anthony J. Sumet.

Nov. 2016

THE REAL
MARY KELLY

THE REAL
MARY KELLY

WYNNE WESTON-DAVIES

BLINK
bringing you closer

Published by Blink Publishing
107-109 The Plaza,
535 King's Road,
Chelsea Harbour,
London, SW10 0SZ

www.blinkpublishing.co.uk

facebook.com/blinkpublishing
twitter.com/blinkpublishing

978-1-910536-09-4

Design by Blink Publishing

Printed and bound by Clays Ltd, St Ives Plc

1 3 5 7 9 10 8 6 4 2

Papers used by Blink Publishing are natural, recyclable products made from
wood grown in sustainable forests. The manufacturing processes conform to
the environmental regulations of the country of origin.

Every reasonable effort has been made to trace copyright holders of material
reproduced in this book, but if any have been inadvertently overlooked the
publishers would be glad to hear from them.

Blink Publishing is an imprint of the Bonnier Publishing Group
www.bonnierpublishing.co.uk

To

Elizabeth Weston Davies

my great aunt, who until recently had no known grave
and whose fate was unknown to her family for 130 years.

Acknowledgements

I would like to thank the many knowledgeable and extremely helpful librarians and archivists that have assisted me in the research for this book. They are the unsung heroes of our nation's history, preserving it and making it accessible to successive generations. In particular I wish to thank Anne Wheeldon of the London Borough of Hammersmith and Fulham, Malcolm Barr-Hamilton of Tower Hamlets Council, and Catherine Richards of the Powys Archives.

The staff of the National Archives, the London Metropolitan Archives, the British Library, The National Newspaper Library formerly in Colindale but now closed whilst the collection is moved to new premises in Boston Spa, West Yorkshire, the Archives of the London Borough of Camden, the Durham County Archives, The Suffolk County Archives, the Buckinghamshire County Studies Centre, the Gloucestershire Public Libraries and the *Archives Départmentales des Côtes d'Armor*, France, have all been unfailingly helpful.

I owe most of my thanks to the encouragement and tolerance of my wife, Julia, who has put up with long hours of what should by rights have been shared time, during which I was immured in my study working on the book or out doing research in the streets of London, or in one of the many archives.

The intrusion into our joint leisure time over the course of five years should have been intolerable but instead she uncomplainingly supported me, sustained me with endless cups of tea and coffee, and proof read countless drafts of the manuscript as the book evolved. My children Jessica and Edward similarly had to put up with less of my company when they were at home for weekends than they deserved but nevertheless gave me unstinting support. To my cousin Jill Nicholls and her son John Tindle I owe thanks for their recollections of Jill's father Ted and his association with Sickert. My brother-in-law Richard Malone and his wife Susan advised me about American vocabulary and usage. Others who have helped with general encouragement and constructive criticism include the late Rosemary Petty of Dallas, Texas, my brother Peter Weston-Davies who was able to confirm many details of family history, his wife Dorinda, and Frances Williams.

To Sara George, herself a noted author of books such as the brilliant *The Journal of Mrs Pepys*, I owe a debt of gratitude for help and constructive criticism in crafting the early structure of the book. Kate Summerscale, the author of the best-selling *The Suspicions of Mr Whicher* was an inspiration and gave me her encouragement, practical support and research suggestions in numerous emails. I am extremely grateful to Keith Skinner, one of the world's leading authorities on the Whitechapel murders and co-author of the most authoritative reference book on the subject, *The Complete Jack the Ripper A to Z*, for his encouragement and for introducing me to his, and now my, agent Robert Smith.

John Julius Norwich kindly confirmed my belief that his grandfather, the eminent surgeon Sir Alfred Cooper, far from being responsible for mutilating Walter Sickert and turning him into a woman-hating monster as other authors have suggested, was ever held in high esteem by the artist for his skill and compassion.

To Professor Harold Ellis CBE, perhaps the greatest teacher of anatomy and surgery of the 20th century and a foremost medical historian, I also owe huge thanks. Not only through his truly inspirational teaching did he launch me and countless others on their medical and surgical careers but his endorsement of my theories regarding the anatomical knowledge of the Ripper gave me the confidence to complete the book. Dr Raymond Prudo, formerly Professor of Psychiatry at McMaster University, Toronto, Canada, gave me expert advice about the possible psychopathology of Francis Craig. Robert Radley, a noted forensic handwriting expert, kindly gave me his opinion on the very small amount of Francis Craig's handwriting known to exist. Personal communications from Professor Alun Evans of the Department of Epidemiology, Queens University, Belfast gave me further insights into the life of E T Craig. Robert David Pool kindly sent me information about his ancestor Sergeant David Pool of the Metropolitan Police who was murdered in mysterious circumstances in France in 1901. Christine Williams, a solicitor and expert in family law, advised me on aspects of divorce law relating to Francis Craig's petition and affidavit.

Finally I would like to thank my agent Robert Smith, himself one of the country's leading experts on the Whitechapel murders, who proved himself to be an excellent mentor and professional colleague and my publishers at Blink, Clare Tillyer, Acquisitions and Rights Director and my editor Joel Simons who helped to make the process of publication a much easier and pleasanter experience than it might otherwise have been.

Contents

The East End in 1888. Spitalfields is centred on Commercial Street with the notorious Flower and Dean and Thrawl Streets running between it and Brick Lane. Whitechapel lies in the centre and, to the south, the area around the docks is Wapping. The two H division police stations at Commercial Street and Leman Streets are within a few hundred yards of three of the murder sites. Francis's lodgings at 306 Mile End Road were about a mile and a half from the most distant site, Mitre Square, where Catherine Eddowes met her death.

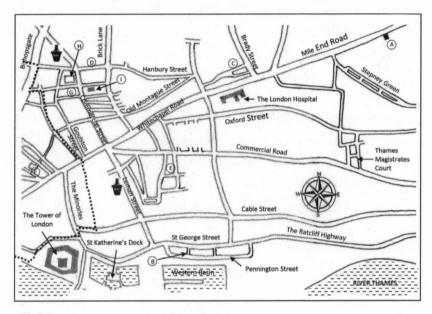

KEY

A 306 Mile End Road where Francis Craig lodged from 1886 until a few months after the murders.

B Breezer's Hill, Elizabeth's home from late 1885 or early 1886 until the end of that year.

C Bucks Row (Polly Nichols, d. 31st August 1888).

D 29 Hanbury Street (Annie Chapman, d. 8th September, 1888).

E Dutfield's Yard, Berner Street (Elizabeth Stride, d. 30th September, 1888)

F Mitre Square (Catherine Eddowes, d. 30th September, 1888)

G Miller's Court, Dorset Street (Elizabeth Weston Craig a.k.a. Mary Jane Kelly, d. 9th November, 1888)

H Spitalfields market

I Christ Church, Spitalfields

The homicidal impulse may have developed from a revengeful or brooding condition of the mind ... the murderer in external appearance is quite likely to be a quiet inoffensive looking man, probably middle-aged and neatly and respectably dressed.

Report to the Metropolitan Police by Mr. Thomas Bond FRCS,
Surgeon and Lecturer in Forensic Medicine to the Westminster Hospital, London.
10th November 1888

CHAPTER ONE

The Mystery

At some time in either late 1885 or early 1886 a young woman arrived in the East End of London.[1] She arrived suddenly and anonymously, and people wondered what such an attractive woman – who was apparently used to living comfortably and riding out in carriages – was doing in the worst stews of the London docks. When she left it again, some two and a half years later, it would be in her coffin and still no-one was any the wiser as to who she was or what had brought her there. Despite that, when her brutally murdered body was found in a squalid room in Spitalfields on the morning of 9th November 1888, she became overnight one of the best-known and most tragic characters in British criminal history. She became famous not because of who she was but because of who had killed her. His name, until now, has also remained a mystery but her murderer's *nom de guerre* is as well-known as any in history. It was Jack the Ripper.

The crowds that turned out for his victim's funeral on 19th November brought the streets of East London to a standstill. Her coffin, carried in a glass-sided hearse behind two black-plumed horses, bore the name Marie Jeanette Kelly but few people then or now believed that that was her real name.

Marie Jeanette, or Mary Jane as most people knew her, took her real identity to her grave in Leytonstone Catholic cemetery. The arc light of the world's press, the investigative powers of the greatest police force in the world and the intense scrutiny of hundreds of writers and criminologists since have never succeeded in penetrating the false persona that a frightened young woman carefully encased herself in 127 years ago.

Her first residence after she came to the East End was in the house of a character famous in the mythology of Jack the Ripper, who until recently has always been known as 'Mrs. Buki'. The first written appearance of Mrs. Buki was in *The Star* on 12th November 1888.[2] *The Star*, which had been founded less than a year before, had already become by far the highest circulation newspaper in Britain. After the news of Mary Jane's murder burst upon the world on 9th November, the newspaper sent one of its reporters into the streets of Wapping in an attempt to shed some light on her shadowy background. Other newspapers and the Press Association did the same but the anonymous newshound from *The Star* succeeded in uncovering more detail than any of the others, possibly because his employer's bulging purse was capable of loosening more tongues.

He reported that the woman, who had previously been employed at an up-market house of ill-repute near Knightsbridge, had 'suddenly drifted into the East-end'. Although the words 'suddenly' and 'drifted' don't belong naturally together, it was clear that most people who knew her believed that Mary Jane had left her previous haunts in something of a hurry – taking refuge in the ano-nymity of the poorest and most crowded part of the capital – but from who or what she was fleeing remained, like the girl herself, a mystery.

The Star reporter went on to say that Mrs. Buki resided somewhere off St. George's Street, the polite name for the westernmost end of the notorious thor-oughfare otherwise known as the Ratcliffe Highway. The Highway, as most locals knew it, was a long road running parallel to the River Thames, skirting the complex of docks that started just downstream of the Tower of London.[3] It ran to the north of the high dockyard walls, many of which are still standing although the docks they once protected have almost all passed into history. In 1886, when Mary Jane arrived on the scene, the Highway consisted largely of chandlers' shops, public houses, opium dens and brothels, all catering to the constantly changing population of seamen whilst their ships were berthed in what was then the largest port in the world. Mrs. Buki apparently ran an enterprise of the last kind and the newcomer, who was, by all accounts, younger and prettier than most of the women who plied their trade around the streets of Wapping, soon became part of her household.

She did not, it seems, stay long with Mrs. Buki and within a matter of weeks moved to a nearby establishment run by a Mrs. Mary McCarthy[4]. Her house was on the corner of Breezer's Hill and Pennington Street, facing the 14ft wall which formed the boundary of the huge and malodorous Western Basin of the London Docks. Even by the standards of the docks it was an unattractive place but no doubt, being close to the dockyard gates, it had the advantage of being one of the first premises of its kind that sailors came across on their first run ashore after a long voyage.

It is from the time of her arrival with Mrs. McCarthy that a clearer picture of the mysterious newcomer emerges. Many of the details are based on the investigations conducted by *The Star* reporter and published on 12th November. They are recollections of events that happened up to three years earlier drawn from a number of different sources and, not surprisingly, the particulars vary according to whom the reporter was talking to. The most voluble was Mrs. Elizabeth Phoenix, who claimed to be Mrs. McCarthy's sister. She had presented herself at Leman Street police station on the evening of the previous day, two days after the hideously mutilated body of a young woman had been discovered in Miller's Court, Spitalfields and the day before the inquest was due to open at Shoreditch town hall[5]. She told the police that she believed that the victim might have been the same young woman who had lodged with her sister in Pennington Street between two and three years previously. Very soon it was established that she was correct and it was probably a policeman from Leman Street who tipped off *The Star*'s reporter in return, no doubt, for a small consideration.

It was by the time she had moved from Mrs. Buki's that the mystery woman had begun using the name Mary Jane Kelly, despite the fact that she had initially told Mrs. McCarthy that she was Welsh[6]. There is nothing surprising in her choice of name. It has been estimated that in 1880 between 70 and 80 percent of the prostitutes in London were Irish, the result like so much other

Irish emigration, of the successive famines that had swept the country since the potato blight had first appeared in 1845[7]. Because of this the word Kelly was frequently used as a synonym for a prostitute and many 'unfortunates', as lower class prostitutes were known, used it whenever they needed an alias.

The stranger soon changed her story to one that sat better with her adopted name, saying that she was in fact Irish, having been born in Limerick, and taken to Wales as a baby when her father sought employment in the iron industry[8]. Few people appear to have been taken in by this however. An unnamed woman who knew her later, when she was lodging at a doss house in Thrawl Street, stated categorically that she was Welsh and that she spoke the language fluently. It is yet another of the enduring riddles that surround the girl who called herself Mary Jane Kelly; if she was actually Welsh why would she have wanted to appear to be Irish? Welsh or Irish however, most people agreed that she was better educated than other girls of her sort and, according to Mrs. McCarthy, she was 'no mean artist'.

Mrs. McCarthy and her sister were puzzled and fascinated by the new arrival. She was a different class of girl from the raddled dockyard prostitutes they were used to. She claimed to have worked in an upmarket brothel run by a Frenchwoman in the West End before coming to Wapping and, shortly before she arrived, to have been taken to France by a gentleman who they assumed was one of her clients[9]. It was incomprehensible to them why a woman who boasted of having lived the life of a lady and of riding around Knightsbridge in a carriage should have exchanged that life for the noisome, dangerous streets of the East End.

The identity of Mrs. McCarthy is well established (although, at the time and until recent research established her true name, she has usually been referred to as Mrs. Carthy or Carty), but that of Mrs. Buki remained a mystery for more than a century. Through a recent brilliant piece of Internet detective work by husband and wife team, Neal and Jenni Sheldon, it is now known that she was in fact a Dutch widow by the name of Boekü, a word for which the nearest English pronunciation is Buki or Bookie[10].At the time that Mary Jane knew her, she lived with a man called Johannes Morganstern, a skinner in the fur trade, who occupied 79 Pennington Street, next door to Mrs. McCarthy's.

The cause of her leaving Mrs Boekü's was most likely to have been arrears of rent, although drink may also have played a part for Mary Jane, who according to Mrs. Phoenix was, 'one of the most decent and nicest girls you could meet' when sober, became a veritable fury on the occasions when she had one too many. Moving next door did not, apparently, enable her to escape her debts and Mary Jane travelled one day to visit the French lady in the company of Mrs. Boekü, to collect a box containing expensive gowns that she had left there. The fact that her former landlady bothered to accompany her troublesome ex-lodger all the way across town strongly suggests that she didn't trust her out of her sight, and since no-one in the East End ever subsequently saw Mary Jane attired in such finery, it may reasonably be assumed that no sooner had she re-trieved the gowns than she was made to hand them over in lieu of the missing rent. It is this report and a similar one by a Press Association reporter quoted in the *Echo* on the same day that are the only independent corroborations of the story that she later told her lover Joe Barnett, of having once worked in a 'gay house'* in the West End.

Breezer's Hill is little changed in appearance today from when Mary Jane knew it. It is a narrow cobbled alleyway which slopes down from the Highway to Pennington Street, overshadowed by tall, red-brick warehouses. Although today the warehouses have been gutted and converted into offices and smart loft conversions it is easy enough to imagine what it might have looked like on a winter's night in 1886 when the few gaslights barely penetrated the swirling fog rolling in from the river. If Mary Jane really had been used to the stuccoed mansions of Knightsbridge – and her visit with Mrs. Boekü suggests that she was – then the greasy cobblestones and soot-stained brickwork of Breezer's Hill must have made a dismal contrast.

Mary Jane stayed at Breezer's Hill during most of 1886, leaving, according to Mrs. Phoenix, towards the end of that year. Exactly what prompted her to move from the comparative comfort of Mrs. McCarthy's is not known but Joe later spoke of an older man, who he assumed to be her father, coming look-ing for her at about that time[11]. When she got wind of it Mary Jane laid low for a few days and later took her leave of Breezer's Hill. There then followed a

A heterosexual brothel in the 19th century.

gap of about four or five months during which her whereabouts are unknown. Both Mrs. McCarthy and, later, Joe Barnett said that it was during this period that she lived with one of her regular clients, a builder's plasterer called Joseph Flemming, in Bethnal Green. Joe also said that she told him that after she returned from France she had lived for a time with a man called 'Morganstone' near the Stepney gasworks[12]. Mrs. Phoenix herself has recently been identified as Elizabeth Felix, who in 1888 was living with a man calling himself Adrianus Felix, but who, it is now known, was actually Adrianus Morganstern, the brother of Mrs. Boekü's consort Johannes. In the East End of London in those days people frequently went under a variety of names, usually to avoid creditors, a fact that makes teasing out the details of their lives a difficult task for later historians. To complicate matters still further a third brother, Maran Morganstern, also lived near the Stepney gasworks so it might have been either brother with whom Mary Jane lodged before or after her time in Breezer's Hill. What seems certain is that Mrs. McCarthy, Mrs. Phoenix, Mrs. Boekü and the Morganstern brothers all knew each other and helped the young woman who called herself Mary Jane during the period after she first came to the East End, before she disappeared again and the last, dark chapter of her life began.

CHAPTER TWO

Mary or Marie?

No known pictures of Mary Jane in life survive. A few fanciful artists' impressions of her were later published in the illustrated newspapers but these differ so wildly that it is clear that their originators had no first hand idea of what she actually looked like. Those that did know her, such as Mrs. Phoenix and Chief Inspector Walter Dew – who encountered her when he was a young policeman on the beat in Whitechapel – described her as attractive and about 5ft 7in in height, quite tall for a woman in those days. Inspector Dew used the word 'buxom' to describe her, although Mrs. Phoenix preferred 'stout'[13]. She had blue eyes and thick hair which, when let down, reached to her waist. It was probably dark in colour although the fact that she was later known by a variety of nicknames including 'Fair Emma' and 'Ginger' suggests that she may have been in the habit of changing it from time to time. She took pride in her appearance and Dew said that she never appeared in public except in a spotlessly laundered apron although, unlike most of the unfortunates, she rarely wore a hat.

If she did live with Joseph Flemming it appears to have been a short-lived relationship because on Good Friday, 8th April 1887, she was in a public house in Spitalfields and there she encountered Joe Barnett. They were immediately attracted to each other and on their second meeting the following day they decided to live together. She told him much the same story that she had told Mrs. McCarthy and her sister, although she said to Joe that she preferred to be called Marie Jeanette in the French fashion rather than plain Mary Jane. She was proud of having worked in a French establishment and she made no secret of that part of her life. She also boasted to Joe about having travelled to France with a gentleman shortly before her arrival in the East End.

Joe was an amiable but feckless man in his early 30s. He had been a fish porter in Billingsgate market until around the time he met Mary Jane, but had lost his licence for some unspecified misdemeanour and now did casual labouring jobs around the various markets when he could get them. They were a well-suited pair, both warm-hearted and generous although not above occasional violent spats when one of them, usually Mary Jane, had had too much to drink.

She told Joe a story that she had not, it seems, imparted to her companions during the Breezer's Hill days or to anyone other than Joe since that time. Her real name, she told him, was Davies on account of her having once been married to a young Welsh miner of that name who had been killed in an explosion two or three years after their wedding. It would turn out later that it was not the first time she had used the story of being a widow. In due course her death certificate would carry both the names Kelly and Davies.

The couple drifted like most of their kind from one common lodging house to another, always within the 'wicked half mile' of Spitalfields, moving on when their arrears of rent led to eviction. Eventually, in the early spring of 1888, they moved into 13 Miller's Court at a rent of four shillings and sixpence a week.

Miller's Court was a foetid cul-de-sac opening off Dorset Street which, like its companions Thrawl Street and the oddly misnamed Flower and Dean Street, was the heart of the most wretched part of the area. Clustered around Spitalfields market they were densely packed with common lodging houses, invariably known to their inhabitants as doss houses, where rooms were let out by the night for a few pennies[14]. At the bottom end of the scale three or four pence would buy a night in a bed shared with a stranger where the sheets were changed, at most, once a week and the ticking on the pillows was greasy and filthy because pillowcases were an unknown luxury. Boots were generally not taken off before getting in to bed for to do so risked having an eminently pawnable commodity stolen in the night.

Unless paid for in advance, rooms had to be vacated by 8am in the morning. There was little temptation to linger after that time as the additional facilities consisted only of an outside privy shared with 50 or more others and a so-called kitchen with a bare table and a few chairs where residents could make themselves a mug of tea, in the unlikely event that they possessed any. It was better than actually sleeping on the pavement but only marginally so.

The residents of the doss houses were mainly casual male labourers in the docks and the various markets, and women who were collectively known as unfortunates. An unfortunate was a woman, usually in her 40s or 50s who, generally through alcoholism, had lost whatever position in society that she had ever occupied and had descended to eking out an existence through a mixture of prostitution, hawking or taking in washing.

Many unfortunates had once been respectably married women before drink took its toll and they were thrown out by their families. Once on the streets of Spitalfields and Whitechapel they became part of a huge drifting population of many thousands, largely unknown or forgotten by the rest of Victorian society. They operated at the very edge of human existence, their only possessions being what they carried beneath their layers of grubby clothes and consisting mostly of broken fragments of comb, shards of mirror, pawn tickets and a little tea or sugar in screws of blue paper. Apart from needing her doss money, an unfortunate's main requirement was the few pence needed to purchase a tot of rum to go into a glass of hot water. A woman who was prepared to go with a man into one of the dark, stinking back alleys or a dimly lit court and stand braced against a wall, back to the customer, ragged skirts hitched up above her waist, could make enough in a day to secure a bed of sorts for the night and, if she was lucky, keep herself mercifully drunk for the rest of the time.

It was a wretched, painful existence and in winter many unfortunates literally starved or froze to death in the gutter. Despite, or maybe because of, their shared privations they were a surprisingly cheerful lot, sticking together through thick and thin, sharing what little they had and gathering, when they could afford it, to sing and make merry in the many public houses which surrounded the markets. There were occasional disagreements to be sure, and short-lived fights over trifles such as a piece of soap were not uncommon, but mostly the unfortunates and their feckless male companions rubbed along in cheerful shared poverty.

To most of those that knew her in the East End it was apparent that Mary Jane sprang from a different, more privileged background. A number of newspapers, particularly those aimed at the popular end of the market, were fascinated by the possibility that her antecedents were socially above those amongst whom she found herself at the end of her life. The *Western Mail* quoted Joe Barnett as saying that her parents were well off and on 17th November the *Graphic* said, 'Lastly, we would remark … that the woman Kelly did not belong to the "gutter class". She was a woman of respectable parentage and superior breeding, who had gradually sunk into the state of degradation in which she was existing when she met her terrible death.'

Despite this, Mary Jane identified with her fellow unfortunates and made friends with a few, although none claimed to know her well. As long as Joe was in work she did not need to earn her living on the streets and he was fiercely opposed to her doing so. But prostitution was a way of life for her, whether it was in a grand house in Knightsbridge or the back alleys of Whitechapel, and when money was tight, which was most of the time, she willingly resorted to it. It seemed to give her what she most valued in life: independence from being reliant on others. Her relative youth and good looks ensured that when she went out on the streets she had no shortage of customers.

Number 13 was a small ground floor room with a door that opened directly into the arched passageway that connected the court with Dorset Street. Two irregularly sized windows looked out onto the yard and the room itself contained only a wooden-framed bed, two small tables and two chairs. The only concession to luxury was a framed print of a popular sentimental picture, *The Fisherman's Widow*, hanging above the small fireplace[15]. The door closed with a spring lock but the only key had been lost and Joe and Mary Jane were in the habit of putting a hand through a window pane – that had been broken in one of their periodic fights – and opening the catch that way[16]. Usually a man's coat hung over the broken window to act as a curtain and keep out the draught.

Almost everything that is known about Mary Jane Kelly comes from Joe Barnett's testimony at the inquest and from interviews that a few of her close companions gave to newspaper reporters in the days following it. The problem is that much of it is contradictory even when the same person is being quoted. For instance, according to the court transcript, at the inquest Joe said that she had six brothers and a sister who all lived at home and another brother serving with the 2nd Battalion of the Scots Guards. The next day's *Telegraph* reported him as saying that she had six brothers in London and *The Times* reported him as saying that she had six brothers and sisters in Wales. With this amount of confusion it is no wonder that attempts to pin down the family of Mary Jane Kelly have proved so elusive.

There are clever details, however, sufficiently interesting and yet slightly unlikely – why seven siblings rather than, say, three? – as to be compelling to subsequent researchers. What was a son of an allegedly Irish family resident in Wales doing in the Scots Guards? The Guards regiments have always been fiercely proud of recruiting in their own territories, the Grenadiers in Nottinghamshire, the Coldstream in Northumberland and Durham, and the Scots north of the border. The Welsh Guards did not yet exist, not being founded until 1915, but there were several Irish infantry regiments and surely a man by the name of Kelly would have found himself more at home in a predominantly Catholic unit than a Presbyterian one?

Then there is the question of his nickname. Mary Jane told Joe that he was known to his army comrades as 'Johnto'[17]. Johnto however is a well-known Welsh diminutive of 'John'. More properly it is 'Ianto' since the letter J does not exist in Welsh, but it is often rendered as Johnto in families that speak both Welsh and English. It seems an odd choice for Scottish soldiers to bestow upon a man called Henry.

Joe and Marie Jeanette, as he always called her, moved into 13 Miller's Court in about March or April of 1888. At first it seems they were able to pay the four shillings and sixpence a week that the room cost but then work began to dry up for Joe who, having lost his Billingsgate fish porter's licence, was doing casual labouring jobs around the other markets and hawking fruit around the streets when all else failed. Soon they began to fall behind with the rent and by early November they were thirty shillings in arrears.

If Joe had been in a secure job no doubt they would have been able to muddle through, but as the nights began to draw in and the already wet summer gave way to a chilly autumn Mary Jane's soft heart got the better of her. Twice Joe came home in the early hours to find that she had allowed another unfortunate to doss down in the small room overnight. It led to a number of explosive rows and when Mary Jane started to talk of going back on the streets in order to obtain money to pay off the rent arrears it became almost too much for Joe. The final straw came when his headstrong partner decided to offer a home to Mrs. Maria Harvey, another unfortunate who had finally been thrown out by her husband.

Joe did the decent thing; instead of throwing Mary Jane out as Mrs. Harvey's husband had done, on 1st November he moved out himself, leaving the room to Mary Jane and arranging to call round from time to time to give her whatever money he had to spare. It must have been heart-breaking for him; he was obviously very fond of the strange Welsh-Irish girl with her stories of Paris and life as a high-class courtesan in the West End, places that were as foreign to Joe as the headwaters of the Amazon.

A few snippets that she told to her other acquaintances also came out at the inquest and many more were reported in the profusion of newspaper accounts after the event. In particular *The Daily Telegraph* reported that she 'was believed to be the wife of a man from whom she is separated' and her friend Julia Venturney, who lived opposite her in Miller's Court, also said that she had confided that her husband was still alive. If indeed she did have a living husband, one can see why she might have chosen to tell the man she was actually living with a different story.

With the present-day advantage of computers and digitised records, a family of the alleged size and composition of Mary Jane's living in Wales between the 1860s and 1880s should be easily identifiable – particularly given that the first names of at least three of them were known – but despite the most intensive search at the time and for more than 120 years since, no family remotely resembling it has ever shown up. Following the Miller's Court murder the police also made extensive enquiries with their colleagues in Ireland, which was then still part of Great Britain, with similarly negative results. Despite saturation press coverage at the time, no member of Mary Jane Kelly's family ever came forward and none were present at her funeral. Nor can any trace of a likely marriage of a Mary Kelly to a man called Davies be found, or of the death in a mining accident of someone of that name and age at around the right time. In fact, surprising as it may seem, there are no plausible Mary Jane Kellys of the right age or of the background she gave recorded in the England and Wales censuses throughout the relevant part of the 19th century. The only possible conclusion is that Mary Jane Kelly never existed and that whoever the mysterious woman was, she was going under a false name and that, of course, throws considerable doubt on the rest of her story.

The only thing that Mary Jane never made a secret about was her profession. She was evidently proud of her past life as a prostitute and boasted of having worked in an upper-class brothel run by a French woman. At the inquest Joe Barnett said, 'She was in a gay house in the West End, but in what part she did not say. A gentleman came there to her and asked her if she would like to go to France[18].' The coroner then asked if she had gone, to which Joe replied, 'Yes; but she did not remain long. She said she did not like the part, but whether it was the part or purpose I cannot say. She was not there more than a fortnight, and she returned to England, and went to the Ratcliffe-highway.'

It is a slightly curious way of putting it but Joe was an uneducated man who was recounting some half-remembered detail from a conversation about events that took place anything up to two years before. By 'part' he could have meant the place or, possibly, the party, meaning the person she went with. What he meant by 'the purpose' is harder to explain. On the face of it, whoever she went with, the purpose would presumably have been to visit an exciting foreign city and have a good time. If, on the other hand, she meant that the purpose was to cement a relationship that she mistakenly thought was casual or temporary into a more permanent arrangement, it is easier to understand. Joe is known to have had a speech impediment and this may account for the lack of clarity in this and other parts of his testimony[19].

The coroner specifically asked Joe if he had heard Mary Jane saying that she was afraid of anyone, clearly attempting to discover if she could have known her killer. His answer was reported in slightly different ways in various papers over the next few days but *The Star* for one reported him as saying, 'Yes, she used to get me to bring her the evening papers and see if there was another murder but beyond that she was not afraid of anyone that I know of.' Some people have taken that to mean that Mary Jane was illiterate and that Joe had to read the papers to her but that doesn't tally with Mrs. McCarthy's opinion of her being well-educated or with her landlord's assertion that she received letters from Ireland on one or more occasions.

How he would have known that they were from Ireland is dubious since, at that time, Ireland was still part of Britain, postage stamps were identical throughout the kingdom and postmarks were often blurred and illegible. Julia Venturney said that she had often heard her friend singing Irish songs but that would not necessarily signify anything since sentimental Irish ballads were immensely popular in the music halls of the time and there was also the possibility that Julia would not have been able to distinguish between Welsh and Irish songs. The song that she was heard singing on the night of her death has since been reported by many as being an Irish song but 'A Violet Plucked from Mother's Grave' was in fact an English music hall song written by Will H. Fox for the Mohawk Minstrels.

There is also some doubt about her age. Joe Barnett said that she had told him that she was 25 but whether that was when they first met or at the time of her death is unknown. Her death certificate says 'about 25 years' but her body was so badly mutilated that in pre-X-ray days it would have been impossible to tell her age to within five or more years either side of this and it is probable that they took this estimate from Joe. Almost all prostitutes habitually deducted as many years from their ages as they thought they could get away with because youth brought with it a premium in the flesh trade. The reporter of a New York newspaper, the *Syracuse Herald*, who appears to have done a particularly thorough job of interviewing the inhabitants of Dorset Street on the day after the murder, quoted her landlord, John McCarthy, as saying that Mary Jane 'looked about 30'.

While many of the British newspapers took their copy from the press agencies, from police statements which were frequently contradictory or from jobbing reporters who seem to have plagiarised each other's work unblushingly, their brothers from America appear on the whole to have done a much more professional job. With the exception of *The Star*'s reporter and the one from the Press Association, few of the British reporters seem to have actually interviewed the people who knew Mary Jane personally. As a result there are many glaring differences between the reports on either side of the Atlantic in the days following the events in Miller's Court.

Although it may now seem surprising, readers of newspapers in the United States were often able to read about the unfolding events in Whitechapel some hours in advance of their cousins in Britain. Whereas the American reporters sent their copy directly to their offices in New York, Chicago or Philadelphia by means of the electric telegraph, the readers in Birmingham, Exeter or Norwich had to rely on the physical delivery of newspapers by rail from London which meant that they were often 12 to 24 hours behind Americans in reading the latest sensational news from the East End.

Amongst the differences in the first hours after the murder in Miller's Court was that of the victim's name. Most of the American papers reported it as Lizzie Fisher, although they added that she was known to her friends as Mary Jane[20]. Many of them, including the *New York World* on 10th November, said that she was, 'tall, not bad looking, with a dark complexion and generally wearing an old black velvet jacket...' *The Boston Globe*, amongst others, reported that she had been in service and that she was a married woman who had been deserted by her husband on account of her dissolute ways[21]. The *Washington Evening Star* agreed with the reporter from the *Syracuse Herald* in quoting people that knew her who said that she looked about 30 when she had arrived in Dorset Street about eight months previously in marked contrast to Joe Barnett's assertion that she was 25. As the late Philip Sugden, one of the most authoritative and painstaking of Ripper historians pointed out in his book, *The Complete History of Jack the Ripper*, most of the early police estimates of the ages of the victims were markedly less than they turned out to be once they had been identified.

A poignant little piece which gives a glimpse of the day-to-day life of Mary Jane and her fellow unfortunates is the interview with her neighbour Elizabeth Prater – who lived in the room above hers – which was published in *The Star* on 10th November, the day following the murder. The interview makes it very clear that Elizabeth Prater was also an unfortunate who earned her living in the same way as Mary Jane.

She told the reporter, whose own comments were added in parentheses:

> 'She was tall and pretty, and as fair as a lily. I saw her go out in the shell* this afternoon, but the last time I saw her alive was about 9pm on Thursday night. I stood down at the bottom of the entry, and she came down. We stood talking a bit, thinking what we were going to do, and then she went one way and I went another. I went to see if I could see anybody. (Mrs. Prater adds with frankness) She had got her hat and jacket on, but I had not. I haven't got a hat or a jacket. We stood talking a bit about what we were going to do, and then I said, "Good night, old dear," and she said, "Good might, my pretty." She always called me that. That was the last I saw of her. (Then Mrs. Prater breaks down, and commences to sob violently) I'm a woman myself and I've got to sleep in that place tonight right over where it happened.'

It is a moving little passage that resonates with sincerity. Elizabeth Prater was 45 and had struggled to bring up a family of her own children and her stepchildren before she was widowed for the second time and sank into the abyss of alcohol and destitution. The heart-rending little detail of her not possessing a hat or jacket in which to face the cold, wet November night and the nice touch of her addressing a woman 15 years her junior as 'Old dear' and in turn being called 'My pretty' by Mary Jane who, one imagines, had all the advantages of youth over the other woman brings their voices echoing back through the years.

The enigma of Mary Jane lingers on. Was she Welsh or was she Irish? Was she 25 or older? Was her name Kelly or Davies? Both names are on her death certificate and the only thing that can be said with any degree of certainty is that her name was not Mary Jane Kelly or even Marie Jeanette Kelly. But if she was not who she said she was, who was she? And why was she so keen to keep her real identity hidden?

*A temporary open coffin used to transport bodies to the mortuary.

28

CHAPTER THREE

Elizabeth

Shortly before Mary Jane arrived to ply her trade around the streets of Wapping, a girl of similar age disappeared from the streets of Bloomsbury. She usually went by the name she had been christened, Elizabeth Weston Davies, although she should more properly have used her husband's name as she had been married eight months before on Christmas Eve, 1884. Her marriage had been an abrupt event, hardly an affair of the heart as she had scarcely known the man before he blurted out a sudden invitation to join him on a trip to Paris and then, almost as an afterthought, the suggestion that they might as well get married first.

It suited Elizabeth; she was an impulsive girl whose world had been thrown into turmoil little more than two months previously when her employer's husband had died unexpectedly, and she had horrified her respectable Welsh family by embarking on a life totally at odds with that which her mother had planned for her. She was the sixth child and fourth daughter of Edward and Anne Davies. Her father had been a slate quarry agent until his premature death in 1875 when Elizabeth was 18. The family lived comfortably enough in Aberangell, a hamlet in the upper Dovey Valley in Montgomeryshire, and

Elizabeth grew up close to her younger brother John, attending the village school with him and not leaving until after her 16th birthday, a remarkably late age for a girl in rural 19th century Britain. At home the family spoke both English and Welsh and she was equally fluent in both.

At the age of 19 Elizabeth's mother had become lady's maid to the 16-year-old daughter of a Montgomeryshire landowner, John Edwards. The building boom of the 1830s and 1840s had propelled John Edwards from being a comfortably off local squire to one of the richest men in Britain by dint of the acres of slate-bearing hillside that he owned. With no sons and only two daughters Sir John, as he had become, was determined to marry them off to suitable young men. As he prepared his younger daughter, Mary Cornelia, for her first London Season in 1846, he engaged an English woman, Elizabeth's mother Anne, to become her personal maid in the hope that it would improve her English and help rid her of her Welsh accent.

Due in large measure to Anne's influence, Mary Cornelia's entry into London society was a triumph and less than three months after her Coming Out ball she married George Vane-Tempest, a dashing young Life Guards officer, at St. George's Hanover Square. The two women remained lifelong friends and in due course Anne and her own husband Edward were to name two of their elder children George and Mary in honour of their employers. At the time of his marriage George bore the courtesy title of Earl Vane but in 1872 he inherited the title and vast estates of his half-brother, the fourth Marquess of Londonderry[22]. With the amalgamation of the Edwards' slate quarries and lead mines, and the Londonderry lands and coal mines, one of the greatest and most prosperous dynasties of Victorian Britain was established.

In due course Anne's friendship with Mary Cornelia was rewarded when her fourth daughter Elizabeth was given the same post that her mother had held nearly 40 years before, lady's maid to the Marchioness of Londonderry. In Victorian Britain ladies' maids were in a specially privileged position compared to other household servants. They were appointed and employed directly by the lady herself and were not answerable to the butler and the housekeeper like the other staff. Like Elizabeth, they often occupied separate and superior quarters to the other servants and sometimes even had servants of their own. It was to this favoured world that Elizabeth travelled when she took up her position at Londonderry House sometime before 1881.

During her time in London Elizabeth was introduced to a new and exciting world. As well as witnessing the glittering social life of her employers, during her free time she also became part of a bohemian, literary and artistic clique that flourished in part of London that is now known as Fitzrovia. Lying between respectable Bloomsbury and the heart of London's burgeoning shopping and theatre-land, it was at various times home to writers like Charles Dickens and Oscar Wilde, artists like James McNeill Whistler and William Powell Frith, and political figures including Karl Marx and, much later, George Orwell. It supported a colourful and constantly changing population of writers, actors, prostitutes, charlatans and eccentrics. Elizabeth was clearly fascinated by it and, having artistic leanings herself, it became a second home to her during her occasional free time.

Amongst this population were two families, the Gilders and the Maundrells, who for most of the 19th century shared houses and relationships, sometimes formalised by marriage and sometimes not. Elizabeth's connection was probably through the Gilders who, like her own family, came from the Dovey Valley in what is now Powys but was then Montgomeryshire[23]. William Gilder had been the Captain and Adjutant of the Royal Montgomeryshire Militia of which John Edwards was the colonel, but in 1838, when bankruptcy struck, he fled with his family to Brittany and took up with an Anglo-French family, the Maundrells[24].

Sexual relationships in Victorian Britain were much more ambiguous than is often assumed today. Far from being the bigoted prudes that history has painted them, upper- and middle-class people, particularly in the capital, frequently engaged in extramarital sex. Businessmen kept mistresses in neat villas in St. John's Wood; aristocratic women like Lady Cardigan were visited discreetly by their lovers in Mayfair mansions; and prostitution, at all levels of society, was at least ten times as common as it is today[25].

The Maundrells were part of this world. They numbered amongst their close friends Thornton Leigh Hunt, eldest son of the poet James, and himself the fiery founding editor of *The Daily Telegraph*. Hunt subscribed to the *Phalanstère* movement, one of the many utopian cults that flourished in the mid-19th century. At its most extreme, it believed that institutions such as marriage and the family should be abolished and replaced by huge communal buildings in which free love – both heterosexual and homosexual – could be practiced in rooms specially set aside for the purpose. Hunt practiced his beliefs at least to the extent of fathering four children by his own wife and three by the wife of his best friend, apparently with the full approval of all concerned. Two of his daughters almost certainly became prostitutes in brothels run by two of the Maundrell sisters.

Ellen, or Héleine as she preferred to call herself, was the eldest child of Robert John Maundrell and Charlotte, daughter of old Captain William Gilder[26]. Born in Brittany in 1846, she considered herself more French than English and eventually, in old age, returned to die in her beloved France. In 1877 she married William Macleod, son of another expatriate, but his life as a Purser in the Royal Navy kept him in the Far East for most of his life and, apart from an only child – Helen Kathleen, born the year after their wedding – they had little in common and the marriage eventually ended in separation[27].

Ellen and her unmarried sister Frederica were highly successful businesswomen[28]. They needed to be since their father, although calling himself a gentleman, never aspired to being anything more than a clerk in the Post Office Savings Bank, and their grandfather William spent his entire life paying off the debts occasioned by his bankruptcy in 1838. The sisters' entrepreneurial drive led them into one of the most profitable business ventures in Victorian London. They ran French brothels.

Like most things French, Gallic prostitution was highly fashionable in the second half of the 19th century. The Prince of Wales had almost made Paris his second home and *Le Chabanais*, the most exclusive of the Parisian brothels, was his invariable choice when in the city. Founded by an Irishwoman by the name, real or assumed, of Madame Kelly, *Le Chabanais* served its clientele the choicest French food and wines as well as the most attractive young women available[29].

The Maundrell sisters could easily pass themselves off as French; there is evidence that Ellen, certainly, was bilingual. In her early life she had been an actress, a term that was more or less synonymous with prostitute in the 19th century, and by the 1880s she was operating a string of middle-class brothels in St. Pancras, Camden and Islington. Usually masquerading as private hotels or coffee houses, they catered discreetly for middle-class men and, although they were known to the police, they were largely left alone. The attitude of Victorian society was that prostitution was inevitable and as long as it was kept off the streets it was tolerated.

At some time in the early 1880s the sisters had accumulated so much wealth that they took the lease of a huge house in the area south of the site of the Great Exhibition of 1851 that had subsequently been developed into what became the fashionable districts of Knightsbridge and Kensington. Number 28 Collingham Place is little changed to this day[30]. It is a stucco-fronted mansion on six floors which today, like many of its neighbours, has been divided into expensive flats. Then it was occupied solely by the Maundrell sisters, their servants and their girls. In the census of 1891 it appeared to front as a school, although with apparently only one pupil – a girl of 18 – and three so-called teachers it appears a little light on customers. The local newspapers including the *Kensington Chronicle* contained dozens of advertisements for the local private schools and educational establishments, many of which appeared week after week, but absolutely none were for 28 Collingham Place.

Elizabeth was settled into her life as lady's maid in one of the most socially important houses in London and, it seems, enjoying the company of her colourful, bohemian friends when on 6th November 1884 her life was turned upside down. George Vane-Tempest, Fifth Marquess of Londonderry, died whilst he and his wife, Mary Cornelia, were staying at their house in Wales. His widow, the Dowager Marchioness, was heartbroken. She announced her intention of never returning to London again and settled down to spend the rest of her days in widow's weeds in her childhood home.

Elizabeth was faced with a stark choice: remain with her mistress and be condemned to a life of quiet service looking after an ageing and reclusive woman in a house that would never again echo to the sounds of parties and laughter or – what? She could have returned to London and no doubt have obtained another post as a lady's maid, although whether her employer would have assisted her in light of what she may have viewed as disloyalty is debateable. But then another opportunity presented itself.

Within days, it seems, of the Marquess's death Elizabeth was installed in the Maundrells' upper-class French brothel in Kensington and enjoying a life such as she personally had never experienced. In order to appeal to the rich clientele the girls were dressed in the latest French fashions and encouraged to adopt French names and manners. Whether any of the customers, which included many well-travelled and sophisticated men from Mayfair and Belgravia, were actually fooled is questionable but it added to the mystique and allure of the sisters' establishment. It is not known what name Elizabeth adopted but Marie Jeanette is as likely as any other. In the few weeks that she remained in the 'gay house', as such places were euphemistically known, Elizabeth revelled in wearing the expensive gowns that her employers provided and riding out in Hyde Park in their carriage, provided no doubt as an effective way of showing off the merchandise.

It ended, abruptly, sometime in December of 1884 when a man, some 20 years older than she was, came into her life. Francis Spurzheim Craig may have been a client of the Maundrells' French brothel but in light of what was to follow it seems more likely that Elizabeth met him elsewhere, most probably at one of William Morris's Sunday soirées at his riverside house in Hammersmith. Morris was a giant of Victorian society. A highly successful artist, writer, designer and a founding member of the Pre-Raphaelite Brotherhood, he was also a left-leaning politician who became the focus of what would eventually become the Socialist movement. Whilst himself living in opulence – in his country house, Kelmscott Manor in Gloucestershire, and his London residence, Kelmscott House in Hammersmith – Morris railed against poverty and inequality. He frequently travelled to the East End, the most squalid part of the capital, and addressed left-wing meetings at places like the International Working Men's Educational Club in Berner Street, Whitechapel.

He also surrounded himself with a bohemian mixture of writers, artists, poets and political activists for whom he held regular Sunday evening meetings at Kelmscott House. Amongst the Morris set were writers such as Oscar Wilde, George Bernard Shaw and H.G. Wells; artists including Dante Gabriel Rossetti and Aubrey Beardsley; musicians such as Gustav Holst and political figures like Friedrich Engels, Sidney Webb and Eleanor Marx, daughter of the more famous Karl. The Maundrells may well have been part of the group for they were certainly friendly with others that were, including the artist Walter Sickert and the journalist and playwright George Robert Sims[31]. Another regular attendee was a serious-minded political thinker called E.T. Craig.

CHAPTER FOUR

The Phrenologist's Son

Edward Thomas Craig lived near to Morris in Hammersmith, although in a much more humble dwelling. At over 80 he was nearing the end of his political life but in his youth he had been one of the founders of the Co-operative movement and a considerable force in left-wing politics. 'E.T.' – as he was always known – and his wife Mary had an only child, a son who like his father earned his living by the pen. Unlike his father, who was a journalist of note and in his time the editor of at least eight newspapers, Francis was merely a humble penny-a-line reporter on local newspapers[32]. At 47 he should already have achieved his life's ambitions and been the editor of a newspaper or an author of some standing with a house and servants, but instead he was still living in genteel poverty with his elderly parents in a two-up, two-down artisan's cottage in the backstreets of Hammersmith.

The Craigs were in no position to afford carriages even if E.T.'s socialist principles had allowed it, so they walked the mile to and from their house at 3 Andover Road to Morris's mansion on the Thames. For his age E.T. was remarkably fit and a lifelong exponent of healthy living. Teetotal, vegetarian and non-smoking, he believed strongly in the virtues of fresh air and body building[33]. He and Francis sold fitness aids such as barbells, massage rollers and bath salts by mail order and the younger man had been trained from his youth to build up his upper body strength. Although no definitely identified pictures of him exist, Francis was probably of medium height but broad-chested and with well-muscled arms. His later writing revealed that he was a keen follower of rowing and it is likely that he had been an enthusiastic oarsman in his youth.

Francis owed both his forenames to his father's lifelong passion for phrenology, a pseudo-science that was pioneered by a German doctor, Franz Gall, and his protégé Johann Spurzheim in the late 18th century. By the first decades of the 19th century it was an established movement held in high regard by scientists, doctors and philosophers and E.T. had been a devotee ever since hearing Spurzheim lecture on the subject in Manchester in 1831. It was much beloved of the early socialists and co-operators because it offered the common man the possibility of gaining insight into his own character and, thereby, the capacity for self-improvement.

E.T. became adept at the art and described himself as a 'Professor of Phrenology' for much of his life, but by the middle of the 19th century most doctors and scientists had realised that it was based on false premises[34]. Feeling the outside of the skull was of no more use than running one's hands over the cover of a book and attempting to interpret its contents. The stubborn E.T., however, characteristically refused to accept the obvious and never lost faith in it. He was belatedly rewarded when he was elected President of the British Phrenological Society in 1888, the year of the Whitechapel murders, at a time when almost all educated people had long since abandoned it.

E.T.'s other two passions were public health and anatomy. In his teens he had been admitted to Manchester Infirmary following an injury[35]. He later gave an account of creeping into the operating theatre after the day's work was done to examine the amputated limbs before they were removed by the hospital porters. In his memoirs he wrote that it, 'awakened a deep interest in the structure and anatomy of the body'. He is known to have taken part in dissections of the human body. In his *Lectures on Phrenology* the doyen of British phrenologists, George Combe, described Craig assisting Dr. John Abercrombie, the foremost neuropathologist of the day, to dissect the brain of a 'Mr. N', an aged diplomat who had suffered a personality change shortly before his death[36]. It is likely that E.T. took Francis to observe dissections and encouraged him to study the subject from popular books such as Sir Charles Bell's *A System of Dissection Explaining the Anatomy of the Human Body*, a detailed practical account of how to cut up the human cadaver and gain access to its innermost secrets.

Although E.T.'s assertive and obdurate personality was well known and frequently commented on by his few friends and many enemies, shadowy is the best description of his only son, Francis Spurzheim Craig. Almost everything that is known about him comes from other people's insubstantial descriptions of him and from the fleeting penumbra he cast on his surroundings. A great deal is known about his parents but Francis, who had no brothers or sisters and no known descendants, left little of himself behind except in such of his journalistic output that can definitely be attributed to him – and that is little enough. It is probable that this absence of a written legacy is largely due to his parents' deliberate sheltering of their awkward son from the normalities of the outside world. For Francis himself was far from being a normal man.

From surviving descriptions of Francis by the few people who knew him at all well and with the benefit of modern psychiatric knowledge it is evident that he suffered from what today would be known as a severe personality disorder. He may possibly have had high-performing Asperger syndrome but, if so, it was certainly overlaid with psychotic features. At his inquest in 1903 he was described as 'most eccentric' and 'very nervous', although his ex-employer, Arthur Lane, also saw another, darker side to him. He was a man, said Lane, who 'took antipathies to people for no apparent cause'. He was given to erratic and unpredictable behaviour, jumping up in the middle of a meal and rushing out into the street shouting, 'I'm off!' In later life he also had what his acquaintances recognised as delusions, fancying that all the world was against him and even – ominously – that the police were after him for murder.

Today his behaviour would be recognised as falling somewhere in the hinterland between 'psychopathy' and a true 'psychosis' on the schizophrenia spectrum. He was a highly intelligent man and with adequate support which, during their lifetimes, he received from his parents, he was capable of functioning almost normally. The problems came when he tried to exist independently.

For most of his life he lived under his parents' roof and they appear to have handled his financial affairs and his day-to-day needs whilst he earned a living as a reporter and, later, an editor. Surprisingly, he seems to have been a good journalist and surviving pieces that he wrote show an intelligent, witty mind that was completely at odds with his face-to-face persona.

At such a distance it is difficult today to put a single label on Francis's specific psychosis. The most likely diagnosis by current standards is probably 'schizo-typal personality disorder' (STPD). The main diagnostic features of STPD are behaviour or appearance that others find odd, eccentric or peculiar; suspicious-ness or paranoid ideas; poor rapport with others; a tendency to withdraw so-cially; and obsessive ruminations, often with sexual or aggressive content. All of these are characteristics that can easily be discerned in what little is known about Francis Spurzheim Craig.

whom

This was the man that Elizabeth encountered late in 1884. Possibly they met and talked as they strolled the gardens of Kelmscott House before the start of a meeting. Despite his age Francis was unmarried and had probably never had a normal relationship with a woman other than his strong-minded mother. He found conversation difficult and his few friends and acquaintances described his curious habit of breaking off in mid-sentence and fleeing the scene when the pressure of making small talk became too much for him[37]. Only when he was talking about a topic that interested him did he become less tongue-tied and capable of sustaining a proper exchange. One such subject was travel, especially to foreign countries[38].

In 1864 Francis had left the sanctuary of his family home for what may have been the first of the only three occasions that he did so in his adult life. It is tempting to think that he might finally have had enough of living under his parents' roof and decided to strike out on his own, but it is more likely that he was urged to do so by his father in the hope that it might prove the making of him. The incentive was probably the American Civil War, the first great conflict of modern warfare, where new technologies like machine guns, anaesthesia and photography were deployed on the battlefield for the first time. The war was attracting reporters and journalists from all over the world and when, on 4th April that year, the *City of London* docked in New York from Liverpool via

Queenstown, Ireland, Francis was amongst the passengers[39]. Where he went and what he did while he was there is not known but he seems to have had a fair degree of exposure to the American newspaper industry because after his return he adopted the less formal, more free-flowing style of his American fellow reporters and for the rest of his journalistic life, intentionally or otherwise, American expressions and forms of spelling crop up in his writing.

Between his return to England in 1866 and 1870 Francis was employed by the *Oxford Journal* and once again he lived with his parents who were resident in the city at the time[40]. Sporadic examples of journalism published under his own name begin to appear from this time although, since they were usually signed only with his initials, F.C., they are difficult to track down. In 1884 he wrote a series of three articles for the *Tricycling Journal* about a journey that he undertook on such a machine from London to Oxford in which he described the landscape and notable sights along the way. He evidently loved the English countryside and in later life he published polemics about the protection of public open spaces and rights of way. He also wrote other accounts of meandering through the rural landscape by canal boat. In all of these there is evidence of the keen eye for geographical detail that must have stood him in such good stead during the three years that he later spent mapping Cambridge and its surroundings.

The census of 1871 is the only one during the entire life of his parents in which Francis was not living at home. They had left Oxford to settle in Cambridge and Francis journeyed to London in an apparent attempt to break into the world of mainstream national journalism. It does not appear to have been met with success. On the night of Sunday 2nd April he was living alone in a private hotel in Essex Street. The street, which is just off the Strand, is close to Fleet Street, then the heartland of the British newspaper industry. It is an obvious place to live for someone trying to make their way in the profession of *his* journalism but in the case of Francis there is a surprising entry under 'Rank, profession or occupation.' It reads: 'No occupation.' Most people who were temporarily out of work would have entered 'Reporter, unemployed' or similar. If they were fortunate enough not to have to work they entered 'Living on own means' or 'Annuitant'. The words 'No occupation' usually indicated someone who was permanently unable to work through mental or physical incapacity.

Even stranger is the entry under 'Where born'. The convention was that a person entered first the county and then the town of their birth and everyone else on the page has done just that. Francis entered 'Cambridge, Ealing Grove'. He had been born in Acton so the entry should have read 'Middlesex, Acton.' Ealing Grove was the name of Lady Noel Byron's boarding school where his parents had taught until 1835, two years before Francis was born and to which they may later have sent their son. It is nowhere near Cambridge. It is almost as if he was deliberately interpreting the question to mean 'Where educated'. Even then there is an anomaly. He may well have attended the school at Ealing Grove but there is no evidence of his having enrolled in, let alone graduated from, Cambridge University.

The whole entry has an air of failure and despair about it. He may have been drunk or even under the influence of drugs when he filled in the census form, or suffering a mental crisis associated with his disordered personality, but what was he doing there? Ten years before, in the census of 1861 when living in Warwick, he had confidently declared himself to be a newspaper reporter and, moreover, the head of the household. It looks as if Francis had suffered some sort of breakdown. The attempted move from provincial reporter on the *Oxford Journal* to journalist in the national press seems to have ended in disaster. Within a few weeks he was back living once again with his parents.

At this time the Craigs were living in modest comfort in New Square, Cambridge. They had a resident, 12-year-old housemaid and one wonders how employing such a child squared with E.T.'s socialist conscience. E.T. was in an inventive phase at this stage of his life. In the Cambridge Working Classes' Industrial Exhibition of 1873 he won the silver medal for the greatest number of new inventions on display, 27 in all, none of which he troubled to patent although several of them were later plagiarised by other people who made considerable amounts of money from them, sending E.T. into periodic frenzies of complaint and litigation.

During this period he earned a large part of his living as a ventilation engineer, environmental health being for him a lifetime obsession and inextricably linked to the welfare of the working man and his socialist instincts. His restless urge to travel took him all over Britain lecturing on sanitation and ventilation.

He became a fierce opponent of the move to install mains drainage and sewage systems, attacking Sir Joseph Bazalgette, the pioneering sanitary engineer, in print and in public speeches on every possible occasion. For E.T. human sewage was much too valuable a commodity to dump at sea and instead the 'guano', as he called it, should be collected and used to fertilise the land. 'Dirt', as he wrote in a letter to the *Oxford Journal*, 'is simply manure in the wrong place.' It was yet another example of E.T.'s misguided and ultimately doomed obsessions, although, as his ideas have recently been adopted by the Green movement, maybe he was just ahead of his time.

The impression that Francis suffered a psychological breakdown in 1871 is reinforced by the fact that when he returned to live under the parental roof he did not resume work as a reporter for some considerable time. Perhaps the failed attempt at breaking in to mainstream journalism had sapped his confidence to such an extent that he could no longer face the prospect of spending days in the company of his fellow men, jostling with other reporters as they competed for the best copy in the local courts. He may initially have spent some time living quietly with his parents, perhaps receiving discreet treatment from a local doctor, for there is no record of his ever having entered any of the county lunatic asylums, either in Cambridge or Middlesex.

Eventually – and no doubt once again through the influence of his father – he was commissioned by William Spalding, a local printer, to undertake a detailed survey of Cambridge and the surrounding countryside. It was to take Francis nearly four years and must have involved a huge amount of pacing the lanes and byways of the medieval city, measuring and surveying the streetscape. Until the end of his life he retained a passion for maps and topography and, apparently, an almost photographic memory for streets and the people who inhabited them.

The map was a success and became the forerunner of similar city plans such as the famous A–Z gazetteer of London. Other than newspapers it is the sole document that the British Library holds that bears his name in contrast to the 17 or so that are listed for his father. '*Spalding's Plan of Cambridge and its Environs Surveyed and Compiled Expressly for W P Spalding by Francis S Craig*' was printed in 1875 and as a result of his endeavours his name is listed in

Tooley's Dictionary of Map Makers. He was later involved in new editions in 1881 and 1885.

Although it was a long way from the type of work he was used to, it apparently enabled him to regain his self-confidence and eventually to return to the world of journalism. By early 1875 Francis had been appointed editor of the *Bucks Advertiser and Aylesbury News* and it is likely that yet again his father's influence had secured the post for him. His parents appear to have moved from Cambridge to Aylesbury with him, probably realising that it could only work successfully if they continued to provide him with a home and the day-to-day support that he needed. They settled in Ripon Street in the Buckinghamshire county town and E.T. lost no time in re-establishing his ventilation business locally, assisted by Francis.

On 25th January 1875 an article entitled 'The Tring Centenarian' appeared in *The Times*. It started: 'Mr Francis Craig writes from Aylesbury' and concerned a local character, Betsy Leatherland, who had recently died at the improbable age of 112. Francis took the side of Sir Duncan Gibb, an eminent London physician who had both examined Betsy in life and conducted her post-mortem examination, and who was apparently certain that the old gypsy woman was indeed the age she claimed even though he said that she 'had the heart and lungs of a young girl of 15'. It was later convincingly shown that she could not have been anywhere near that age and Sir Duncan's reputation suffered accordingly but by that time Francis had not only sold the story to *The Times* but had managed to have it syndicated by at least 15 other newspapers the length and breadth of Britain. It is clear that, despite his social shortcomings, he was a man who knew very well how to use the newspaper world to his own advantage.

But it was not to last. The *Bucks Advertiser*, which was owned and published by a local printer and insurance agent, Robert Gibbs, had a rival Aylesbury publication – the *Bucks Herald* – also published weekly on Saturdays. On Saturday 29th May 1875, the hammer blow fell. The *Herald* published a long letter on its correspondence page above the signature 'Honesty'. It has all the hallmarks of being a put-up job by the *Herald's* own editorial staff rather than being a genuine letter from one of its readers but was no less effective for that. Below the title 'Coincidence of Great Minds', it started:

Sir – Being an occasional reader of your contemporary, the *Bucks Advertiser*, I could not fail from time to time to notice the similarity of tone and expression that exists between its leading articles and those of *The Daily Telegraph*; but I was scarcely prepared for the most perfect piece of unblushing impudence that occurred in last Saturday's issue. Having read an *original* (query, editorial) from a person signing himself "W. S." on "The Labourers' Meeting at Wingrave," I had a suspicion that I had seen something like it before. Turning over my file of *The Daily Telegraph*, I find the so-called original communication of the *Bucks Advertiser* there appearing, in last Wednesday's issue, as leader! To show the completeness of the plagiarism, I send the two herewith and trust that you will print both in parallel columns. Your readers will note that, with the exception of a few verbal alterations to make it local, it is a pure reprint.

The editor had then done as requested and placed the two pieces side by side so that, although the *Telegraph* piece made references to Yeovil and Somerset, it was immediately obvious that Francis had indeed lifted it almost verbatim and substituted Buckinghamshire for Somerset and Wingrave, near Aylesbury, for Yeovil.

Even worse was to come. Below the two columns the correspondent continued:

P.S. – Since writing the above, a friend, to whom I showed it, has brought me some additional coincidences, culled from the editorial portion of the *Advertiser*, designated "The Week," which you can add to your contemporary's "crib" from the *Telegraph* –

The twin columns continued showing that, as well as *The Daily Telegraph* plagiarism, Francis had also stolen large chunks of copy from both *The Morning Post* and *The Times* over the course of the preceding two weeks. It did not need to go further back than that, the point had been made and the damage done.

The letter concluded:

> Whilst congratulating your contemporary upon the *adaptive* pow-
> ers he possesses, as here evinced, would it not be more candid to
> his readers to quote the sources whence he derives his inspirations,
> to say nothing of common fairness to the daily leader writers?
>   Yours truly,
>   HONESTY

Francis was no doubt summoned to Mr. Gibbs's office within minutes of the
Herald hitting the streets on that Saturday in May. The following week the
Herald carried a terse announcement which stated:

> "HONESTY"
> With reference to a letter under that signature, which appeared in
> our paper last week, we are requested to state that the services of
> Mr F Craig as editor of the *Bucks Advertiser and Aylesbury News*
> have been dispensed with.'

Francis had been caught red-handed committing one of the worst crimes in the
cut-throat world of journalism. That he thought he could have got away with
such obvious and prolific theft of his fellow hacks' work without being quickly
caught out shows a remarkable lack of judgement, consistent with his unworldly
personality. It almost put paid to his career in the world of newspapers and must
have made him a figure of derision in the streets of the small market town.

This event would have had an even more serious effect on Francis than it
might on most other men. A major present day long-term study known as the
Collaborative Longitudinal Personality Disorders Study has found that stressful life events have a seriously deleterious effect on people with STPD, pushing
them further towards the criminality and violent behaviour that are associated
with the schizophrenia spectrum. In Francis's case it seems that it lay bottled
up, festering away until 13 years later when another, even more stressful, event
caused it to erupt with disastrous consequences.

Exactly what happened to Francis and his parents during the next few years is unclear, although there is evidence that he worked with his father in his ventilation business for at least a couple of years. They placed advertisements for the Craig system of ventilation in many local newspapers across Britain and managed to get laudatory articles on the benefits of their ventilators published in some of them, such as one in the *Luton Times and Advertiser* on 3rd June 1876. By that time it appears that they had moved to London and their address is given as 19 Seymour Street, Euston Square[41].

It seems that by 1876 their ventilation business was starting to slow down, due probably to the many rival systems that were beginning to appear in the newspaper advertisements. In that year the family moved from Marylebone to Hammersmith, transformed in the 40 years since the Craigs had lived in nearby Acton from a village in open countryside to the west of London to a suburb in a continuous sea of red brick houses that stretched from Paddington to Ealing. The population of London had more than doubled to nearly 4 million in that time and its land area had grown in proportion. To serve the burgeoning suburban population, a large number of new local newspapers had sprung up, and it was probably the new opportunities that these offered that drew Francis along with his by now ageing parents. E.T. was now 74 and, although still very active in writing dozens of pamphlets and his memoirs, he had largely given up his ventilation and sanitary engineering activities.

Francis may have done well – either out of the mapmaking enterprise or the ventilation business – because it was apparently he who bought the house to which the family moved, 2 Redmore Road, not far from the Broadway, the new commercial centre of Hammersmith. It is perhaps more likely that his parents, realising that their life expectancy was limited, bought the house and settled it on Francis to provide a secure future for him after they had gone. Francis is shown as the owner in 1878 but by 1880 E.T. is also resident and shown as paying his son five shillings a week to rent two unfurnished rooms on the first floor. Such an arrangement was not unusual at the time because the Representation of the People Act of 1867 had given the vote to any man over the age of 21 who either owned or rented and occupied property worth more than £10 a year. By paying his son five shillings a week E.T. was effectively also buying his right to vote.

The Craigs stayed at 2 Redmore Road for the next seven years. Even though it was a substantial house on three floors, it must have been crowded for the 1881 census showed that they shared it with two other families, a total of nine people. Curiously, although Francis apparently owned the house, his father is shown as head of the household and a journalist in the 1881 census whilst Francis is merely a reporter. It is probably indicative of the subservient role that Francis played to his father throughout their lives but it also shows that he had been unable to find work as an editor in the six years since his sacking by the *Bucks Advertiser*.

In 1884 the family moved to a smaller house a couple of streets away in Andover Road (since re-named Perrers Road). Despite his advancing years, E.T. threw himself once more into left-wing politics. In 1878 his old friend William Morris had bought a house on the Thames in Hammersmith which he re-named Kelmscott House. There he established a branch of the Socialist Democratic Federation, which met in the coach house every Sunday evening, and E.T. is known to have attended these *soirées*, almost certainly assisted on the mile walk to and from Andover Road by Francis.

And there Francis might have remained – living the life of a low profile reporter on the local newspapers, helping his father to pack and dispatch the health salts, massage rollers and barbells which they now sold by mail order and avoiding the human contact that he found so difficult – until, suddenly and mysteriously, Elizabeth came into his life.

He loved Paris and Elizabeth was naturally keen to hear more about the city of which she could only pretend to be a citizen. Quite how it came about is impossible to say but soon after their first meeting Elizabeth found herself agreeing not only to visit the French capital in the company of this strange, reticent individual but also to becoming the wife of a man old enough to be her father.

Elizabeth had just passed her 28th birthday but could pass for a woman five years younger and indeed she habitually deducted several years from her real age in official documents such as the census and her marriage certificate. For a woman in Victorian England it was an advanced age at which to still be unmarried and it is likely that she eagerly grasped at the unexpected opportunity. Francis no doubt told her that he was a journalist with high expectations of soon becoming the editor of a newspaper. He probably did not tell her that he had been sacked in disgrace from his first appointment as editor nine years previously.

However their meeting came about, it was a union doomed to failure. Francis probably saw it as a chance to live independently, free from what he felt was the overbearing influence of his parents, although in reality he was barely able to function without them. For Elizabeth it was an opportunity to marry and have children before it was too late and, perhaps, to travel to some of the exotic places that Francis told her about during their encounters in William Morris's garden. Neither of them could have known the terrible consequences of such a sudden and ill-thought out match.

CHAPTER FIVE

Marriage

Elizabeth and Francis were married at Brook Green register office on Christmas Eve 1884. The somewhat strange choice of day appears to have come about through Francis taking advantage of his parents being distracted by other events since it is known that they opposed the match and he would not have wanted them on the scene. Probably, being more worldly than their son, they recognised Elizabeth for what she was.

The days before Christmas 1884 were busy ones for E.T.. The socialist Henry Hyndman had set up the Socialist Democratic Federation in 1881 and Morris and his followers were early members. However, by 1884 the autocratic behaviour of Hyndman led Morris and his supporters to challenge him for the leadership. It culminated in a vote being taken late on the evening of 27th December at the Federation's headquarters in Westminster following which Morris, E.T. Craig and a number of others, exasperated by Hyndman's intransigence, broke away and formed the rival Socialist League[42]. E.T., and probably his wife Mary too, were almost certainly away from home for much of the time over the days before and after Christmas, and Francis seems to have taken advantage of their absence to marry Elizabeth by special licence. The shock of his son's rebellion coupled with the late nights and hard work surrounding the Hyndman machinations proved too much for the 81-year-old man. Within a few days he suffered a massive stroke from which he never fully recovered[43]. It was too late to affect Francis however. He and Elizabeth had already fled the nest and Francis would not see his parents again for nearly five years.

In 2011 a bundle of old documents tied with pink tape surfaced at The National Archives which suddenly threw a searchlight's glare on the strange marriage of Francis Spurzheim Craig and Elizabeth. They included a petition for divorce and its supporting sworn affidavit[44]. There are many signs that Francis had embarked upon the venture with some hesitancy. The petition itself was dated 6th March 1886 but the word 'Sixth' was later crossed through and altered to 'Eighth' and initialled 'FSC' in the margin. Almost certainly it had been drawn up ready for him to sign on the sixth but he had not turned up until two days later. There are other little amendments that make no material difference to the document but show that he was in an uncertain frame of mind.

It commenced with the words, 'The Petition … Sheweth that your Petitioner was on 24th day of December 1884 lawfully married to Elizabeth Weston Davies Craig then Elizabeth Weston Davies Spinster at the Office of the Registrar of Marriages, Brook Green Hammersmith in the County of Middlesex the said Elizabeth Weston Davies Spinster describing herself as Elizabeth Weston Jones Widow,' but Francis has inserted the word 'falsely' with a carat mark between the words 'Spinster' and 'describing' and initialled the alteration in the margin. It doesn't alter the sense in any way but suggests that Francis was trying to justify his actions to himself and others.

It was written in the elaborate copperplate hand of a solicitor's clerk and addressed 'To the Right Honourable The President of the Probate Divorce and Admiralty Division of the High Court of Justice (Divorce).' After establishing the fact that the marriage had taken place legally it goes on to state that he and Elizabeth had 'lived and cohabited at 3 Andover Road, Hammersmith, 7 Lemon's Terrace Stepney Green and 12 Argyle Square, all in the County of Middlesex.'

Then comes the bombshell. Using the tendentious legalese no doubt dictated by his solicitor, Francis goes on to state: 'That I am informed and verily believe that on the night of 19th May 1885 the said Elizabeth Weston Craig was seen to enter a house and private hotel, 53 Tonbridge Street in the company of a young man 20 – 24 years at 10 o'clock at night[45].' It does not say whether she was seen by Francis or someone else, although if Francis himself had witnessed the act it would probably have said so since it is likely to have carried more weight in a court of law. Nor does it state whether by that date Elizabeth had actually left him although it seems highly likely that she had, since she would hardly have been abroad by herself at that time of night as a respectably married woman.

There seems little doubt that Francis had been totally unaware of his intended's occupation at the time of their marriage. It was not unusual for a sexually experienced single woman to describe herself as a widow at the time of marriage in the 19th century for to do so conveniently explained her non-virginal state on the wedding night. She would then either have had to give her maiden name as her married name or invent a different married name. Elizabeth had chosen the latter course, changing her own name Davies for the equally common Welsh name Jones whilst retaining her middle, family name – Weston. The next time she decided to tell a partner that she was a widow she would revert to Davies as her married name[46].

It was a ruse that, like the marriage, did not last very long. The marriage certificate itself shows that Elizabeth's deception was not confined to her name. She also gave a false age, 26, which was two years less than her actual age. Again this was common in the 19th century when few checks were made against birth certificates and indeed many people, including Francis, had been born before civil registration of births, marriages and deaths commenced in June 1837.

The rest of the details on the certificate are more or less accurate except that Elizabeth failed to put 'deceased' after her father Edward's name and Francis aggrandised his occupation by describing himself as a journalist rather than a reporter[47]. The witnesses are shown as E. and L. Warren. These were Edward Warren, a local rate collector who was perhaps the nearest to a true friend that Francis ever had and who would later give evidence at his inquest, and his wife Louisa. Then as now it was customary for close members of the bride and groom's families to act as witnesses so the fact that no-one from either family did so suggests that none were present.

Although the exact date of Elizabeth's leaving him is not given in the divorce petition, it seems clear that she had departed by 19th May 1885. In the space of just over four months they had lived in three different houses as well, perhaps, as having spent a week or two in Paris.

3 Andover Road was the house that Francis shared with his parents and Elizabeth had also given it as her address at the time of the marriage although it was probably just an accommodation address since it is highly unlikely that the Craigs would have permitted their son to share their tiny house with a young woman of whom they strongly disapproved. 7 Lemon's Terrace was a cottage in a row of dwellings erected by a speculative builder of that name at the Mile End Road end of Stepney Green. In 1885 it was in an area densely populated by Jewish immigrants from the Russian Empire who had fled the pogroms of 1871 and 1881, and it was close enough to Stepney gasworks to be affected by the sulphurous stench when the wind was in the wrong direction. It is difficult to see why Francis would have chosen to take his new bride there unless it was to put as much distance as possible between himself and his parents. At any rate they did not, it seems, stay there long before moving to the much more salubrious surroundings of Argyle Square, a pleasant leafy oasis in solidly middle-class Bloomsbury.

Exactly what caused such a rapid disintegration of the marriage is not clear although, with the benefit of knowing more about the character and personality of Francis it is possible to deduce some of the possibilities. He was, as became abundantly clear at his inquest, a strange, tongue-tied man who found normal conversation almost impossible. Yet Edward Warren disagreed with another witness that he was 'sensitive'. Warren believed that Francis possessed a firm personality and was capable of standing his ground. If he was anything like his father he would have been stubborn to the point of intransigence. Elizabeth for her part was also possessed of a temper that could be explosive at times, especially if she was under the influence of alcohol, which was not infrequently. It was a recipe for disaster.

From the divorce petition it is clear that by May 1885, little over four months since the marriage, Elizabeth had left Francis. Years later Edward Warren would say that Francis's wife disappeared about three months after the wedding and

Arthur Lane, proprietor of the *Indicator* and Francis's ex-employer, said that the marriage was 'very brief, for his wife drank, and deserted him'.

Whatever the actual precipitating event, it is clear that a reclusive man who had lived with his parents for almost his entire life and a hot-headed, lively, upper-class courtesan who had spent much of the last ten years living in one of the grandest houses in London and mixing with well-known artists, writers and bohemians were not well matched. An age gap of 20 years and the fact that Francis is known to have been very abstemious whereas Elizabeth, if not an actual alcoholic, frequently drank too much, did not help. Francis's decision to take such an unsuitable woman as his bride may have had more to do with a desire to break free from the suffocating influence of his parents than any real expectation that it could possibly work.

Despite that, Elizabeth's desertion dealt Francis a savage blow. There is evidence from his later writing that he was very fond of children. He was an ardent supporter of the National Society for the Prevention of Cruelty to Children and frequently wrote in heart-rending terms about cases of child cruelty and neglect. Christmas was a time of special significance to him and he wrote wistfully about Christmas trees and tables groaning with presents 'as in good days of old'. It seems likely that Francis's Christmases in a small household dominated by an austere, teetotal father were anything but the Dickensian dream that he conjured up and possibly he yearned for a home with children and merriment such as he had never known. Whatever the truth, his reaction to Elizabeth's departure was extreme.

His first response was to seek the help of his old friend Edward Warren. He prevailed upon the kind-hearted, easy-going man to give up his job for a few days to accompany him back to St. Pancras to comb the streets in a vain attempt to find his errant wife[48]. It was to no avail and Warren soon had to relinquish the task and return to his own family in Fulham. Francis did not give up however. It is clear from the petition that he next recruited the assistance of private detectives to search for Elizabeth. It was not a cheap undertaking and on Francis's meagre wages as a penny-a-liner it must soon have eaten into his reserves.

His efforts eventually bore fruit but in a way that Francis might not have wished. At about 10pm at night on the evening of 19th May Elizabeth was spotted entering a private hotel at 53 Tonbridge Street in the company of a man of between 20 and 24 years of age. The inference was obvious and it must have come as a shattering blow to Francis. Elizabeth was working as a prostitute.

She had not moved very far. Tonbridge Street was only a few hundred yards from their lodgings in Argyle Square. Her lack of caution seems to indicate that she was either unaware of Francis's attempts to find her or maybe she presumed that once he discovered the truth he would not bother to pursue her further. If so, she did not know her husband.

The initial sighting unlocked a series of others. Elizabeth, it was discovered, was living at the Monmouth Hotel and Coffee House, 161 Drummond Street, just west of Euston Station and either Francis himself or, more likely, the private investigator on his behalf quickly established through enquiries at the local police station that it was a well-known brothel. There followed a number of other sightings in and around Holloway and Camden of Elizabeth in the company of various clients. One man in particular was a regular. Elizabeth was spotted on several occasions during June, July and early August with one 'Harry McBain, Baker' and finally she spent the nights of 17th and 18th August 1885 with him at 26 Caledonian Road, Kings Cross. The address is that of another coffee house that rented out rooms, often a cover for a brothel and like other addresses that were later named in Francis's divorce petition it was owned and operated by Elizabeth's old employer Ellen Macleod.

Harry McBain was in fact Henry McBlain and his name is given correctly on the outside of the petition but misspelled throughout the actual document[49]. He was a retired 58-year-old ship owner and timber merchant, an Ulsterman who had made a modest fortune in Canada before retiring to London. Why he is described as a baker in the petition is a mystery although there was a large bakery within a few hundred yards of his house in St. Augustine's Avenue, Camden Town and possibly he owned or had a financial interest in it. He may have known the Maundrells through his daughter Annie, who was a clerk in the Post Office Savings Bank for which Ellen's father Robert had also worked.

The persistent attention of Francis or his agents eventually proved too much for Elizabeth. It must have been a nerve-shredding experience to be stalked night and day, never knowing when Francis would step out of an alleyway and beseech her to return to him. There may have been tearful rows in the open streets, a constant barrage of notes and letters, maybe even attempts to drag her back to their home by force. It may also eventually have proved too much for Mrs. Macleod. It could not have been good for business to have that sort of caper going on anywhere near her discreet establishments and involving one of her girls. It may have been she who finally told Elizabeth to pack her bags and leave the neighbourhood.

Whoever made the decision, the sightings in August are the last recorded ones of Elizabeth in North London and in fact the last ever of her under that name; after that she disappeared, not just from the scene but from history as far as most of her family and those that knew her are concerned. How long Francis went on looking for her in that area or paying others to do so is not known but at some time in the next few months the focus of his search moved further east.

On 6th March of the following year Francis visited Mr. R.H. Owens, a commissioner for oaths, at his chambers in Serle Street, Lincoln's Inn Fields, to swear an affidavit to a petition for divorce against his wife Elizabeth. His solicitor, Arthur Ivens, whose own chambers were at 107 Great Russell Street, opposite the British Museum, had drawn up the petition based on the evidence that Francis had supplied him with which terminated abruptly after the sightings of 17th and 18th August the previous year. The document bears a momentous piece of information, although one which is easily overlooked on a first reading. It starts with the words: 'I Francis Spurzheim Craig of 306 Mile End Road in the County of Middlesex ...' At some point in the previous months he had moved from the home he had shared with Elizabeth in Argyle Square back to the East End.

It is improbable that he would have done so as long as he thought that Elizabeth was still in the Bloomsbury area, so it seems that he had received some information which revealed that she had moved east. When and how this had occurred is impossible to say. Maybe he or someone acting for him had talked to other girls who knew her and had been told that that was where she had gone. Even if she had sworn her fellow prostitutes to secrecy, a few shillings or a glass of gin may have been all that was needed to loosen their lips.

The informant, whoever she was, very probably worked from the same brothel as Elizabeth. The divorce petition states that '... on the 10th January 1885 the said Elizabeth Weston Craig wrote a letter from the Monmouth Hotel and Coffee House, 161 Drummond Street, Euston Square in which she stated that she had been staying there since leaving the East End…' It is a tantalising but odd snippet. On 10th January 1885 the pair had only been married for 17 days. It hardly seems long enough for them to have lived and cohabited at three different addresses and then to have separated, let alone to have also spent some time in Paris[50].

There may be two explanations. It is conceivable that there is a mistake about the date. It may be that the letter was written in January 1886; early in the New Year, people frequently continue mistakenly to use the old year when writing cheques or letters. More likely is the possibility that Elizabeth had resumed her old trade during the day whilst Francis was at work and was using the Monmouth Hotel as her base. The intended recipient of the letter is not known. Almost certainly it was not Francis or that would have been stated in the petition. Possibly she had written it to a friend or family member so that they could safely write to her at that address and Francis had intercepted it or it had somehow come into his possession[51]. In that case, 'since leaving the East End' would indicate that they had only lived at Lemon's Terrace, Stepney, for a matter of days.

Why had Elizabeth reverted to prostitution so soon after their marriage? Had life with Francis proved so intolerable that she had quickly realised that there was no future in it? Did she need the money? Francis was paranoid about his finances, frequently believing that he was facing ruin when there were no grounds for such an idea. A doggerel poem that he wrote in December 1889 called *An Editor's Christmas* which was published in the *Indicator*, of which he was then the editor, talks of a table being strewed with 'The bills and the notes for which he was sued'. Creditors, real or imagined, seem to have haunted Francis throughout his life. Elizabeth, who had until her marriage been financially independent and apparently well-off, at least for the few weeks whilst she was working in the West End gay house, suddenly found herself reliant on a man who could have been the model for Ebenezer Scrooge. If so, it was a situation that a girl of as independent a nature as Elizabeth would have quickly found intolerable.

The combination of living with such an odd man and the loss of her independence no doubt led to the first of many rows. Elizabeth may have resorted to drink which would have worsened an already precarious situation. Francis's deepening paranoia may have caused him to employ the services of private detectives to keep his wife under observation until, unable to stand it any longer, she walked out on him.

When the trail finally went cold in August 1885 it apparently did not take Francis long to discover that Elizabeth had moved to the East End, whether the information was imparted by one of her former friends or not. As with all port cities, the area around the docks was a magnet for prostitutes. Sailors on their first run ashore after a long voyage, their pockets bulging with several months' accumulated pay, were easy prey and the Ratcliffe Highway which ran parallel to the north bank of the Thames teemed with brothels. Moreover the East End, which had the highest population density in Britain, was an ideal place in which to disappear if that was your wish. It seems that Elizabeth had had enough of being stalked and accosted by Francis or his lackeys. Probably she only intended to make it a temporary exile; the upmarket West End was her more natural environment. She no doubt hoped that after a few weeks or months it would be safe for her to move back to old haunts by which time Francis might have lost interest or found it impossible to pick up the trail again. At any event, if that was her intention, she badly underestimated the extent of his obsession. Nor could she have known that his craving to have his wife back had gradually changed into a bitter, festering resentment. It was the classic case of love turned to hatred.

CHAPTER SIX

The Trail Goes Cold

When Francis pursued Elizabeth to the East End in late 1885 or early 1886 he took lodgings at 306 Mile End Road. The house no longer exists because the south side of the road suffered extensively in the Blitz of 1940 and the area was rebuilt as a huge estate of council owned flats in the 1950s[52]. The north side survives however and it is easy to see that the buildings opposite would have consisted of a mixture of 18th and 19th century terraced houses mostly with commercial premises at street level and two or three floors of family accommodation above. In the census of 1891 the house is occupied by William Hasted and his family. Hasted was a printer and may have had his shop on the ground floor. As a reporter Francis would have needed to come and go at all hours and no doubt he had his own key to the street door so that he could let himself in whenever he wanted without disturbing the family.

The Mile End Road is an eastwards extension of Whitechapel Road and both were part of the old Roman road that left the city via the Aldgate and travelled in an almost straight line to the garrison town of Colchester some 65 miles distant. It was a wide thoroughfare which served as a major artery to London, and night and day a stream of wagons brought produce in from the farmlands of East Anglia, and fish from Ipswich and Lowestoft to the markets of the capital. Since the three great city markets of Billingsgate, Spitalfields and Leadenhall were re-stocked overnight ready to open in the early hours of the morning it was a place of constant bustle and noise, never free of human or animal traffic at any hour. Just as they still do today, market traders set up their stalls along the pavements of the Whitechapel Road selling fruit and vegetables, coffee and all manner of wares from cut-price portmanteaux to tin baths. At night the road was lit by occasional gas street lamps and the hissing naphtha flares of the stall holders.

Soon after Francis's arrival, a few hundred yards to the east and on the opposite side of the road from his lodgings, a remarkable building project began to take shape. Known as 'the People's Palace of Delights', it was the result of a collaboration between the novelist and historian Walter Besant and the philanthropist Edmund Currie. It was intended as an alternative to the public houses, music halls and gin shops which were seen by enlightened Victorian society as the root causes of the poverty and wretched condition of the working classes of the East End. It was to provide a place where both men and women could have free access to libraries, exhibitions, lectures, concerts, dances, a swimming pool and a winter garden and be refreshed with nothing more intoxicating than tea. After it was opened by Queen Victoria in 1887 it proved to be a great success and the hordes of people who flocked to it throughout the day and much of the night would have added to the constant comings and goings past Number 306. The ornate building, rebuilt after a fire in 1931, still stands and today is now part of Queen Mary University of London.

No doubt Francis chose his lodgings carefully. They were within easy walking distance of the Thames Magistrates Court at Arbour Street, the busiest police court in the country, which served the area east of the City of London and north of the Thames which took in the London docks, Wapping, Whitechapel and Spitalfields. They were also little more than a mile from the Ratcliffe Highway which, Francis probably guessed, was where he might find his errant wife; not so close that there was a danger that she might spot him first and do a bolt before he pinpointed her but sufficiently near for him to keep the area under discreet surveillance.

Apart from the possible near miss in 1886 his search for Elizabeth does not seem to have met with success for the better part of two years. It was likely that she was altering her appearance during this time; Mary Jane acquired several nicknames during her sojourn in the East End – including 'Ginger', 'Black Mary' and 'Fair Emma' – which suggests that she was changing her hair colour as well as her name. There does not seem to be a consensus about the natural colour of her hair. Several people described her as fair although that may have referred to her complexion rather than her hair. In the pictures of Mrs. Barrett that Walter Sickert painted and which some people believe to have been his later recollection of Mary Jane, she is always depicted with dark hair and blue eyes. After her death some newspapers stated categorically that she had fair skin and ginger hair while others, including the *New York World*, said just as emphatically that she was dark complexioned. The only existing photograph of her, a macabre death bed scene showing her terribly mutilated corpse on the bed in Miller's Court, appears to show dark hair but it is possible that it was so saturated with her blood that it is impossible to tell.

As 1886 and 1887 dragged on, the notes in the divorce papers make no reference to her having been spotted and in May 1887 Francis appears finally to have run out of money. He dismissed his solicitor, Arthur Ivens, and thereafter is recorded as acting for himself, although there are no notes of anything new happening in relation to the petition until August of the following year[53].

While working in the area and hunting for Elizabeth, Francis had ample time to become familiar with the streets of Whitechapel, Wapping and Spitalfields. His mapmaker's training gave him an eye for the urban landscape and an ability to see the warren of streets, courts and back alleys laid out in plan form almost as if he was swooping above them like a London pigeon. He in turn would have become a familiar sight to the policemen of H Division at their stations in Commercial Street, Leman Street and Commercial Road. Policemen and reporters have always had an affinity, each providing the other with scraps of information and rubbing shoulders in the police and coroners' courts and, off duty, in the pubs and watering holes of the district they serve. Despite his natural aversion to face-to-face conversation and small talk Francis would inevitably have got to know the local Bobbies on the beat and become familiar with the set patterns of their daily lives and the rhythms of policing the Metropolis.

What they made of him is difficult to say. He was an educated man with a quirky sense of humour and maybe he was able to entertain them with stories of his time in America, but with one possible exception he probably made few real friendships during his time in Whitechapel. The poem he wrote and published in the *Indicator* after he left the East End gives some clues as to his existence during this period. It is a maudlin piece called *An Editor's Christmas* which has been mentioned already and is quoted in full in a later chapter. In it he describes, in cod rhyming couplets, making his way back to a lonely fifth-storey room after a day's work, his shoes, full of holes, letting in moisture from the slush-covered pavements. He sat trying to read and darn his socks by the light of a solitary candle until he fell asleep and 'dreamed him of fame' and 'the success for which he had prayed'. In his sleep he sees a Christmas tree and a table piled with bank notes and 'presents and gifts as in good days of old'.

It is probably an accurate description of the way Francis was living during the three years he spent in Whitechapel and the longing references to fame and success almost certainly reflect his state of mind for much of his life. Although he yearned for recognition he thought of himself as a failure and that was probably reinforced by his father who, as all who knew him agreed, was an arrogant and bombastic man obsessed with his own self-importance. The poem goes on to describe the editor wandering the streets for the news, 'feeling the pavement through the holes in his shoes'. The cost of searching for Elizabeth by using private detectives, and engaging a West End solicitor to start a costly divorce action, were more than enough to reduce a penny-a-line reporter to penury and the self-pitying lines of the poem vividly portray his plight.

As he fruitlessly tramped the streets and alleys of the East End searching for Elizabeth during 1887 and on into 1888 the resentment and bitterness seem to have grown. The initial desire to have her back had long since given way to a determination to take his revenge on her and the people that he held responsible for her downfall. But once again she had given him the slip. The fact that he himself remained in the area suggests that he knew that she was still around. Whether small snippets of information were reaching him or whether her failure to reappear in her old haunts in the West End reinforced his conviction is not known but he had certainly not given up as the events of 1888 would show.

Elizabeth seems to have kept in touch with at least one member of her family during this time. There is a persistent story that Mary Jane Kelly was visited in the East End by her brother Johnto[54]. It was suggested by Joe Barnett that this was a nickname for her brother Henry, who was allegedly serving with the 2nd Battalion of the Scots Guards, although no such person has ever been identified. Elizabeth's younger brother was known to his family as Johnto and he certainly knew that his sister was a London prostitute for he passed that information on to his own son John many years later. When John senior came to London around 1884 he boarded with a Welsh dairyman who originally hailed from a village a few miles from the Davieses in Montgomeryshire. His lodgings were in Leigh Street, St. Pancras, only a few hundred yards from Francis and Elizabeth's rooms in Argyle Square, and it is very likely that the brother and sister were in touch at that time and may have remained so after she decamped to Whitechapel. If so it may be the explanation for the Johnto story, although Elizabeth's brother had no known connection with the Scots Guards[55].

If the first two years of Francis's residence in the East End were uneventful, things were hotting up by the start of 1888. The East End was always a crime-ridden area but in the early part of the year it excelled itself in violence and cruelty directed at women. First, on Saturday 25th February, an unfortunate called Annie Millwood was attacked in the street and stabbed multiple times in her legs and lower body by an unknown assailant. She survived, as did Ada Wilson who opened the door to a stranger on 28th March and was stabbed twice in the throat when she was unable to hand over any money.

A much more serious attack took place on 3rd April, Easter Monday, when another unfortunate, Emma Smith, was set upon by a gang of youths in Brick Lane, Spitalfields. She was beaten and savagely gang-raped before having a blunt object rammed so forcibly into her vagina that it perforated into her abdominal cavity. She survived for four days before inevitably succumbing to peritonitis, a condition for which in 1888 there was no surgical remedy[56]. The reports in the newspapers shocked not only the East Enders, who were almost inured to such things, but a wider, national audience who were just starting to realise that all was not well in a part of the capital of which most preferred to forget the existence. The attack was attributed to a so-called 'High Rip' gang, groups of disaffected, unemployed youths who preyed on prostitutes, knowing that the police and the general public held them in such low regard that they were almost beyond the protection of the law.

Then, on 7th August another unfortunate was murdered on a public staircase in George Yard Buildings, Spitalfields. This latest in the series of attacks on unfortunates in the district was the first to fully capture national attention but that would not happen until after reports began to appear in the press following the inquest which opened at the Working Lads' Institute on Thursday 9th August.

CHAPTER SEVEN

The Breakthrough

The Working Lads' Institute, 285 Whitechapel Road, had been opened by the Prince and Princess of Wales three years before. The Alexandra Room, named after the Princess, was a large reading room with tall windows overlooking the street and, because Whitechapel had no coroner's court of its own, it had been selected by Mr. Wynne Baxter, the coroner for the Southern division of East Middlesex, as a suitable place in which to hear inquests. Under normal circumstances the room was easily large enough to accommodate the jury and officers of the court as well as members of the public and the three or four local reporters that might normally be expected to attend an inquest. That was certainly the case on 9th August. The *East London Advertiser* commented that 'there was scarcely any one present except the authorities and those connected with the case, the public being conspicuous by their absence'.

Baxter himself was away, taking a summer cruise through the fjords of Scandinavia, so the inquest was conducted by his deputy, Mr. George Collier[57]. Mr. Collier was a very different character from his bluff and forthright senior colleague. During the entire proceedings he was 'painfully quiet' according to the *Advertiser*. Although reports of the first day of the inquest appeared in at

67

least 14 local and national newspapers in the days that followed it is apparent that most of them are syndicated copies of the same second-hand account. Almost all, including the nationals such as *The Times*, *The Manchester Guardian*, *The People* and *The Daily News*, reported the police surgeon's name as 'Keleene' (it was actually 'Killeen'), indicating that they used the same source for their stories. Only two local papers, the *East London Advertiser* and the *East London Observer*, contain accounts of the inquest that were obviously written by reporters who were actually present. Both of them paint vivid and colourful accounts of the scene, describing the dress and the voices of the witnesses in detail. Of the two, the report in the *Advertiser* bears most resemblance to the later journalistic style of Francis Craig. There is his typical use of quotation marks to indicate that he is making a joke as in his description of the jury as '20 good and true men of this county'. When giving the cause of death both the *Advertiser* and the *Observer* used the American spelling 'hemorrhage', and in a later account in the *Advertiser* of Polly Nichols's funeral the reporter spells the word 'ruse' as 'rouse', which although pronounced to rhyme with 'blues', is an American spelling still in use today[58]. It is slender evidence that Francis was the *Advertiser*'s correspondent but he was resident in the district served by both the *Advertiser* and the *Observer* and it is highly likely that he was writing for one or other of them. On balance the *Advertiser* seems the more likely.

On the first day of the inquest the identity of the victim had not been established although several people had come forward and given conflicting names. The first witnesses were people who lived in George Yard Buildings, on the staircase of which the body had been discovered. The building was one of a series of 'model dwellings', community housing put up by public and private subscription to house the working poor of London and the major cities of Britain in the 19th century. The apartments all shared semi-open communal staircases which served as convenient places for the destitute to sleep and for prostitutes to take their clients since the meagre gas lighting was extinguished at 11pm.

Monday 6th August was a bank holiday and a married couple, Mr. and Mrs. Mahoney – who had been out celebrating – had come in a little before 2am. They had not noticed anything on the stairs although, as Mrs. Mahoney pointed out, it was so dark that they might easily have missed seeing a body unless they had tripped over it. Alfred Crow, a cab driver, was the next witness. He had noticed a body lying on the staircase when he returned home at 3.30am but took no notice as he was used to seeing vagrants sleeping there. An hour and a quarter later John Reeves, a dock labourer, descended the stairs on his way to work. By that time it was light and he saw the body of a woman, her skirts pulled up over her head, lying in a pool of blood. He did not stop to look further but hurried off to find a policeman.

Dr. Timothy Killeen, the police surgeon, arrived at the scene at 5.30am and his evidence was listened to in shocked silence by the small audience in the Alexandra Room. The woman, who Dr. Killeen estimated to be about 36 (she was actually 40)[59], had been slaughtered by 39 separate stab wounds to the stomach, lower abdomen and chest. Following the post-mortem examination that he conducted later the same day, he ascertained that the abdominal wounds, several of which had pierced the stomach, liver and spleen, had all been inflicted by a sharp, short-bladed knife like a penknife but a large chest wound which had penetrated the sternum and just nicked the heart could only have been done with a strong, rigid instrument such as a sword bayonet or a dagger. The cause of death, he stated, was haemorrhage from the various stab wounds.

The coroner listened gravely to Dr. Killeen's evidence and then addressed the jury. Since there was doubt about the woman's identity he was going to adjourn the inquest for a fortnight. He added that the man who could have inflicted 39 wounds on a poor defenceless woman must have been a perfect savage.

When Francis left the Working Lads' Institute that day an idea seems to have taken root in his mind. Before the inquest resumed on 23rd August he had visited a solicitor – exactly who is not known since he had dismissed Arthur Ivens in May of the previous year – sworn an affidavit and on Monday 20th, presented it in person to the High Court of Justice: Probate, Divorce and Admiralty Division, in the Strand. It sought leave to strike out Paragraph 5 of his petition and to make certain other alterations. Permission was duly granted by the Registrar, Mr. D.H. Owen, and the following day Francis returned to file the amended document and the supporting affidavit[60].

It was an extraordinary thing to do. The petition had in effect lain dormant since being filed in March two years before, as all attempts to serve it on

Elizabeth had failed because of her disappearance. Why had Francis suddenly gone to the trouble and the significant expense of swearing an affidavit and making radical changes to a document that he had probably not given much thought to for more than two years? To have gone to that degree of inconvenience and expense at any time would have been odd but for a hard-up newspaper man to have taken several days off right in the middle of the most sensational murder investigation of the time seems almost incomprehensible.

The clue lies in Paragraph 5. It is the one in which he names Mrs. McLeod [sic] as the owner and proprietor of the various brothels in the Kings Cross and Holloway districts in which Elizabeth was alleged to have entertained her clients, including Harry MacBain [sic]. Why would Francis suddenly have decided to spare the reputation of a woman who he held responsible for Elizabeth's behaviour and ultimate disappearance? He could not have been worried by the threat of her bringing a suit for libel since the divorce petition was protected by legal privilege and, in any case, since it had not yet been made public, she would have had no way of knowing that she had been named in it. It seems much more likely that Francis wanted something from her.

That something was the whereabouts of his wife.

The time and money that he had spent using private detectives to track down Elizabeth after she had left him in March or April 1885 had alerted him to Ellen Macleod's activities and he may even have met her in his fruitless efforts to get Elizabeth to return to the marital home. He undoubtedly knew how and where to get in touch with her and it seems that at some time between 21stAugust and the night of the first Ripper murder ten days later he visited Ellen Macleod and made her an offer. In return for her telling him where to find Elizabeth he would strike her name and the addresses of her brothels from the divorce petition. Should he succeed in finding her and having the petition served, in due course when the case came to court Ellen Macleod would not have to suffer the indignity of having her name made public.

It probably seemed like a reasonable offer to Ellen. As far as she knew, Francis simply wanted to divorce his errant wife and he needed to know her address for that reason. Did she in fact know it? Mary Jane Kelly was known to have received letters from time to time and presumably she sent some also.

She had also visited her ex-employer in the West End in the company of 'Mrs Buki' to retrieve her French gowns so it seems possible, if she and Elizabeth were one and the same, that the two women had kept in contact. It may even have been the case that Elizabeth used Ellen Macleod as the conduit between herself and her own family.

Whether the changes to the petition were actually made remains in some doubt. The copy that is held by The National Archives bears a few minor initialled corrections but they look as if they were made when the document was first drawn up in March 1886[61]. In that document Paragraph 5 remains resolutely un-struck out. The affidavit, an almost identical document, has crosses besides Paragraphs 5 to 9 – those in which Ellen and her premises are named – but they too have not actually been struck out. Maybe he made the changes in his own copies and that was enough for Ellen. She was satisfied and Francis, apparently, went away with what he wanted.

The stage was now set for the next act.

CHAPTER EIGHT

Rehearsal

By the time the inquest on the woman whose body had been found on the staircase of George Yard Buildings resumed on 23rd August she had been identified as Martha Tabram. Her story was typical of so many of the other East End unfortunates. From a respectable working-class background she had married Henry Tabram, a furniture warehouse foreman, at the age of 20. The couple had two sons but by the time she was 23 Martha was already drinking heavily and her husband threw her out. She drifted into Whitechapel where she scraped a living through hawking, occasionally living with an unemployed carpenter called Henry Turner and, inevitably for one in her situation, eventually resorting to street prostitution.

After evidence of identification had been given by Martha's former husband and her sister-in-law, a witness was called who was able to throw what at first appeared to be a good deal of light on the affair[62]. She was Mary Ann Connelly, another prostitute, who went by the working name of 'Pearly Poll'. It was something of a misnomer since Mary was a big, raw-boned, masculine woman with a voice ravaged by years of alcohol and tobacco which, like many of her friends, she smoked in a cut-down clay pipe. By all accounts she also had a truculent and unhelpful manner. She gave evidence that she and Martha, who she knew as 'Emma', met at about 10pm on the evening of 6th August. It was the Summer Bank Holiday and the public houses and music halls of the East End were packed with people eager to catch a last few hours of carousing before returning to work the next day. They met up with a pair of soldiers and visited several pubs, drinking a mixture of rum and beer, before splitting up to complete the transactions with their respective clients. Mary and her soldier – apparently a corporal – went in one direction down Angel Alley and Martha took her private to the staircase of George Yard Buildings, no doubt a secluded spot she had used many times in the past.

A local policeman later remembered having talked to a soldier, who he believed to have been a Grenadier Guard, near the entrance to George Yard. The soldier had told the constable that he was waiting for a friend who had 'gone with a girl'. Since Dr. Killeen, the police surgeon who had examined the body on the staircase and later conducted the post-mortem, specifically suggested that the wound that had penetrated the breast bone and punctured the heart had been caused by a strong bladed weapon like a soldier's bayonet, it was a promising lead[63].

Mary Ann Connelly was extensively questioned by the police and asked if she would attend an identity parade. This was carried out at the Tower of London, the nearest military barracks, where it was assumed that the soldiers had come from. She was unable to pick out anyone from the ranks of the Scots Guardsmen mustered on the parade square and then apparently remembered that the two soldiers had been wearing caps with white bands. That immediately identified them as Coldstream Guards and Mary was asked if she would attend another identity parade at their depot at Wellington Barracks near Buckingham Palace.

She agreed somewhat reluctantly and the next day she picked out two soldiers as having been the ones that she and Martha had been drinking with. As it turned out both men – one of whom had spent the night with his wife – had rock solid alibis and at that stage the police concluded that Mary was unreliable, uncooperative or both. Inspector Reid, the detective who was in charge of the investigation, confirmed to the court that Pearly Poll had been unable to help them any further but that investigations were continuing.

The inquest jury duly returned a verdict of wilful and felonious murder by person or persons unknown and the police investigations continued. A week later there had been no further progress and press interest was beginning to wane when two apparently unrelated events occurred which were to change the course of criminal history.

Francis was no doubt in court to hear the Tabram verdict. A very full account of the proceedings, quite possibly written by him, appeared in the *East London Advertiser* on 23rd August. By that time he knew where Elizabeth was living and his desire to avenge himself on her had been re-ignited. But now it was not divorce he sought.

He wanted her dead.

Three years had passed since she had walked out on him. In that time his obsession to have her back, to resume their life together and maybe to raise a family had gradually changed to a festering resentment, but the passage of time did not cause her to fade in his memory. The obsessive rumination typical of STPD meant that she had rarely been out of his mind during that time. He had wasted three years of his life, almost bankrupted himself in looking for her, forfeiting his self-respect and the goodwill of his parents. She had made him look a fool by disappearing after he had spent a great deal of money in preparing a divorce petition which could then not be served because she had done a moonlight flit. Gradually the bitterness had built up until now all he could think about was taking the ultimate revenge on her; nothing less would do.

As he sat listening to the closing witnesses and the coroner's summing up, Francis must have been thinking about how he could achieve his objective and yet not be detected. As a court reporter he knew that invariably and with good reason the first person the police suspected in the case of a married woman's murder was the husband. Although Elizabeth had made things easier by disguising her identity, he did not know how much she may have told her friends since she had been in the East End. Had she mentioned that she was married? Had she indeed mentioned either her maiden name, Davies, or her married name Craig to anyone? Were there letters that, if found, could lead to her true identity being discovered and, through that, the facts of their marriage? Above all, what had become of her wedding ring? Until the late 20th century men in

England rarely, if ever, wore a wedding ring but married women always did and, to symbolise the union of the couple, it was frequently engraved on the inner surface with the date of the wedding and the names or initials of both partners[64]. If Francis had given Elizabeth such an object it was essential that it should be found and removed.

Slowly a plan crystallised in his mind. Martha Tabram was the third unfortunate to be murderously attacked in a small area of the East End in less than eight months. If the sequence continued – particularly if the next ones could all be connected by a distinctive pattern that made them appear to be the work of one man, and that man was seen as a lunatic – then Elizabeth's death as one of the series would be less likely to be connected with an ex-husband, even if the fact that she had once been married should later come to light.

The idea that a man would kill other innocent people in order to disguise his real motive and the identity of the intended victim may at first seem extraordinary yet it is probably as old as murder itself. At the time it seems to have been too bizarre a concept for the Metropolitan Police, for they do not even seem to have considered the possibility. However, a psychopath sufficiently motivated to kill one person may have no compunction about killing others if he thinks it will assist him in carrying out his mission whilst remaining undetected. There have been examples throughout history.

In September 1949 Albert Guay, a French Canadian, planted a dynamite bomb in his wife's suitcase before she checked in for a flight from Quebec to Baie-Comeau. In the ensuing mid-air explosion 23 innocent people were killed along with the intended victim on whose life Guay had taken out a large life-insurance policy[65]. Six years later Jack Graham murdered the 43 passengers and crew of United Airlines Flight 629 soon after it took off from Denver, Colorado in an identical way, hoping to profit by his mother's will and life-insurance policy[66]. In Texas in 1974, Ronald Clark O'Bryan, another psychopath, murdered his own 8-year-old son Timothy using candy poisoned with cyanide, apparently in order to profit from a $20,000 life-insurance policy. Hoping to disguise the object of his murderous intent he also handed out poisoned candy to four other children, including his daughter, under cover of a Halloween 'trick or treat' outing. Fortunately none of the other children sampled the poisoned sweets and as a consequence his plan was laid bare[67].

In O'Bryan's case, unlike Francis, he had no particular animosity against any of the intended victims, he was simply killing for profit. Francis, on the other hand, was driven by a bitter hatred of his wife and a desire to exact vengeance at almost any cost, although not, apparently, that of his own neck. He also had good reason to dislike prostitutes in general, since he no doubt considered that it was prostitution that had effectively taken his wife from him. Killing both Elizabeth and at the same time taking with her a few women of a class that most people considered to be outside normal society was a price he may have considered well worth paying.

It was an outrageous plan but then, as we have seen, Francis was not a normal man. As his future employer Arthur Lane said, he was a man who took antipathies against other people easily and for no reason[68]. As his writing was later to show, he suffered from a smouldering resentment against a world that he felt had treated him unfairly; he was crushed by a sense of failure. Add to that a corrosive malice towards a woman for whom he had once held a fatal obsession but who had, in his mind, cruelly and wantonly abandoned him, and the lives of a few other unfortunates were to him of no consequence[69].

The idea of embarking on a campaign of mass murder almost certainly came to him during the three weeks in which Martha Tabram's inquest took place. He could have visited Ellen Macleod at any time during the past three years but his hurried visit to the High Court on 20th August suggests that a plan had suddenly formed in his mind and he needed to get on with it whilst Martha's murder was uppermost in the consciousness of the Press and the general public.

Six types of serial killer are generally recognised by criminologists: Visionary, those who have schizoid or psychotic tendencies and are driven to commit their crimes by hearing voices; Missionary, those who have a mission to rid the world of a particular type of person; Lust; Thrill; Power-Seeker – which are all self-explanatory – and Gain[70]. The last category best fits Francis, although he may also, to a certain extent, have exhibited some aspects of all the others, except perhaps Lust. Gain serial killers murder to achieve a particular end, which may be monetary or otherwise, and once their goal has been achieved, they stop. That is what distinguishes them from the others and it is what makes the Ripper stand out in the canon of murder. Of course, their underlying personality disorder persists and, should the need arise, they remain capable of killing again many years into the future.

If this was what was passing through his mind during the Tabram inquest, he would also have realised that he would have to devise a suitable *modus operandi* to ensure that there would be no possible doubt that the sequence of killings from that moment on were the work of one man and that that man's motive was directed against a recognisable class of victim rather than against one target in particular. He knew that there was little to connect the killings of Emma Smith and Martha Tabram other than the fact that they were both unfortunates. The next ones had to be different and the only way to ensure that was to carry them out himself.

His choice of method was dictated by his upbringing. His father's passion for anatomy and his participation in dissections is well documented. In the 19th century you did not have to be a doctor or medical student to indulge your interest in the workings of the human body. Attendance at lectures in anatomy, observations of, or even taking part in, dissections was open to any man (women were excluded until the latter part of the century) who was willing to pay a fee at any one of the 20 or so medical schools in the country or at any of the private schools of anatomy that existed during much of the century. The last private school of anatomy in Britain was Thomas Cooke's in Bloomsbury, and that didn't close its doors until 1918[71].

With his enthusiasm for education, particularly self-education, it would have been natural for E.T. Craig to have introduced his son to the dissecting room at an early age. Whether or not Francis had ever wielded the knife himself, by the time he was in his teens he was probably used to seeing his father laying open the abdomen and demonstrating the organs of the body, following the course of the great vessels as they ascended from the thoracic cage into the neck and, especially, attempting to confirm his phrenological beliefs by slicing into the yielding substance of the brain.

It may not have taken Francis long to decide that leaving the bodies of his victims bearing the unmistakeable stigmata of the dissecting room was a good way of making them appear to have been the work of a deranged anatomist. That way the attention of the police would be directed towards the thousands of doctors and medical students that lived in the capital rather than towards an inky-fingered reporter. There was, however, no way in which they could be made to look as detailed and meticulous as actual medical dissections. Medical students then, as now, take a full year to dissect a single human cadaver, spending perhaps eight to 12 hours a week on the task and working in groups of four. Francis was going to have, at best, only a few minutes, working alone, on the ground and in semi-darkness. The most he could hope to do was to give his work a passing resemblance to a medical student's dissection but he trusted that it would be sufficient to link the killings together as the work of one man[72]. But the dissections, such as they were, would be done after they had been killed.

Since, of necessity, all but one of the actual killings would take place in the open, they had to be accomplished as quickly and cleanly as possible – leaving the victim no chance to cry out or to struggle. His knowledge of anatomy was good enough to know that a swift cut through the soft tissues of the neck dividing both carotid arteries and the windpipe in one sweep of the knife was enough to achieve this. Ideally they should be lying supine on the ground when it was done, so that there was less chance of being sprayed with blood.

Francis's lodgings at 306 Mile End Road were in the heartland of the Jewish East End. Directly opposite was the old Beth Holim Jewish hospital, behind which lay the Sephardic burial ground, first opened when Oliver Cromwell allowed the Jews to return to England in 1656. It is tempting to think that as Francis pondered his strategy he may have gained inspiration by witnessing a *shochet*, or Jewish ritual slaughter man, at work. There were many butchers and slaughter houses that used the ritual method of slaughter, or *shechita*, by which animals were rendered kosher and fit to be eaten by observant Jews. If he persuaded a friendly *shochet* to allow him to witness the methods they used, he would have discovered that the most highly favoured was the *shechitamunachat*, in which the animal was lain upon its back on the ground before the long *challaf* or ritual knife was drawn in single sweep through all the soft tissues of the neck severing the carotid arteries, the jugular veins, the oesophagus, the trachea and the vagus nerves which supply the heart. That way the heart stopped almost instantly and bleeding was minimal. A slight hesitation, or failure to sever all the vessels in a single sweep, risked spraying the *shochet* with blood as well as rendering the animal *neveleh* or unfit to eat. Later the police surgeons who disagreed on many details concerning the killings were unanimous on one thing. The Ripper's victims were all killed lying flat on their backs, four of them on the ground and the last on her bed.

But in order to use this method Francis would have to get his intended victims to lie flat on the ground, not something that they were likely to do voluntarily given the filthy and often muddy condition of the Whitechapel streets. His father, E.T. Craig, published a pamphlet in 1892, called, in his typically over-verbose style, *History of a great discovery in the Prevention of Premature Death by the Power to Restore Fluidity of the Vital Current in cases of Inflammation of the Blood when Dying*. It contains detailed instructions for the application of *tapotement* (tapping or percussion) to the veins and arteries of the neck, the anatomy of which is shown in great detail in accompanying illustrations which may have been done by either E.T. or Francis, both of whom were accomplished draughtsmen[73]. E.T. would have known, and may have warned his son, that the technique carried a certain degree of risk if not performed by an expert. On either side of the neck, an inch or so below the angles of the jaw, the two carotid arteries which carry most of the blood to the brain divide into their two major branches. At this point, called the 'carotid sinus', they lie just in front of the transverse processes of the third and fourth cervical vertebra. If both are pushed back against the bony prominences, simultaneously the circulation to the brain is cut off and instantaneous loss of consciousness results. Even sudden brief pressure on one or other of the carotid sinuses can stimulate the baroreceptors which detect blood pressure and may result in a catastrophic drop in arterial pressure and loss of consciousness. Using these so-called pressure points to render a victim unconscious was a technique taught to commandos in the Second World War and is still taught to Special Forces soldiers today. It can leave very characteristic bruising of the neck which is nothing like the bruising left by manual strangulation[74].

The final parts of the preparations would have been the acquisition of a suitable weapon and the selection of the murder sites. The first was easy. In 1888 there were more than 40 surgical cutlers' shops in London, most of which were clustered around the great hospitals and medical schools of the capital. Across the river near Guy's Hospital were the shops of Laundy and Down, around St. Batholomew's lay Evans, Ferguson and Arnold, and in the Whitechapel Road itself, not half a mile from Francis's lodgings, was Krohne and Seseman's. The knife used in the Ripper murders, although never found, was described in detail by the police surgeons. It had a narrow, pointed blade about 7 or 8in long and was lethally sharp. It was a perfect description of a surgeon's amputation knife, designed over centuries for cutting with lightning speed through the skin, muscles and sinews of the leg in the pre-anaesthetic days when split seconds could mean the difference between life and death.

The blades of amputation knives, being made of the highest quality tempered carbon steel, snapped easily and they frequently had to be replaced in the sets that all surgeons and many general practitioners owned. Replacements were therefore sold singly in pasteboard cases about a foot long and an inch wide, with an internal cork to protect the needle-sharp tip of the blade. Weiss's catalogue of 1889 shows that a knife of this sort could be had for eight shillings and sixpence[75]. Weiss also sold an amputation knife with a choice of a 7 or 8-inch blade that partially retracted into the handle, reducing its overall length to about 10in for portability. Such a weapon would have been ideal for carrying concealed up a sleeve or in a pocket.

Keeping the blade suitably sharp would not have been a problem. Even in the hirsute second half of the 19th century most men shaved at least part of their face and neck and most owned at least one cut-throat razor which had to be kept keen on a leather strop or a whetstone. Francis, like his father, was apparently clean-shaven except for bushy sideburns. He would have been perfectly familiar with the daily ritual of keeping a blade in good order.

Francis was more than just a creature of habit. If later accounts of him are to be believed he verged on being an obsessional compulsive. Having decided on his course of action he would certainly have selected a number of possible sites for his forays and then have reconnoitred them more thoroughly than any military commander. His three years as a reporter in the East End combined with his map-maker's eye must already have familiarised him with most of the warren of streets, alleyways and courts of the area, but now he would have looked at them with a new sense of purpose. He needed places that were frequented by the unfortunates yet quiet enough to allow him five or more minutes in which he could be reasonably sure of being undisturbed. They needed to have a little light but sufficient shadow that if he was seen the observer would not be able to recognise him easily later.

They also needed to have more than one exit so that if he was surprised he had a fair chance of being able to make his escape. It is safe to bet that he selected and recce'd more locations than he was likely to need and meticulously walked the different routes to and from them, measuring the time that it would take him to regain the sanctuary of 306 Mile End Road before the discovery of a body and the resulting hue and cry made the streets too dangerous. Francis though had one enormous advantage: his profession as a reporter gave him a good excuse to be out in the streets at all hours of the day and night. Almost certainly he was known to all the local policemen who would have been used to seeing him in the local police court most days and for him to have been found in the vicinity of a crime scene was the most natural thing in the world. He was simply doing his job.

The relationship between the police and the press during the events of 1888 was not a happy one. Senior officers, particularly the unpopular Commissioner of the Metropolitan Police, Sir Charles Warren, were singled out for ridicule for their bungling inability to catch the right man and this made them defensive and antagonistic. Warren himself, like many senior police officers at the time, had been a regular soldier and had carved out a highly successful career in the Royal Engineers. He had spent a large part of his early military life in Africa and the Middle East and used his surveying and engineering skills to good effect in conducting the first modern excavation of the Temple Mount in Jerusalem, a feat for which he was appointed a Fellow of the Royal Society. A vertical shaft that he discovered and which was once thought to be part of the water supply of the city is known to this day as Warren's Shaft. He also succeeded in uncovering what had happened to Edward Palmer's ill-fated political expedition to the Sinai peninsula in 1882, discovering that Palmer and his two companions, who had been carrying a great deal of money to buy the allegiance of the local Bedouin tribesmen, had been robbed and brutally murdered. He succeeded in recovering their bodies, which were then shipped back to England,

and in bringing the killers to justice. For this and other of his exploits he was knighted and it was probably the element of detection involved in the Palmer expedition that led to his being considered a suitable person to take charge of the Metropolitan Police[76].

Soon after standing unsuccessfully for election to Parliament in the Liberal interest, Warren was invited to take the post of Commissioner of the Metropolitan Police in 1886. From the outset he did not hit it off with his immediate colleagues. He was ridiculed for designing for himself a ludicrously over-ornate dress uniform and, probably because of his Liberal sympathies, he never succeeded in gaining the support of Henry Matthews, the Tory Home Secretary. Very early on he clashed with James Monro, the Assistant Commissioner. Monro, who had a legal background, had been expecting to succeed to the role of Commissioner himself and was understandably peeved when Warren was appointed over his head. It led to continuous bickering between the two men which culminated eventually in both offering their resignations to Matthews.

The Home Secretary accepted Monro's resignation but sweetened it by allowing him to retain control of the Special Branch and to report directly to him as part of the Home Office. In doing so he removed a highly efficient investigative tool from the control of the Metropolitan Police. In Monro's place Robert Anderson, another lawyer, was made Assistant Commissioner and Superintendent Adolphus 'Dolly' Williamson was appointed Chief Constable in charge of the Criminal Investigation Department. All three men were in the confidence of Henry Matthews and they habitually met behind Warren's back. Effectively it meant that he was out of the loop for much of the Ripper investigations, which did not enhance his chances of success.

Probably at Francis's level things were different and the beat policemen were more easily disposed towards a local reporter that they trusted than towards the hordes of out-of-town newsmen and even ones from America and further afield that began to arrive in droves by the middle of October.

His appearance was also in his favour. There are no known pictures of Francis Craig, although there are many of his more famous father. There is a contemporary newspaper illustration of Annie Chapman's inquest that shows a man looking very much like a younger version of E.T. Craig, of which more later, but descriptions of him at his own inquest used words like 'nervous', 'sensitive' and 'reticent'. He was apparently an inoffensive, unremarkable looking man, a man who by his own account was shabby and down at heel during this period of his life. He wore the standard dress of the clerical, lower middle-class man, an Inverness coat and a billycock hat[77].

Mr. Thomas Bond, Lecturer in Forensic Medicine at the Westminster Hospital and police surgeon to the Metropolitan Police, probably came nearest to it than anyone when he described him thus: '… the murderer in external appearance is quite likely to be a quiet inoffensive looking man, probably middle-aged and neatly and respectably dressed.[78]' It could hardly have been a better description of Francis.

By Thursday 30th August the stage was set. A mild-mannered, inoffensive looking reporter, 51 years of age, although he probably looked younger, had armed himself with a viciously sharp amputation knife and, driven by a blinding hatred of a much younger woman who he felt had done him a grievous wrong, was about to embark on the most notorious rampage in criminal history.

CHAPTER NINE

Polly

At about 8.45pm on the evening of 30th August 1888 a large fire broke out in the London docks. It started in a bonded warehouse at the South and Spirit Quay of St. Katherine's Docks and every available steam fire engine in the city and East End of London was sent to deal with it[79]. At well past midnight, they were still engaged in what was increasingly beginning to look like a losing battle to stop the fire from spreading to the brandy stores in the basement and causing an explosion that would threaten the very fabric of Tower Bridge, now two years into construction a few hundred yards upstream. Most of the men that could be spared from the City of London Police and H Division of the Metropolitan Police had been sent to the docks to control the huge crowds of spectators whose numbers had been swelled by people coming out of the theatres and music halls. Fortunately they were able to use the high dock gates to keep most people at a relatively safe distance, but their very numbers were causing severe congestion in the narrow streets where the horse-drawn engines from further and further afield were struggling to get through.

It was a squally night with occasional spats of rain and the blaze cast an angry reflection on low clouds whipped across the sky by the brisk west wind.

Every now and then a great shower of sparks shot up into the night as another roof timber collapsed and the roar of the crowd gathered by the riverside swept over the rooftops of Whitechapel like the sound of a wave on a distant beach. Since no-one's life was threatened, except perhaps those of the firemen, the crowd was in high good humour. Even though the next day – Friday – was a working day, no-one seemed to be in a hurry to leave the scene and return to their homes. They cheered loudly as each new steamer arrived, horses at the gallop and smoke already belching from the brass chimney.

Then, shortly after 1am, a rumour started to spread that yet another fire had broken out at Shadwell about half a mile downstream. This time it had started in an engineer's shed in the Ratcliffe Dry Dock and it quickly spread to Gowland's coal store. Before long 800 tons of fuel were ablaze and the whole East End of London was lit up as if morning had come early.

With all the available engines in East London already pumping water from the Thames at St. Katherine's Docks, new appliances were sent from across the river, from Southwark, Lambeth and even as far afield as Wandsworth and Peckham. London had seen nothing like it since the Great Fire in 1666 and would see nothing like it again until the Blitz 52 years later.

It took all night to get the fires under control and the engines were still pumping foul-smelling river water to damp down the smouldering ruins of the warehouse the following afternoon[80]. Fortunately there had been no loss of life and, much to the disappointment of the spectators, the brandy did not explode. In the early hours people started to drift back to their homes to catch some sleep in what remained of the night for a working day would dawn within a few hours.

To this day the coincidence of two such conflagrations starting so close to each other and within four hours has not been explained. Arson is the obvious conclusion but little effort seems to have been made by the authorities at the time to follow this up. That is, perhaps, understandable, because within a few hours the police of H Division had other things on their minds, an event that relegated reports of the fires to positions of lesser importance in the local and national newspapers the following day. Few people apparently, either at the time or since, made any serious connection between the fires and what was to follow.

Yet if a man, for his own particular purposes, wished to clear the streets of as many observers and policemen as possible, what better way than to cause two simultaneous diversions on such a spectacular scale? It is also worth remembering that personality disorder and schizoid tendencies are frequently associated with fire-setting[81].

A little after 3.40am on that Friday morning a woman's body was found in Bucks Row, Whitechapel, about a mile north of the fires. The Row, which has since been re-named Durward Street, consisted of a terrace of labourers' cottages facing warehouses and a coal yard across a narrow cobbled street. The body was half on, half off the pavement when it was spotted by Charlie Cross, who was taking a short cut on his way to work. At first he thought the dark shape was a tarpaulin that had fallen from a passing wagon. Being a carman for Pickfords, he knew the value of a tarp and crossed the street to take a closer look.

As he drew near he saw that it was a woman and his initial presumption was that she was drunk – a not uncommon state of affairs in the streets around Whitechapel in the early hours of the morning – but as he got closer he saw that her skirt was lifted exposing her upper thighs. As he stooped to take a closer look he heard another man hurrying by on the other side of the street. He called him over and together they tried to ascertain whether she was dead, as Cross assumed. The other man, one Robert Paul, thought that he detected a slight movement of the chest, indicating that she might still be breathing but 'very little if she is'[82].

They were both anxious not to be late for work so they decided to continue on their way and tell the first policeman that they encountered. Cross paused for a moment to pull her skirt down in an effort to restore a little dignity to the woman who they both instinctively recognised as one of the area's unfortunates.

There were very few policemen around because of the fires and they had to walk nearly half a mile to Hanbury Street before they met PC Jonas Mizen. They told him what they had found and he set off at once in the direction of Bucks Row. By the time he arrived, two other policemen had also found the body. They quickly established that the woman was recently dead and only just beginning to cool, but whether any of them noticed at that stage that her throat had been cut is in some doubt. One of them went to fetch the nearest police surgeon, Dr. Rees Llewellyn, who lived a few hundred yards away at 152 Whitechapel Road. Police surgeons were not employed full-time by the police but were (and still, for the most part are) local general practitioners appointed to act for the police as and when necessary. In 1888 few of them had any forensic training or experience.

Dr. Llewellyn arrived within minutes of being summoned. He confirmed death and that the woman's throat had been cut but made no further detailed examination. He was struck by the relatively small amount of blood that had spilled into the gutter, 'About a wine glass and a half' he later recalled in evidence[83]. He ordered that the body be taken to the parish mortuary at the Whitechapel workhouse in Old Montague Street, where he would examine it later, and at about 5am the dead woman was removed on a police hand cart.

It was only when the two mortuary attendants, themselves elderly residents of the workhouse, undressed the body and prepared it for the police surgeon's arrival that they found to their profound shock that the woman's abdomen had been slit open in two long incisions, one in the midline and the other extending from the groin to the left flank. Through the longer of the two, glistening coils of intestines were spilling out. They quickly summoned the superintendent who wasted no time in sending for Llewellyn immediately.

The inquest on the body found in Bucks Row was opened the following day, Saturday 1st September 1888, at the Working Lads' Institute in Whitechapel Road only a few hundred yards from the scene of the murder[84]. The coroner, Mr. Wynne Edwin Baxter, who had recently returned from his Norwegian holiday, sat facing the room beneath a gilt-framed portrait of Princess Alexandra. Baxter was a big man in every way and his broad shoulders and huge walrus moustache made him unmistakeable. To his right sat the expert witnesses and the clerk of the court and to his left the ranks of the all-male jury, women not being permitted to sit on juries until 1919. Facing the coroner were two rows of chairs reserved for the press and behind them sat the relatively few members of the general public that were allowed admission[85].

By the time the inquest opened the stamps of the Lambeth workhouse on some of her grey underwear had helped to identify the woman found in Bucks Row as Mary Ann Nichols. Mary Ann, or Polly as she was generally known,

88

was typical of the unfortunates who had reached that position in life through drink. She had been born Mary Ann Walker in 1845, the daughter of a locksmith. After marriage to William Nichols, a Fleet Street printer, she had five children but had begun drinking heavily even before the birth of the youngest in 1877. In 1880 they separated with William having custody of the children and, until he was able to prove that Polly was living as a prostitute, paying her a small allowance.

From then until 1888 she lived a life punctuated by spells in and out of various London workhouses and casual wards and sleeping rough in Trafalgar Square[86]. In the summer of 1888, in a last despairing attempt to rescue a daughter that he loved despite everything, her father found her work as a servant to a religious, teetotal couple in Wandsworth. At first it looked as if it might work and she wrote a touchingly enthusiastic letter to him asking for news of her children, but a few days later she stole some clothes from her employers and headed for the nearest pawnbrokers. By the end of August she was living in a low grade doss house in the notorious (and inappropriately named) Flower and Dean Street, Spitalfields[87]. On the night of 30th August she didn't have the four pence needed to secure her bed for the night so she embarked into the darkness to earn it, joking to the warden, 'I'll soon get my doss money – see what a jolly bonnet I've got now!'

After evidence of identification and the finding of the body had been heard, Dr. Llewellyn gave a detailed account of his post-mortem examination although, apparently in collusion with the coroner, he omitted to give a full account of the abdominal wounds, in particular not mentioning the protrusion of the bowels. As the full details had already appeared in many of that morning's newspapers, it seems unnecessarily fastidious. It was not a course of action that Baxter would take at the next inquest. Nor did Dr. Llewellyn comment in his report that a ring appeared to have been removed from one of Polly's fingers although, apparently, the fact was noticed by several other people. In light of what was to follow it may have been a significant omission.

The shocking details of Polly Nichols's death stunned most of those present in court and ensured that the news of the fires was relegated to second place in newspapers around the world the next day. The absence of any signs of a struggle, and the fact that in a narrow street of labourers' cottages where people were asleep no-one had heard anything, seemed strange and sinister. It was almost as if a malign, supernatural presence had been lurking in the shadows of Bucks Row and the people of the East End shivered and locked their doors and windows even more securely that night.

CHAPTER TEN

Annie

On Monday 3rd September the inquest on Polly Nichols was adjourned for two weeks to allow the police to make further investigations and for Dr. Llewellyn, the less than competent police surgeon, to make another and fuller post-mortem examination. In particular the coroner had asked him to discover whether any of Polly's internal organs were missing, a detail that had apparently not occurred to him during the first autopsy. But on 8th September, before it had resumed, another murder took place in the backyard of 29 Hanbury Street, less than half a mile from the Working Lads' Institute, and Coroner Baxter was obliged to open a second inquest.

Number 29 Hanbury Street was a one of a long terrace of dilapidated houses that had long since outlived their purpose but were still used as overcrowded slum dwellings by the wretched inhabitants of Spitalfields. Originally they had been the houses of prosperous Huguenot silk weavers but the growth of the silk mills of Cheshire, coupled with repeal of the duty on imported French silk in 1860, spelled the end of the hand-woven silk industry in East London. By 1888 most of the weavers' houses were unfit for human habitation yet were still homes to hundreds of people. In September 1888 number 29 – a house that was suitable for maybe six people to occupy comfortably – housed 17, including Mrs. Harriet Hardiman and her 16-year-old son, who both lived in a noisome room on the ground floor which they also used for cutting up and selling cat meat. Several other families each occupied a single room in the three-storey building and, in common with most other houses in the street, the front door was never locked to allow them to come and go as they pleased.

The new victim was another unfortunate called Annie Chapman. She was 47 years old and, like Polly Nichols, alcoholic and of very short stature. Her body was found within an hour of her death by an elderly lodger, John Davis, coming down the steps from the back door of number 29 to use the privy at the end of the yard. The body lay just to the left of the steps, between them and the paling fence that divided the yard from that of the next door house. This time there was no chance of missing the finer points of the crime. Annie lay sprawled on her back, her head very obviously all but severed from her body and her entrails draped up over her right shoulder like a macabre necklace.

In a highly agitated state Davis ran out into Hanbury Street and blurted out the terrible news to the first men that he came across before rushing onwards to Commercial Street police station to summon help. Within minutes the police were on the scene and a crowd had begun to gather in the street outside. Unlike that of Polly Nichols, a very full post-mortem examination was carried out by Dr. George Bagster Phillips – the senior and highly experienced police surgeon to H Division – both in the yard before the body was moved and later in the Old Montague Street mortuary.

Davis had found the body just before 6am and a little over an hour before, when it was just becoming light, John Richardson, the landlady's son, had sat on the steps to trim a piece of loose leather from the sole of his boot. He was certain that Annie's body had not been there at that time. Albert Cadosch, a 28-year-old Frenchman who lodged next door at number 27, had been in the backyard a little after 5.30am. He had heard voices from the next yard and then something heavy falling against the 6ft fence, but he did not attempt to look over it as he was already late for work. It seems certain that Annie met her death between 5.30am and 6am when it was fully light and many people were up and about. The murderer it seemed had taken Annie through the hallway of 29, the front and back doors of which were never locked, had carried out his execution and then made his escape without anyone having seen or heard anything unusual. For the second time in little over a week the mysterious killer had struck, carried out his dreadful mutilations and disappeared in the space of just a few minutes.

When the news became known of what was by now the fourth murder of an unfortunate in the area in five months, public concern began to rise nationally as well as locally. When the inquest opened on Monday 10th September, there was little enough space in the improvised courtroom for the coroner, his officers, the court officials, the jury and the witnesses, let alone the public and representatives of the press. Crowds built up on the pavement of Whitechapel Road soon after the doors opened, as people of all ages and classes jostled and pushed each other, hoping to gain admittance. After the shocking revelations of the last case, everyone wanted to hear for themselves the evidence of the police surgeon. They were to be disappointed, however, because the coroner's officer, Mr. Banks, had instructed the police not to allow members of the public access to the building[88].

A contemporary drawing of the scene at Annie Chapman's inquest still exists[89]. It was done by a courtroom artist working for the *Pictorial News* and is undoubtedly an accurate depiction of the scene. Such artists were employed much as they are today – to record scenes in courtrooms in which, then as now, photography was not allowed. Combining it with the detailed descriptions of the event, which appeared in the local papers the following Saturday, it is possible to account for most of the people in the picture. Coroner Baxter sits on the far side of a heavy, leather-skivered table beneath the portrait of Princess Alexandra after whom the room was named. Always an imposing figure with his black walrus moustache, on that day he wore a white waistcoat, crimson silk tie and check trousers[90]. To his left, facing the end of the table, sat the jury of 18 men. Immediately to his right was Dr. George Bagster Phillips, the senior police surgeon to H Division, and at the end of the table, facing the jury, were the two representatives of the police. According to the *East London Advertiser* these were Inspector Abberline and Inspector Helson, although the *East London Observer* says that Inspector Joseph Chandler, the police officer from Commercial Street police station who took charge of the scene of the crime in the yard of 29 Hanbury Street, was there rather than Abberline.

The Real Mary Kelly

Frederick George Abberline is one of the best-known figures in the Ripper story, having played a role in almost every dramatic portrayal – in fact and fiction – of the events of 1888. He joined the Metropolitan Police in 1863 at the age of 20 and was a high flyer from the start[91]. He was promoted to sergeant within two years and soon transferred to the newly formed detective branch later to be known as the Criminal Investigation Department or CID. He was stationed in Whitechapel at Leman Street police station for 14 years before being transferred in 1887 to Scotland Yard. With his knowledge of the area and the local villains, when the killings of 1888 started he was a natural choice to be sent back to be put in charge of the investigations on the ground. He was later commended for his discreet handling of the notorious Cleveland Street homosexual brothel scandal that erupted in 1889 and which was one of the causes of Queen Victoria's grandson, Prince Albert Victor, figuring in so many of the later conspiracy theories surrounding the Ripper saga. With the possible exception of Abberline's predecessor, Jack Whicher, probably no other factual detective of the Victorian era is better known[92].

Neither of the men in the picture however looks much like contemporary drawings of Abberline, of whom no known photographs exist. Abberline had mutton chop whiskers which connected with a neatly trimmed moustache, whereas the figure in the *Pictorial News* illustration has no moustache and is wearing a monocle in his right eye. The other, bearded, figure, who is presumably meant to be Helson, is partly obscured by Mrs. Amelia Palmer (mistakenly called Farmer in the picture), a fellow resident of the Dorset Street doss house from which Annie Chapman had sallied forth for the last time in the early hours of Saturday morning. She is standing at the table facing the coroner as she gives evidence of identification. Next to her, seated at the table with his back to the viewer, is a bearded man who is probably Mr. Banks, the coroner's officer.

But it is one of the remaining figures in the picture who is perhaps the most interesting. Three men are seated at a table in the foreground, their backs to the artist. They are gentlemen of the press. There were about 20 or 30 reporters present in the court that day according to accounts in the newspapers, contrasting with the two or three that had attended Martha Tabram's inquest only a month earlier. The three that are visible are seated in the front row and only the middle

Another portrait of 'Mrs Barrett'. Sickert depicts her as an older woman – perhaps Elizabeth as she might have been had she lived? (© *Tate, London 2015*)

Dorset Street, Spitalfields. A photograph taken a few years after the events of 1888, but looking very much as it would have done then. (© *Evans Skinner Crime Archive*)

The backyard of 29 Hanbury Street. Annie Chapman's body was discovered between the steps from the back door and the fence. (© *Evans Skinner Crime Archive*)

The scene at the inquest on Annie Chapman on 12th September as captured by the artist from the *Pictorial News*. The reporter in the centre of the three on the press desk in the foreground may be Francis Craig. Compare him with the portrait of his father on the next page.
(© *Evans Skinner Crime Archive*)

E. T. CRAIG,

Educationalist and Social Reformer.

A BIOGRAPHICAL SKETCH

WITH

PHRENOLOGICAL DELINEATION.

[*Reprinted from the* PHRENOLOGICAL MAGAZINE *for February,* 1883.]

PRICE ONE PENNY.

LONDON: L. N. FOWLER,
PHRENOLOGICAL AND GENERAL PUBLISHER,
IMPERIAL BUILDINGS, LUDGATE CIRCUS, E.C.

The "Phrenological Magazine," Monthly, price 6d.

E.T. Craig, Francis's father from the title page of one of his books. Whilst there are many portraits of his more famous father, there are none known of Francis except for the possible drawing of him at the inquest of Annie Chapman. (© *Public domain*)

Inspector Frederick George Abberline. There are no known photographs of the famous detective but many, widely differing, drawings. (© *Evans Skinner Crime Archive*)

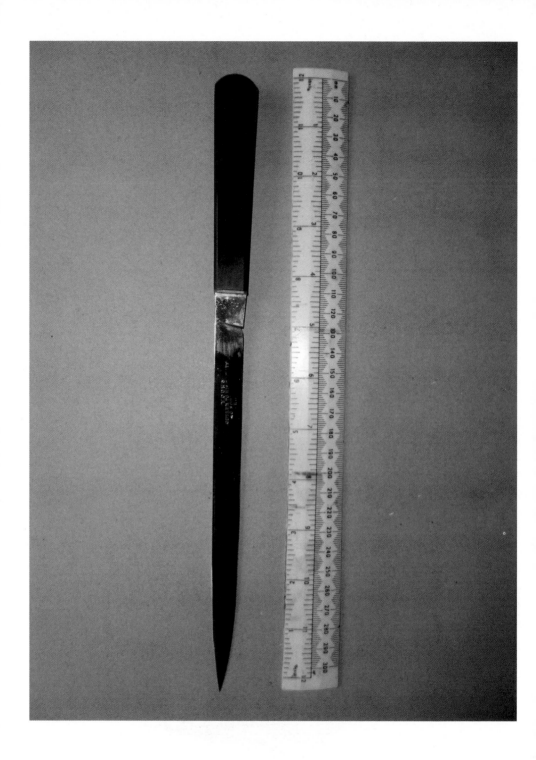

A Liston amputation knife c. 1880 with a smooth ebony handle and a narrow 7-inch blade. It was a weapon of this type that Dr Bagster Phillips said was used to kill and dissect Annie Chapman and the other victims. (© *Wynne Weston-Davies*)

pet theories materially impeded the police and led to a closed-mind attitude to certain lines of investigation. He was a larger than life character, both physically and in the breadth of his interests and activities. A solicitor, born into a prosperous printing family in Lewes, Sussex, of which he was later to become mayor, he had a career as a coroner that lasted more than 40 years. As well as East Middlesex, it included Sussex, the City of London and the Tower of London, the latter no sinecure because he later presided over the inquests of 11 German spies executed there during the First World War. He played a large part in the civic affairs of London and Lewes, was a prominent Freemason, an antiquarian, a microscopist and a notable authority on Milton.

Baxter did not like dissent or room for doubt in his court. When he finally retired in 1920 he is said to have boasted, 'Thirty thousand inquests and not one exhumation.' When Coroner Baxter committed a body for burial they stayed buried. *it*

It was not until late on Thursday 13th September, the third day of the inquest, that the police surgeon Phillips was finally called. When he rose to give his evidence, only one person present in the expectant courtroom could have known that the Ripper himself was amongst the audience who craned forward to catch his every word. Phillips was a quietly impressive figure –54 years old and with nearly 30 years' experience as a police surgeon he was undoubtedly the most expert of the various doctors directly involved in the Ripper murders – yet his evidence was always understated, never seeking to make a flashy point or to divert any attention onto himself. In fact many of the important points that he made were probably lost on his audience precisely because they were so low key. A contemporary described him as, 'Ultra old-fashioned both in his personal appearance and in his dress … His manners were charming: he was immensely popular with the police and the public, and he was highly skilled.'

However much Phillips would have liked to de-sensationalise his evidence, the facts made it impossible. The court was hushed as Phillips quietly read from his notes:

'The left arm was across the left breast, and the legs were drawn
up, the feet resting on the ground, and the knees turned outwards.
The face was swollen and turned on the right side, and the tongue

protruded between the front teeth, but not beyond the lips; it was much swollen. The small intestines and other portions were lying on the right side of the body on the ground above the right shoulder, but attached. There was a large quantity of blood, with a part of the stomach above the left shoulder. The throat was dissevered deeply. I noticed that the incision of the skin was jagged, and reached right round the neck.

'Having received instructions soon after two o'clock on Saturday afternoon, I went to the labour-yard of the Whitechapel Union for the purpose of further examining the body and making the usual post-mortem investigation[94]. The body had been attended to since its removal to the mortuary, and probably partially washed. I noticed a bruise over the right temple. There was a bruise under the clavicle, and there were two distinct bruises, each the size of a man's thumb, on the fore part of the chest. The stiffness of the limbs was then well-marked. The finger nails were turgid. There was an old scar of long standing on the left of the frontal bone. On the left side the stiffness was more noticeable, and especially in the fingers, which were partly closed. There was an abrasion over the bend of the first joint of the ring finger, and there were distinct markings of a ring or rings – probably the latter[95].'

Once again there was reference to one or more rings having been removed. Phillips also mentioned that, in searching the yard he had found a small piece of coarse muslin, a small-tooth comb, and a pocket-comb in a paper case together with 'various other articles' lying by the fence as if they had been carefully arranged. It was not the last time that this almost obsessional little detail of the murderer's behaviour was noticed, but no-one appears to have attached any particular significance to it at the time.

He then went on to give an account of an examination of the victim's brain and the deep cuts which had almost severed the head from the body before hesitating. He had obviously come to what, for him, was a difficult moment. 'There are various other mutilations of the body, but I am of opinion that they occurred subsequently to the death of the woman and to the large escape of blood from the neck,' he said, adding in a voice close to desperation, 'I am entirely in your hands, Sir, but is it necessary that I should describe the further mutilations? From what I have [already] said I can state the cause of death.'

Baxter disagreed: 'The object of the inquiry is not only to ascertain the cause of death, but the means by which it occurred. Any mutilation which took place afterwards may suggest the character of the man who did it. Possibly you can give us the conclusions to which you have come respecting the instrument used.'

The doctor was clearly upset with the turn events were taking. 'You don't wish for details. I think if it is possible to escape the details it would be advisable. The cause of death is visible from injuries I have described.'

'Supposing any one is charged with the offence,' argued Baxter, 'they would have to come out then, and it might be a matter of comment that the same evidence was not given at the inquest.'

'I am entirely in your hands,' murmured the unhappy Phillips.

The coroner agreed to postpone the point for the moment and asked Phillips to give his opinion as to the cause of death. No doubt relieved, even temporarily, the doctor continued, 'From these appearances I am of opinion that the breathing was interfered with previous to death, and that death arose from syncope, or failure of the heart's action, in consequence of the loss of blood caused by the severance of the throat.' In response to a question regarding the instrument used and whether it was the same as the one used to cause the abdominal wounds the doctor said, 'Very probably. It must have been a very sharp knife, probably with a thin, narrow blade, and at least six to eight inches in length, and perhaps longer.' He was giving a description of a very particular sort of knife and the coroner asked whether it was the sort of instrument that a medical man might use for a post-mortem. Phillips replied, 'The ordinary post-mortem case perhaps does not contain such a weapon.' In this he was totally accurate but also, perhaps deliberately, misleading.

What he had described was a long-bladed amputation knife and, since amputations are not part of an ordinary post-mortem, the cases of instruments in use at the time for that purpose did not contain them. He knew that but the coroner, who was not medical, did not. Had he been asked whether the knife was the sort of instrument that a medical man might use for an operation, he would have had to agree. He went on to dismiss the possibilities that it could have been an instrument used by a military man, such as a bayonet or a knife used by someone in the leather trade. He conceded that it could possibly have been a knife used by a slaughter man but only if 'well ground down,' in other words if the blade had been made narrower. As a physician and surgeon of 30 years standing Phillips surely knew exactly what sort of knife had been used, but why he chose not to volunteer the information can only be guessed at.

The next question that Baxter asked was one of the most important in the whole enquiry. 'Was there any anatomical knowledge displayed?'

Phillips's considered reply was critical. 'I think there was. There were indications of it. My own impression is that that anatomical knowledge was only less displayed or indicated in consequence of haste. The person evidently was hindered from making a more complete dissection in consequence of the haste.' The doctor had spotted several tell-tale clues including possibly the most important. He had used the words 'making a more complete dissection'. In other words he had recognised that the person who carried out the act was not merely seeking to kill and randomly mutilate but to explore the body in a rational, scientific way. Such a person, in his opinion, must have done it or witnessed it before and under more conventional circumstances.

Baxter pressed on: 'Was the whole of the body there?'

It was the moment Phillips had been dreading. He hesitated before replying, 'No; the absent portions being from the abdomen.'

The coroner asked whether the missing portions were such that it would have required anatomical knowledge to extract, to which the doctor answered, 'I think the mode in which they were extracted did show some anatomical knowledge.'

At that point, whilst the whole courtroom was at a state of almost unendurable expectancy, the coroner adjourned the inquest for a further week. When it reconvened on 8th October and the police surgeon was recalled to give evidence, it was immediately apparent that he and the coroner were on a collision course. Phillips was deeply unhappy about revealing any detailed account of the abdominal mutilations in open court. In that he was absolutely right by the conventions of the time. It was the job of the inquest to establish only the identity of the victim, the cause of death and to deliver an opinion as to whether that death was natural or unlawful. The details of what happened to the body after death had taken place were at that time no part of a coroner's brief. The reserved, old-fashioned doctor was fiercely opposed to allowing the spectators in court and, through the ranks of reporters, the wider public outside to be party to the distressing facts. A confrontation between the two men was inevitable.

Before asking him to give evidence, Baxter – clearly anticipating the other man's viewpoint – said, 'Whatever may be your opinion and objections, it appears to me necessary that all the evidence that you ascertained from the post-mortem examination should be on the records of the Court for various reasons, which I need not enumerate. However painful it may be, it is necessary in the interests of justice.'

Phillips replied, 'I have not had any notice of that. I should have been glad if notice had been given me, because I should have been better prepared to give the evidence; however, I will do my best.' After the coroner asked him if he would like to postpone his evidence Phillips continued:

'No. I will do my best. I still think that it is a very great pity to make this evidence public. Of course, I bow to your decision; but there are matters which have come to light now which show the wisdom of the course pursued on the last occasion, and I cannot help reiterating my regret that you have come to a different conclusion[96].'

'When I come to speak of the wounds on the lower part of the body I must again repeat my opinion that it is highly injudicious to make the results of my examination public. These details are fit only for yourself, Sir, and the jury, but to make them public would simply be disgusting.'

'We are here in the interests of justice and must have all the evidence before us,' said Baxter sententiously, adding, 'I see, however, that there are several ladies and boys in the room, and I think they might retire.' *The Daily Telegraph* recorded that two women and a number of newspaper messenger boys left the court at that point, the latter no doubt under extreme protest.

Phillips then threw down the gauntlet: 'In giving these details to the public I believe you are thwarting the ends of justice.'

It was an extraordinary accusation for an otherwise reserved professional man to make to a coroner in his own court and it indicates the extreme pressure that Phillips must have been feeling. It had no effect on Baxter, however, who replied: 'We are bound to take all the evidence in the case, and whether it be made public or not is a matter for the responsibility of the press,' displaying, like countless others after him, a touchingly misguided faith in the finer sentiments of the press when set against the sale of newspapers.

There was no contest and as if to settle the matter the foreman of the jury eagerly added that they too wished to hear the full account. The newspapers reported that several jurors joined in with, 'Hear, hear' at that point as if calling for an encore at the local music hall rather than hearing evidence in a court of law. After a few further exchanges Phillips made one final attempt to change the coroner's mind: 'I am of opinion that what I am about to describe took place after death, so that it could not affect the cause of death, which you are inquiring into.'

He was finally and humiliatingly crushed by Baxter saying, 'That is only your opinion, and might be repudiated by other medical opinion.' It was a calculated insult, meant to imply that Phillips's professional view that death had been caused by an incision that severed the neck to the depth of the vertebral column might actually be mistaken.

With remarkable restraint Phillips replied, 'Very well. I will give you the results of my post-mortem examination.'

In the event the account that followed was so unpleasant that most newspapers did not publish the details. Annie Chapman had been literally disembowelled. The perpetrator had opened the abdomen through a midline incision which bypassed the navel, leaving it on a small flap of skin and muscle. At that point the intestines had been freed from their attachments to the posterior abdominal wall and then strung out in a loop over Annie's right shoulder, no doubt to make it easier to access the pelvis for what came next. It was a manoeuvre that only a surgeon or someone with understanding of dissection of the body would have been familiar with[97]. Had the attachment – known as the root of the mesentery – not been divided, the intestines would have remained tethered in a slithery mass in the abdominal cavity, on top of and completely obscuring the deep recesses of the pelvis and its contents which were the main objects of the operator's attention. A non-medical person, even a butcher, might simply have cut through the bowels and removed them piecemeal, but in doing so a large quantity of liquid intestinal contents would have been released to drain into the pelvis, completely submerging its contents and befouling the operator in the process. By performing what is known as a surgical mobilisation of the intestines, the killer managed to avoid perforating the bowel, but this required considerable knowledge and skill as Phillips recognised.

What the murderer's objective was then became apparent. The police surgeon described in measured tones the excision of the victim's womb, ovaries and the upper third of the vagina in 'one sweep of the knife'. When questioned by the coroner as to how long such a procedure would have taken, he said:

'I think I can guide you by saying that I myself could not have performed all the injuries I saw on that woman, and effect them, even without a struggle, under a quarter of an hour[98]. If I had done it in a deliberate way, such as would fall to the duties of a surgeon, it would probably have taken me the best part of an hour. The whole inference seems to me that the operation was performed to enable the perpetrator to obtain possession of these parts of the body.'

It is an astonishing statement but almost certainly true. Even the detail about taking the upper third of the vagina displays a profound degree of anatomical knowledge. Had the operator sliced through the obvious place, the narrow waist between the uterus and the vagina, he would have left the cervix behind since it protrudes several centimetres into the vault of the vagina. No-one without a thorough knowledge of human anatomy could have known that.

The coroner asked what had happened to the organs and Phillips reluctantly confirmed that they were missing. For the first time the public became aware that the killer not only explored the anatomy of his victims, he also removed intact specimens in the same way that medical students often did for more detailed and leisurely examination in their lodgings. But still the police, the general public and perhaps Phillips himself were disinclined to believe that the culprit could be an aspiring or qualified member of the medical profession despite almost overwhelming evidence to the contrary.

Whitechapel was home to the London Hospital, one of the 12 great teaching hospitals of the capital and within easy walking distance of two more: Guy's and St. Bartholomew's. Medical students were ten a penny in the drinking haunts and music halls of the East End[99]. Phillips was adamant both in his written notes and his oral testimony. The killer had detailed anatomical knowledge and some elementary surgical skills but, in his opinion, was not a fully trained doctor. Although clearly reluctant to face the possibility that such a brutal man could be a qualified doctor, a medical student remained a distinct but unspoken possibility.

The coroner then revealed to the court that he had been contacted by one of the London medical schools to say that an American doctor had recently approached it offering to buy human uteruses for £20 each, a considerable sum of money at the time. Despite police investigations the would-be purchaser was never traced and eventually it was discounted as a red herring. Baxter, however, did not waste the opportunity to remind Phillips that had he not insisted on the revelation regarding the removal of the organ from Chapman's body being made in open court, the information regarding the American doctor would not have surfaced.

The two inquests continued in parallel until on 23rd September the jury at the inquest into Polly Nichols's death duly returned a verdict of wilful murder by person or persons unknown. Three days later Annie Chapman's jury did the same.

But if anyone thought that that was the end of the affair they were soon to be spectacularly disabused.

CHAPTER ELEVEN

Jack Introduces Himself

On 27th September, 19 days after the discovery of Annie Chapman's body in the backyard of 29 Hanbury Street and three days before the murders of two more unfortunates – Elizabeth Stride and Catherine Eddowes – on 30th September, a letter was received by the Central News agency. Central News was one of three main press agencies operating in London at the time, the others being Reuters and the Press Association. They did not themselves publish newspapers but gathered news via their own reporters or freelancers like Francis and then sold the stories on to other newspapers throughout Britain and around the world.

The letter had been posted the same day and bore a London EC postmark, which meant that it could have been posted within a few hundred yards of the Central News offices in Ludgate Circus and certainly no more than half a mile distant. The envelope was addressed in red ink to 'The Boss, Central News Office' and contained a letter that has since become the most notorious in the history of crime[100]. In the same handwriting as the envelope it read:

'Dear Boss,

I keep on hearing the police have caught me but they wont fix me just yet. I have laughed when they look so clever and talk about being on the right track. That joke about Leather Apron gave me real fits. I am down on whores and I shant quit ripping them till I do get buckled. Grand work the last job was. I gave the lady no time to squeal. How can they catch me now. I love my work and want to start again. You will soon hear of me with my funny little games. I saved some of the proper red stuff in a ginger beer bottle over the last job to write with but it went thick like glue and I cant use it. Red ink is fit enough I hope ha. ha. The next job I do I shall clip the ladys ears off and send to the police officers just for jolly wouldn't you. Keep this letter back till I do a bit more work, then give it out straight. My knife's so nice and sharp I want to get to work right away if I get a chance. Good Luck. Yours truly
Jack the Ripper

Dont mind me giving the trade name

PS Wasnt good enough to post this before I got all the red ink off my hands curse it No luck yet. They say I'm a doctor now. ha ha'

Despite the apparently sensational nature of the letter the editor, John Moore, to whom as 'The Boss' it had apparently been directed, did nothing about it for two days before asking one of his journalists, Tom Bulling, to forward it with a covering note to Chief Constable Adolphus 'Dolly' Williamson, head of the CID at Scotland Yard. Bulling's note read:

'The Editor presents his compliments to Mr Williamson & begs to inform him the enclosed was sent to the Central News two days ago, & was treated as a joke.'

The police did not treat it as a joke, at least not initially. It was immediately photographed and within a few days copies were circulated to police stations throughout the country as well as being released to the press, clearly in the hope that someone would recognise the handwriting. Unfortunately it was written in the standard educated copperplate of the time and no positive leads resulted. It was, however, entirely unlike the free scrawling handwriting of Bulling who has subsequently been credited with its authorship.

The text of the letter was published in *The Daily News* on 1st October. On the morning of the same day a plain postcard written in the same hand was delivered to Central News. It was postmarked 1st October and, like the letter, it too had been posted in London EC. Now known as the 'Saucy Jacky' postcard it read:

'I was not kidding Dear Old Boss when I gave you the tip youll hear about saucy Jacky's work tomorrow double event this time number one squealed a bit couldn't finish straight off. had not time to get ears for police thanks for keeping last letter back till I got to work again

Jack the Ripper.'

It was written in red crayon and smeared with what was intended to look like blood but was actually red ink. It included a couple of almost perfect thumb prints, unfortunately a few years too early to have been of use, for the Metropolitan Police did not adopt fingerprinting as a forensic tool until 1901 even though it had been in widespread use as a method of identifying individuals in British India and other parts of the world for nearly half a century before that. Had anyone thought to take thumb prints from the journalists at Central News it might at least have been a useful way of eliminating them as the author of the card.

With its clear reference to the 'double event' that took place a day earlier, the writer was clearly seeking to establish that he was the author of both missives as well as the murderer of all four women. There was a feature about the first 'Dear Boss' letter, the postcard and possibly two communications that followed it, one on 5th October and one eight years later, which may have been written by the same person, which was quickly noticed and commented upon. They contained words and expressions that originated in America and were not in common usage in Britain at the time. These included the words 'boss', 'quit' and 'fix me', expressions that are much more familiar to today's audience, used to films and television from across the Atlantic, than they were at the time. Many people, including the police, concluded that the writer was either American or had spent enough time there to absorb the local journalese.

There is in fact a distinctly journalistic flavour to both messages. The absence of sentence structure and apostrophes is typical of reporters at the time who tended to use this style when taking down speech verbatim in the interests of speed but would have restored the syntax when transcribing it later before submitting their copy to an editor. Unlike most of the letters that followed, there are no spelling mistakes in them, suggesting that the writer was a reasonably educated man.

At the time that the first 'Dear Boss' letter and the following postcard were received the police authorities were convinced that they had been written by the murderer even though they later changed their mind. The fact that it was considered worthwhile to disseminate it so widely shows how seriously the police took the communications at the time. It seems extraordinary therefore that no attempt was apparently made to trace journalists or reporters in the area who were either American or who had visited the country. It was presumably no secret to Francis's fellow hacks that he had spent time there some 20 years before.

It is of course entirely possible, indeed likely, that at some time Francis was interviewed by the police. By late October there was a concerted effort to trace and interview all single men living alone in the area, although it may not have extended quite as far as his lodgings in the Mile End Road which were about a mile from the epicentre of the murders. Unfortunately the records of exactly who was interviewed were not kept.

It has been suggested that the postcard was the work of a copycat seeking to cash in on the notoriety of the letter published in *The Daily News*, but it is difficult to see how that could have been the case. Although the text of the letter had been published, the facsimiles of both were not published until 4th October, so the author of the postcard, unless he had been particularly close to either the police or Central News, could not have been able to reproduce the handwriting so accurately without actually being the same person.

There was also the issue of whether the author of the postcard which introduced the words 'double event' into the folklore of the Ripper murders could have known about the crimes at the time that it was written unless he was also responsible for them. It was received at Central News on the morning of 1st October and was postmarked the same day although it could have been posted late the previous day, after the last collection, and lain in the box overnight. The bodies of the two women were discovered in the early hours of the previous day, 30th September, and the rumour mill had ensured that the news was widespread in the East End by the afternoon of that day, so it would have been perfectly possible for someone bent on mischief to have written and posted it by the following morning. What is much less likely is that an imposter would have known that Liz Stride 'squealed a bit' and her killer was unable to conduct his customary mutilations since those details did not become public until her inquest. There is also the fact that the writer said that his recipient would find out about the double murder 'tomorrow', suggesting that the postcard was written, even if not posted, on the 30th – the actual day of the murder – when even fewer of the residents of East London were in possession of the facts.

Publication of the letter and the postcard did, though, have one unfortunate effect. It unleashed a flood of other letters that continued for years afterwards. They were the first of hundreds of letters, postcards and telegrams sent to the police, to various newspapers, private individuals and to no-one in particular. Some reports say that there were more than a thousand but the total retained by the Metropolitan and city police and now in the National and the London Metropolitan Archives is 210. At first they were taken seriously by the police and the first letter and postcard sent to Central News are still considered to be amongst the most likely to have been written by the actual killer. As time went on and letters were received from all over the country and from other countries including the United States, France and Portugal, it became obvious that the vast majority of them were hoaxes or written by people with serious psychological issues. Only two writers were identified and prosecuted for wasting police time, both women.

The most immediate effect that the letter had was to put the name Jack the Ripper firmly into the language. It was a brilliant choice, whether invented by the actual killer or a hoaxer. It is instantly memorable and it quickly passed into general usage. It has the look and feel of something invented by a journalist or an advertising copywriter and it immediately linked the earlier killings with the ones that were to follow in the minds of the police and the general public. There have been many other serial killings before and since of much greater magnitude and – in some cases – of equal ferocity, but none have dwelled in the popular imagination as firmly as the Ripper murders.

Its origin is not hard to perceive; through much of the 19th century there had been numerous sightings of a mysterious character known as 'Spring Heeled Jack', a devil-like creature in human form clad in a long black cloak and spewing forth blue and white flames from his nose and mouth. He supposedly terrorised people, particularly adolescent girls, by jumping out at them in the darkness, scratching their flesh with steel talons and, for some reason, slapping their faces, before escaping in gigantic 10ft bounds.

The sightings took place mostly in London – although a few were reported from other places including Aldershot and Colchester – since jittery army sentries seemed to have a special propensity for spotting him, perhaps with a little assistance from their off-duty comrades[101]. They had commenced in Hammersmith and that borough remained a particular focus of reports for many years. Putting Jack together with the concept of ripping, no doubt taken from the 'High Rip' gangs that had terrorised prostitutes in the East End for some years and who were thought to be responsible for Emma Smith's terrible injuries, produced the perfect epithet. Whether it was the creation of the actual murderer or that of a journalist (or both), it was destined to become one of the best-known expressions in the English language.

There has been an enormous amount of debate as to whether this letter and the subsequent letter and postcard sent to Central News were genuinely written by the Ripper or were creations of one or more of Central News's own journalists to further its own business. This was the explanation eventually favoured by the police but there are a couple of facts against it. If Central News was seeking publicity why did it withhold the letter for two days when a greater impact might have been obtained by releasing it immediately? Secondly, since it was an agency rather than a newspaper, it is hard to see what advantage it would gain from such an exercise. It had no direct circulation to boost and passing the letter to the police rather than to its clients, the newspapers, would not seem to be potentially as commercially advantageous.

There is a small piece of verisimilitude in the letter that few people seem to have commented on. Probably not one person in a thousand, then or now, has ever tried to write with blood. Most people are unaware of the nature of blood that has been stored without an anticoagulant for a period of hours or days in a bottle, whether ginger beer or otherwise. What happens is that an initial, jelly-like clot forms and as this further solidifies, the serum separates from it. Serum is exactly like glue. It is rich in fibrin which gives it the same sticky consistency. It is probably not a detail that a person would invent unless he had actually tried writing with old blood. Many of the other hoaxers that came later wrote in red ink claiming that it was the blood of one of the victims when, patently, it was not. A journalist at Central News would surely have done the same and not inserted the detail about the ginger beer bottle.

George Robert Sims, the popular journalist and playwright whose name has been firmly associated with the Ripper saga for more than 120 years, made a very astute point in part of an article he wrote under the pen name 'Dagonet' in *The Referee* on 7th October 1888:

'The fact that the self-postcard-proclaimed assassin sent his imitation blood- besmeared communication to the Central News people opens up a wide field for theory. How many among you, my dear readers, would have hit upon the idea of "the Central News" as a receptacle for your confidence? You might have sent your joke to the Telegraph, the Times, any morning or any evening paper, but I will lay long odds that it would never have occurred to communicate with a Press agency.

Curious, is it not, that this maniac makes his communication to an agency which serves the entire Press? It is an idea which might occur to a Pressman perhaps; and even then it would probably only occur to someone connected with the editorial department of a newspaper, someone who knew what the Central News was, and the place it filled in the business of news supply. This proceeding on Jack's part betrays an inner knowledge of the newspaper world which is certainly surprising. Everything therefore points to the fact that the jokist is professionally connected with the Press. And if he is telling the truth and not fooling us, then we are brought face to face with the fact that the Whitechapel murders have been committed by a practical journalist – perhaps by a real live editor! Which is absurd, and at that I think I will leave it.'

There is an uncomfortable awkwardness about the abrupt ending which makes one wonder if Sims knew, or suspected, more than he was prepared to let on. He was not the only one who realised that the author of the letter and the post-card that followed it four days later was almost certainly a working journalist or reporter. Very few of the general public even knew of the existence of press agencies at that time and a hoaxer who was not a professional pressman would almost certainly have chosen to send a letter to one of the national newspapers or to the police. It is astonishing that, having correctly deduced that the writer is professionally connected with the press, Sims immediately dismisses the pos-sibility that he could also be the murderer.

There are other features of the letters that are worth noticing and which might tend to connect them to a particular type of man. There is a quirky, almost eccentric, humour to them, black though it is. The writer uses the expression 'ha ha' repeatedly to indicate that he has made a joke, even underlining it for further emphasis. It is typical of a person with a particular sort of personality disorder who finds it difficult to pick up visual cues and to read other people's reactions in face-to-face conversation.

If Francis did write them, the question is why? Most probably he wanted to clearly establish a link between the murders that would distract attention from his real objective, the killing of a particular victim. They enabled him to put for-ward an alternative motive, his dislike of prostitutes. Finally, they also provided him with an opportunity to trumpet his own prowess. For a man whose life might until then have been dogged by failure, they were a means of demonstrating to the world that he could single-handedly outwit the Metropolitan police and the powers that be.

The police did not have long to wait before the prophecies contained in the first letter came true. On 30th September, the day after Central News handed the letter over to Scotland Yard, the horror was elevated to a new level.

CHAPTER TWELVE

The Double Event

The murder of Elizabeth Stride in an entranceway off Berner Street was the only one of the five Ripper murders that was botched. On the face of it, it was not a good choice of site for such an enterprise, although Francis probably had a personal reason for choosing it. Berner Street was a short road that ran down from the bustling Commercial Road to Ellen Street. It was generally quite busy, with a number of small shops which stayed open until after midnight on most evenings. About halfway down on the right-hand side was a three-storey building that housed the International Working Men's Educational Club. To its left was the entrance to Dutfield's Yard, where a number of commercial enterprises had their premises. On the first floor of the building housing the club was a lecture hall with windows looking on to the yard and in which, on the night of 30th September, a political discussion for a large audience of mostly Polish and Russian Jews was taking place. When the serious part of the evening wound up at about midnight, a number of participants stayed behind to sing Russian songs.

Perhaps it was the sound of music, singing and laughter emanating from this building that made Francis decide that the narrow entrance to the yard, shielded from the street lights – which were in any case very sparse – was a good site for his next adventure. There was another possible reason: he was already familiar with the club. As well as Jewish anarchists, it was also frequently used for lectures by socialists. Only two days before Stride's murder William Morris had lectured there, as he had on many previous occasions and Francis – as both a family friend and a local reporter – was almost certainly present[102]. He may have made a note of the darkened alleyway and the yard beyond and realised that it would make a good venue for his purposes.

In this he miscalculated. Apart from the danger of being observed by any one of a number of people who were out and about in Berner Street despite the light drizzle, or the coming and going of members of the club, he had not apparently realised that the yard itself was in use day and night by traders and their horses. It was one of these – Louis Diemschutz, a market trader dealing in cheap jewellery and who was also the club steward – returning to the yard at about 1am to drop off his stock, who apparently disturbed the killer in the act. As the pony turned into the shadowy entrance, it shied away to the left and refused to move on.

Diemschutz dismounted and discovered Stride's body lying just inside the entrance against the right-hand wall. As it was soon established that death had taken place only minutes before and blood was still running over the cobbles from the wound in her neck, it now seems likely that her attacker had retreated into the darkness of the yard when he heard the approach of the pony and cart. If so, he was able to make his escape almost immediately as Diemschutz then rushed into the club to raise the alarm.

Within minutes Berner Street was thronged with people and two police surgeons, Dr. Frederick Blackwell and the ubiquitous George Bagster Phillips, were examining the body as it lay in the alleyway. Dozens of police were fanning out throughout the surrounding streets in the hope of apprehending anyone suspicious who seemed to be heading away from the area.

Elizabeth Stride, another unfortunate who had moved to England from her native Sweden 22 years previously had, like her two predecessors, died as the result of a wound to the throat inflicted by a sharp, narrow-bladed knife. Unlike them the initial incision had only partially severed the left carotid artery and not touched the vessels on the right of the neck. Death was not, as in their cases, almost instantaneous through syncope – the sudden stopping of the heartbeat – but instead was the result of blood loss from the partially severed artery. A large quantity of blood was found flowing away from the body in the direction of the drain in the yard, which indicates that the heart was beating for some time after the wound was inflicted. In addition, bruising on the face and chest suggested that she had put up some degree of resistance. It was almost certainly the arrival of Diemschutz's pony and cart that prevented Elizabeth Stride from suffering the same mutilations as the other victims. Had they arrived ten seconds earlier she may also have escaped with her life and have been able to give the only good description of the killer in history.

As it was, the murderer then demonstrated another example of his audacity and intelligence, not to mention a better understanding of the workings of the London police than most of its citizens possessed. London has not been a single city since the early Middle Ages. The historical City of London, roughly equivalent to Roman Londinium, covers a square mile within the boundary of the old city walls. To this day it is an autonomous and almost self-governing entity with its own police force and, officially, off-limits even to the sovereign without the express permission of the Lord Mayor. It is the financial heart of Britain and in 1888, just as today, relatively few people lived within its confines but flooded in by the hundred thousand to work there during the day. At night it was relatively unpopulated, the dark echoing canyons of thoroughfares like Bishopsgate, Poultry and Threadneedle Street silent except for the measured footsteps of policemen patrolling their beats.

Beyond the confines of the City, in what is generally called Greater London but which is in reality a conglomerate of hundreds of old towns and parishes such as Westminster, St. Marylebone, Whitechapel and Bow, a single police force, the Metropolitan Police, operates. The word London does not occur anywhere in their title or the description of their remit; instead it is charged with policing the Metropolis. The policing of London as such is the exclusive responsibility of the City of London Police and they guard the title jealously.

The City police force – both then and now – has its own Commissioner, appointed not by the government of the United Kingdom but by the Corporation of the City of London. Whilst there was no absolute rule that forbade a

Metropolitan policeman to enter City territory in the course of investigating a crime or in hot pursuit, it rarely happened and permission to do so was usually sought or, more commonly, the responsibility was passed from one force to the other. In the early hours of 30th September 1888, with Whitechapel in turmoil, the City of London was the one place that Francis knew would be a safe haven.

He must also have been sufficiently conversant with the local geography to know when he had passed from the Metropolis and into the City. Apart from the ceremonial entrance to the City at Temple Bar and boundary markers on some of the major roads, only subtle indicators tell a person whether they are within the purlieus of the City. The wrought iron lamp posts and the manhole covers carried, as they still do, a small shield with an embossed heraldic dragon – symbol of the City – but apart from that there was almost no way of knowing whether you were beyond the reaches of the Metropolitan police. Francis apparently knew, however, for he was only a hundred yards inside the City boundary when he encountered Catherine Eddowes and decided to make her his next victim.

Catherine, yet another unfortunate, but unlike her predecessors, thin and scrawny rather than well-built, had been released from protective custody less than 45 minutes earlier. She had been put in a cell in Bishopsgate police station by the City police, having been found entertaining a small crowd by giving a drunken imitation of a fire engine in Aldgate High Street some hours before. Having sobered up enough to falsely give her name as Mary Ann Kelly (and, in so doing, indicating how common an alias it was amongst the unfortunates), she had been released into the night, cheerily replying to the Gaoler, PC Hutt, when she was asked to close the door behind her, 'All right. Goodnight Old Cock.[103]' She appears to have wandered about for the next half an hour until she fetched up about half a mile south on the corner of Duke Street and Church Passage, one of the three entrances to Mitre Square. Somewhere along the way she had encountered a man.

Mitre Square was a small cobbled area, actually more triangular than square in shape, enclosed on three sides by the tall warehouses and offices of City companies including Kearley and Tonge, a large tea and provisions merchants[104]. On the south-west side there was vehicular access to the square from Mitre Street, and in the two opposite corners pedestrian passageways to Duke Street and

St. James's Place. It was a secluded spot which, like much of the area, would have been thronged during the day – with workers taking short cuts through the warren of city streets and vans and drays making deliveries to the warehouses – but which by night was almost deserted. The night watchman at Kearley and Tonge and the beat constable passing through every 15 minutes were almost the only nocturnal inhabitants of Mitre Square.

Three Jewish friends had left the Imperial Club in Duke Street at 1.35am and noticed a woman talking to a man on the corner of Church Passage. Only one of them, Joseph Lawende, apparently got a reasonable look at them. At the mortuary they later identified the woman as Catherine Eddowes from her clothing. Lawende described the man as being about 30, 5ft 7in tall (although *The Times* said 5ft 9in) with a fair moustache and wearing a loose fitting pepper and salt coloured jacket, a grey peaked cap and a red neckerchief. He thought that the man had the appearance of a sailor. After nothing but a fleeting glance they hurried on by. In that part of London, after the events of the past few weeks, even men in groups didn't linger in the streets in the early hours more than they had to.

Ten minutes later, at 1.45am, Constable Edward Watkins entered the square from Mitre Street in order to complete a circuit of it before leaving by the same route. The square was lit by only two gaslights, one at the entrance to Church Passage and the other on the western side towards the entrance to the alley leading to St. James's Place. The south-eastern corner was in deep shadow and in its furthermost recess PC Watkins made out an even darker shape. He turned up the light on his bullseye lantern and shone it into the corner.

Catherine Eddowes's body lay on its back, the three skirts and the grey petticoat that she was wearing pulled up, leaving her naked from the chest down. Her left leg lay straight in line with the body; the right was drawn up and bent at the knee. Dark blood was still trickling across the paving stones from a gaping wound in her neck, but what caused Watkins to recoil in horror was the jagged wound running from the ribcage to the pubic bone from which a loop of intestines had been pulled to be draped over her right shoulder. Some authors have ascribed Masonic significance to placing the intestines over the right shoulder in the cases of both Annie Chapman and Catherine Eddowes, but the truth is that the small bowel mesentery that the killer had divided runs obliquely from the lower right to the upper left of the posterior wall of the abdomen and so the right shoulder is the direction in which the small intestines most easily lie when mobilised[105]. Another piece of gut was lying free on the pavement between her body and left arm.

The ashen-faced policeman ran to Kearley and Tonge's warehouse on the opposite side of the square and shouted through the partially open door to alert the night watchman. 'For God's sake, mate, come to assist me … here's another woman cut up to pieces.' The watchman, George Morris, was himself an ex-copper and wasted no time in hurrying towards Aldgate to summon help. Watkins returned to guard the body, no doubt glancing into every darkened corner of the square and starting at every sound, real or imagined.

Within minutes there were policemen and doctors swarming around the body and the acting Commissioner of the City Police, Major Henry Smith, had been roused from his bed. The first medical man on the scene was George Sequeira, who had been called because he was known to be the nearest resident doctor to Mitre Square. He made no detailed examination of the body beyond confirming that, in the quaint wording of the time, 'life was extinct'. Within a few more minutes the City Police surgeon, Dr. Frederick Brown, arrived and carried out a more detailed examination. Whilst he was doing so one of the policemen called attention to several objects that had been placed, apparently deliberately, by the side of the body. These included a mustard tin containing two pawn tickets, a thimble and three shoe buttons. Once again it seems to be an indication that the killer had been looking for something but perhaps had been disturbed by the sound of PC Watkins's boots as he approached up Mitre Street. When Brown had completed his examination of the body at the scene he gave orders for its removal to the City mortuary in Golden Lane, where he later carried out one of the most detailed post-mortems of any of the five victims.

Later, when the body was undressed in the mortuary, a portion of the right ear lobe dropped out of the clothing. Many commentators have seized on this and linked it to the references to cutting the ears off and sending them to the police contained in both the original 'Dear Boss' letter and the postcard that followed. It seems more likely that this and at least some of the facial injuries that Catherine suffered were accidentally incurred in the semi-darkness as the killer held the long-bladed knife in one hand and frenetically explored her abdomen with the other.

But even as the body was being removed to the mortuary it appeared that the night's excitements were not yet over.

At 2.55am that morning, a little over an hour after the discovery of the body of Catherine Eddowes, Metropolitan Police Constable Alfred Long was patrolling down Goulston Street, Whitechapel, about quarter of a mile north-east of Mitre Square. The east side of the street was made up by the Wentworth Model Dwellings, public amenity housing that consisted of a single, long, five-storey apartment building with several communal staircases served by passages that opened directly on to the street. In one of these entrances he spotted a piece of cloth and as he went to investigate he saw a chalked message on the black painted wall immediately above it. He picked up the piece of cloth and found that it appeared to be saturated with a mixture of blood and faecal material. He blew his police whistle to summon help and when others arrived it was soon established that the cloth exactly matched a piece that had been cut, apparently with a sharp knife, from Catherine Eddowes's filthy apron.

It was an enormously important piece of evidence. It was assumed that the killer had used it to wipe his hands and, possibly, the knife after he made his escape from Mitre Square. Even more importantly, it was the first indication that the police had of the Ripper's direction of travel after completing his night's work. Goulston Street is about quarter of a mile east of Mitre Square and its southern end, near to where the piece of cloth was found, runs into the Whitechapel Road. It seems that the Ripper was heading for the Whitechapel Road and moving in a north-easterly direction. The police seem to have made little use of the information.

Successful serial killers are usually intelligent. It is now known they rarely live at the centre of their area of operations since simple geometry would make it too easy to track them down. Instead they tend to live at the periphery or even just outside it. It is also the case that the first killing in a series is usually closest to the killer's base. As confidence grows, so he ranges further afield[106]. Of course such statistical knowledge was not available to the Metropolitan police in 1888. Had it been so, they might have concentrated their house-to-house search along the axis of the main artery of the East End, the Whitechapel Road. An area between half a mile and a mile from Bucks Row and including a street or so either side of the Whitechapel or Mile End Road would have been a good place to look.

A potentially even more disastrous mistake was to do with the chalk message on the wall of the Wentworth Model Dwellings. It became known in Ripper mythology as the Goulston Street graffito. There is now no accurate representation of it. Two policemen – Detective Constable Daniel Halse of the City of London Police and PC Alfred Long of the Metropolitan Police, the man who had discovered the piece of apron and the writing on the wall – both wrote the words down in their notebooks. Unfortunately the two versions did not agree. Halse wrote, 'The Juwes are not the men that will be blamed for nothing.' Long had it as, 'The Juews are the men that will not be blamed for nothing.' Both versions contain a double negative but they are syntactically different. The first is a message of defiance suggesting that the Jews were ready to take a stand against false accusations. The second seems more accusatory in tone, implying that the Jews were trying to evade their responsibilities. Of course they may have had nothing to do with the Ripper murders but the close proximity of the piece of apron meant that few people, including the police, doubted that the two things were connected. Judging by the clear evidence that Halse gave at the inquest later, compared with Long's confused and hesitant testimony, it is likely that Halse's version is the more accurate.

Goulston Street was densely populated with immigrant Jews. If the Ripper wanted to foment anti-Jewish feeling, he could not have chosen a better place to do so. The police were already focusing their investigations on Jewish men and as a manoeuvre to throw them further off the scent it could hardly have been improved upon. More importantly it may have been another example of the murderer's handwriting and as such it could have been compared to the writing on the 'Dear Boss' letter. It should have been a breakthrough.

Major Henry Smith, the acting Commissioner of the Citypolice, was alerted to the discovery. He appreciated the importance of it immediately and ordered a police photographer to the scene to record the writing *in situ* even though, technically, Goulston Street was not within his jurisdiction. Unfortunately Sir Charles Warren, the Metropolitan Commissioner, arrived before the photographer. He was horrified. Throughout his brief police career he seems to have been haunted by the possibility of crowd violence getting out of control. The previous year he had been responsible for the vigorous suppression by 2,000 police and 400 troops of a Socialist and Irish Home Rule demonstration in Trafalgar Square which resulted in the deaths of three demonstrators. It became the first of three such notorious events in Anglo-Irish political history to be known as Bloody Sunday. Now, faced with such a potentially inflammatory slogan in the heart of a Jewish area at a time when the local population was in a state of near-hysteria, he made an astonishing decision. He ordered that it should be immediately scrubbed from the wall.

His subordinates and officers of the City Police pleaded with him in vain. It was pointed out that the entrance could be screened with a tarpaulin, extra men could be drafted in to keep spectators away. It was even suggested that the word Juwes could be erased to lessen the impact of the slogan. In fact, since it was written in words in which even the capital letters were only three quarters of an inch high, an observer would have had to be very close indeed to read it in the darkness of the entranceway[107].

It was to no avail. Warren was adamant, the graffito must go. A bucket of water and scrubbing brushes were sent for and, before anyone had thought to check the accuracy of the two policemen's notes, the words were expunged forever. This action by the most senior policeman in England was so extraordinary that many historians since have concluded that there must have been a darker reason for it and it has added further ammunition to the already considerable arsenal of the conspiracy theorists. His own reports seem to confirm that a genuine fear of crowd unrest, either by disgruntled Jews or by an anti-Semitic mob (or both), overrode basic police procedure and led to him making an over-hasty decision[108]. Whichever it was, it almost certainly sealed his fate, because in little over a week he had sent in his second resignation to Home Secretary Henry Matthews, and this time it was accepted.

The murder of two victims on the same night raised the whole affair to a new level. Where before there had been a certain prurient interest by the British middle classes in the murder of a series of unfortunates in a seamy part of London, there was now a worldwide focus on the case. There was general incredulity that a single individual seemed able to hoodwink the entire might of the Metropolitan Police, hitherto regarded as the finest and best-equipped force in the world. The Irish Troubles of recent years had resulted in the formation of the non-uniformed detective branch, later to become the Criminal Investigation Department and the model for similar forces around the world, yet even this seemed impotent to stop a single man from committing the most heinous of crimes right under its own nose.

The use of science in solving crime was just beginning. Photography, the chemical detection of blood stains, toxicological examination of stomach contents and tissue samples were all being employed in the investigation of crime and had already resulted in the conviction of such celebrated poisoners as Dr. Edward Pritchard and Mary Ann Cotton[109]. The problem for the police was that they had no-one to use the techniques on. Even when they had opportunities to use the most modern of technology such as photography they were squandered as the events in Goulston Street had shown.

CHAPTER THIRTEEN

From Hell

By 3rd October the 'Double Event' had become the main story in newspapers worldwide. Reporters booked passages to London from all parts of the globe and the telegraph wires were hot with syndicated stories sent out by the agencies. No-one doubted that the Ripper would strike again and soon. As the thirst for news became insatiable so, seemingly, did the Metropolitan police become more obdurate in their refusal to cooperate with the reporters. It became a war in which the world's press pilloried the police and in return the police refused to allow the reporters access to the murder sites or to view the bodies in the mortuaries. The comment in *The Boston Daily Globe* of 9th November was typical of many in newspapers both domestic and foreign:

> Accurate circumstances of the affair are difficult to discover. The police are as usual placing every obstacle in the way of the investigation of reporters …

The Real Mary Kelly

On the following day *The New York Sun* said:

> 'Each time a miserable creature belonging to the most degraded
> class of women is mutilated in an inconceivably horrible fashion;
> the murderer has disappeared; the police do nothing but observe
> secrecy – a secrecy easily melted with a half crown, by the way ...'

In general the City Police seem to have been better disposed towards the gentlemen of the press and, as a consequence (and probably deservedly), came in for far less criticism than the increasingly unpopular Sir Charles Warren and the Mets.

As well as the saturation of the East End by police drafted in from other divisions, all over London the local residents were by this time taking an active part in attempting to track down the Ripper. Several local vigilante groups sprung up, the best known of which, the Whitechapel Vigilance Committee, had been formed on 10th September. George Lusk, a local builder and restorer of music halls, was elected president[110]. He seems to have been a man of some self-importance and soon drew attention to himself by writing letters to the national newspapers. He then asked for police protection for himself and his family because he became convinced that his house in Mile End was being watched by a bearded stranger. If it was, the man was never apprehended or identified.

A little more than two weeks after the 'Double Event', at about 5pm on 16th October, Lusk received in the post a 3in square cardboard carton and a crudely written letter. The box contained half a human kidney. As with so many of the events of that autumn, Lusk's first reaction was that it was a hoax and that it was the kidney of a dog. Instead of handing the items to the police, immediately he put them into his desk drawer and it was not until two days later when he mentioned them to members of the Vigilance Committee that it was decided that they should seek another opinion. Accordingly it was taken to the surgery of a local general practitioner, Dr. Wiles. He was not there and his assistant Mr. F.S. Read looked at the specimen instead. He correctly identified it as a human kidney and advised that it should be taken to Dr. Thomas Openshaw, curator of the pathological museum at the London Hospital.

There are several versions of Openshaw's reaction. Some reports have him declaring that it was 'the ginny left kidney of a forty five year old woman' but other and probably more accurate reports give a much more considered and circumspect reply. Openshaw, as an experienced histopathologist, would have been well aware that it is totally impossible to tell from microscopic appearance the sex of a kidney, and the age could only be guessed at in the broadest of terms. Moreover, unlike the liver, alcohol – whether gin or otherwise – leaves no stigmata on the kidney.

He was, however, able to give several valuable pieces of information. Firstly, the kidney had been preserved in spirits of wine within a short time of being harvested. This was the medical term for rectified ethyl alcohol which was an unusual preservative for human tissues at the time. Most hospitals and dissecting rooms used formaldehyde for this purpose and this left a pungent and unmistakeable odour on anything with which it came into contact. Spirits of wine could, however, easily be purchased at any pharmacy and the term could even be used to mean any ethanol-based spirit, such as gin or brandy.

The second useful piece of information was that about an inch of the renal artery was still attached to the specimen. Since it was already known that two inches remained in Catherine Eddowes's body and the total length of an adult left renal artery is about three inches, this strengthened the possibility that her body could have been the source of the organ.

In order to try to confirm that the half kidney came from the murdered woman, the microscopic findings of Dr. Openshaw were compared to those of Dr. Brown, who had conducted the post-mortem on Catherine Eddowes. Brown had reported that the remaining right kidney had shown 'slight congestion of the bases of the pyramids'. Dr. Openshaw and Dr. Sedgwick Saunders – a pathologist employed by the City of London Police who had also examined the Lusk kidney – agreed that it showed early signs of Bright's disease. This expression is almost never used today since it is far too imprecise, but then it signified any type of kidney disease. Whether Brown's congestion and Openshaw and Saunders's signs of Bright's disease were the same is now debateable and, without the microscopic sections to compare, impossible to resolve.

The letter too has been subjected to microscopic analysis over the ensuing years. The crude handwriting looked nothing like the neat script of the 'Dear Boss' letters but since the wording appears to be a none-too-successful attempt to portray the author as illiterate and, possibly, Irish, it could have been a deliberate ruse. The letter read:

> 'From Hell
> Mr Lusk
> Sor
> I send you half the Kidne I took from one woman prasarved it for
> you tother piece I fried and ate it was very nise. I may send you the
> bloody knif that took it out if you only wate a whil longer
> Signed Catch me when you can
> Mishter Lusk'

Too many others have pointed out that the misspellings of 'knife' and 'while' are far from convincing, as well as the inconsistency of writing 'Mr' and 'Mishter' to require any further detailed analysis here. It is fairly clear that, whoever the author was, it was a deliberate attempt to make it appear to have come from a semi-literate and probably Irish source.

It seems unlikely that Francis was the author. If he wanted to make an impact and demonstrate his connection with the body in Mitre Square, he would surely not have waited two weeks to do so if the kidney was already in his possession. Nor is he likely to have introduced a new suspect in the form of a semi-literate Irishman into the field. He had already established a strong persona in the form of Jack and a new suspect could only weaken his objective of connecting the crimes and linking them to a single killer. It is more likely to have been the result of a prank by a student who had ready access to the dissecting room of his medical school, and comic Irishmen were popular fare in the music halls in which medical students tended to spend rather more of their time than in the lecture theatres.

The inquest on Elizabeth Stride was opened by Wynne Baxter at the Vestry Hall in Cable Street, St. GeorgeintheEast on Monday 1st October and that on

Catherine Eddowes by Mr. Samuel Langham, coroner for the City of London, at the coroner's court, Golden Lane on Thursday 4th October. Baxter opened his proceedings by saying that although the victim's name had been given on the inquest notice as Elizabeth Stride, there was some doubt in the matter and until official identification was complete it would be better to refer to her as an unknown woman. The reason for this uncertainty would soon become apparent.

The early witnesses, all men who had been present in the Working Men's Educational Club together with Louis Diemschutz, the discoverer of the body, gave evidence first. There was no disparity in their testimony and all were agreed that the death must have occurred within a few minutes of the pony and cart turning into the entrance to Dutfield's Yard shortly before 1am. They were also agreed that no-one had heard a sound from the yard during the relevant period. Three tenements occupied by Jewish families fronted on to the yard and the residents of these too had heard nothing. There had been a certain amount of noise from the clubroom, where a few people who had remained after the end of the political discussion were singing Russian songs, but it was generally agreed that had anyone cried out it would surely have been heard by someone.

Then there was a bizarre turn of events which made it clear why the initial identification of the body as being that of Elizabeth Stride was now in some doubt.

Mary Malcolm – the wife of a tailor who lived in Red Lion Square, Holborn – testified under oath that the murdered woman was her sister, Elizabeth Watts. *The Daily Telegraph* reported that she was deeply affected by the experience of giving evidence[111]. She had visited the mortuary three times and, despite initial doubts, she had finally been convinced that the body was that of her sister by the finding of a small black mark on her leg caused, so she said, by an adder bite in childhood. She too had been bitten by the same snake and she displayed her hand for Baxter's inspection. The coroner glanced at it and dismissed it as being 'nothing but a scar'. Mrs. Malcolm then went on to blacken her sister's name with a catalogue of her vices – including prostitution, alcoholism, admissions to lunatic asylums and feigning epilepsy in order to be absolved from her misdoings. For her own part she painted a picture of a dutiful and caring sister who had seen her errant sibling regularly twice a week and helped her out with small sums of money and cast off clothing.

Since a substantial number of other people had already identified the victim as Long Liz Stride this was surprising, but Mrs. Malcolm would not be budged despite cautions and prolonged questioning. The coroner, who obviously had access to the witness statements made to the police, asked her, 'Did you not have some special presentiment that this was your sister?'

Malcolm replied, 'Yes ... I was in bed, and about twenty minutes past one on Sunday morning I felt a pressure on my breast and heard three distinct kisses. It was that which made me afterwards suspect that the woman who had been murdered was my sister.' The coroner pointed out to the jury that he was allowing this 'evidence' to be heard only because of the doubt about the identity of the victim. It was a less than subtle way of telling the jury that he personally placed no store on the veracity of the witness. The down-to-earth Baxter clearly had no truck with psychic visitations and spectral kisses in the small hours of the night. In the event he was proved correct because when the inquest was resumed for what would be the last time on Tuesday 23rd October, the outraged sister – now called Mrs. Elizabeth Stokes – appeared and said that, far from turning up twice a week for a regular handout from her sister Mary, she had not seen her for years. The indignation she expressed regarding the blackening of her character by her own sister knew no bounds although, as the coroner's subsequent summing up showed, she was probably little different in character from the picture her sister had drawn. Whatever Mary Malcolm's motives were, or indeed whether she was genuinely mistaken, has never been determined because she disappeared from the scene and never subsequently spoke of the matter.

The police had interviewed many people in Berner Street and the surrounding area in the hope that someone may have seen Long Liz in the company of a man in the hours before she died. Several of these, including Mrs. Fanny Mortimer who lived opposite the International Working Men's Educational Club, gave initially negative reports but later their memories seemed to improve under the relentless interest of the reporters, invariably helped by small monetary incentives[112]. In the end the police authorities decided that only three accounts were consistent and reliable enough for the witnesses to give evidence at the inquest. These were the beat policeman PC William Smith who passed the couple in Berner Street about 30 minutes before the killing; William

Marshall, a workman in an indigo warehouse who was standing by the door of his house at 64 Berner Street for some time and noticed the couple as they walked past him at about 11.45pm; and James Brown, a dockside labourer who passed a couple on the corner of Fairclough Street – where he lived – and Berner Street as he went to a local shop to buy something for his supper at about 12.45am.

They were all certain that the woman was Elizabeth Stride, who they each individually identified in the mortuary. PC Smith observed that she was wearing a flower on her coat when he saw her but the other two were not sure. All three said that the man was about 5ft 7in in height, Marshall thought that he was 'rather stout' and 'middle aged' whilst Brown put his age at about 28. All described him as wearing a black or dark coat, Smith and Brown describing it as 'cutaway' and Marshall as 'long'. Brown was not sure whether or not he was wearing a hat, Smith said that he had on a dark felt deerstalker hat and Marshall that he wore a round hat with a peak, adding, 'It was something like what a sailor would wear.'

Marshall gave perhaps the best description and, under a certain amount of pressure from the coroner, agreed that the man he had seen was of a clerical type, 'I should say he was in business, and did nothing like hard work.' He was decently dressed and mildly spoken with an educated accent. As the couple strolled past him with the man's arm around her shoulder he heard him say, 'You would say anything but your prayers.' Brown did not hear him speak as he passed them on the corner of Fairclough Street where the man was standing leaning on a wall with one hand, but heard the woman say, 'Not tonight but some other night.'

It is of course impossible to say whether all three witnesses saw the same man over the course of an hour although it is reasonably certain – since Elizabeth Stride had a striking Scandinavian beauty not easily forgotten – that it was the same woman. However, as the coroner pointed out, the descriptions of the man are sufficiently alike, taking into account the variations that occur within any group of witnesses to the same events that it probably was. The noteworthy thing that all three were agreed on was that he was clean-shaven. In 1888 that was unusual for a man. Surveys of group and crowd photographs of the time show that fewer than 20 per cent of men did not sport either a beard or a moustache; indeed it was compulsory that all men in the army and the police wore moustaches, as group photographs of the police and the army at the time show. In the army it was not until 1916, when the need for men outweighed sartorial considerations, that this rule was dropped. Francis, assuming the man in the Chapman inquest picture is him, belonged to the clean-shaven minority of men at the time.

There is a discrepancy in age between Marshall who thought he was middle aged and Brown who put him as 28, but by his own admission, Brown only got a fleeting glance in a poorly lit section of the street. How easy it is for a witness to be mistaken about age can be seen from the evidence that Louis Diemschutz gave after identifying the body of Elizabeth Stride in the mortuary. After a careful look in, presumably, good lighting he put her age at 28. She was in fact 45. Importantly, the descriptions match the one given by Mrs. Long, who almost certainly saw the Ripper outside 29 Hanbury Street talking to Annie Chapman. On that occasion he was wearing a billycock hat but on the night of 29th September he was wearing either a hat with a small peak or a deerstalker. Both hats are soft enough to have been carried in a pocket or stuffed inside his coat so the possibility also exists that he may have alternated between the two.

Marshall, Smith and Brown were not the only people who claimed to have seen Long Liz and her putative killer that night. Mrs. Fanny Mortimer, the housewife living almost opposite the club, originally told the police that she had heard and seen nothing, but later – when interviewed by various newspapers including the *Evening News* – she gave a much more lurid account of the evening's events. 'I was just going to bed Sir when I heard someone cry out "Come out quick; there's a poor woman here that's had ten inches of cold steel in her."' A few minutes later she was amongst the small crowd who gathered in the narrow entrance to the yard to stare at the body huddled by the wall and the trail of blood still congealing in the gutter through the cobblestones. 'Then I see a sight that turned me all sick and cold. There was the murdered woman a-lying on her side, with her throat cut across till her head seemed to be hanging by a bit of skin. Her legs was drawn up under her, and her head and the upper part of her body was soaked in blood. She was dressed in black as if she was in mourning for somebody.' It was just the sort of stuff that the reporters wanted to hear and they were prepared to pay well for it. It is also so inaccurate as makes it unlikely that Fanny Mortimer had been near enough to see the body at all. Of all the victims, Liz Stride had the smallest neck wound and, at that stage, it was partially covered by her scarf.

She also mentioned a young man she had seen hurrying along Berner Street a few minutes before the murder carrying 'a shiny black bag'. The young man in question – Leon Goldstein – came forward as soon as he heard about the account in the newspapers and proved to be a commercial traveller in cigarettes, dummy packets of which he carried in his bag. Another of her sightings, which she did not apparently mention to the police, was that of a couple, 'A young man and his sweetheart were standing at the corner of the street about twenty yards away, before and after the time the woman must have been murdered, but they told me they did not hear a sound.'

The most celebrated of the apparent sightings was that made by Israel Schwartz, a Hungarian Jew, who was hurrying down Berner Street on his way home. Schwartz did not speak good English and he gave his evidence at Leman Street police station through an interpreter. He described seeing a man pulling a woman out of the entrance of Dutfield's Yard at about 12.45am and throwing her down on the pavement. The woman, who, like Stride, was dressed in black, cried out three times, 'but not very loudly'. At that moment the man called out 'Lipski' to another man smoking a pipe on the opposite side of the street. This alarmed Schwartz since Lipski had become a well-known anti-Semitic term of abuse in the locality since the poisoning of Miriam Angel by Israel Lipski in a house in an adjoining street the previous year[113]. Schwartz apparently took to his heels and was pursued for some distance down Berner Street by the pipe smoker before the latter broke off the chase.

This evidence would seem on the face of it to be the most critical of all since it appeared to implicate at least one other person in the murder. The newspapers reported it with varying details the following day; in one account the pursuer was wielding a knife rather than a pipe and in another the assailant pulled the woman back into the alleyway after throwing her to the ground. For some reason Schwartz was not called to give evidence at the inquest. This may have had something to do with the difficulties in giving evidence through an interpreter but is more likely to be because – since no-one else had reported the incident – the police decided that Israel Schwartz should join Fanny Mortimer and later Matthew Packer, as an unreliable witness.

Finally, with the problems of identification over and the facts surrounding the finding of Elizabeth Stride's body established, the court was able to turn its attention to the medical evidence. The first doctor to testify was Dr. Frederick Blackwell, the nearest police surgeon to Berner Street. When he had arrived at about 1.16am the body was still warm to the touch. He gave a graphic description of the placid expression on the face of the deceased, an expression which is still apparent in the mortuary photographs. He also mentioned the check silk scarf wound around the neck and tied in a bow on the left side. The incision, he said, commenced 2in below the angle of the jaw on the left, just below the scarf which showed signs of having been cut by the knife along its lower edge. The great vessels on the left of the neck had been partially severed and it was from these that the considerable stream of blood which stretched along the gutter to a drain near the back door of the club had been flowing. The cut continued across the neck, completely dividing the windpipe, and terminated an inch below the angle of the jaw on the right but without damaging the major vessels on that side. A juror asked whether there would have been any possibility of the victim crying out after the incision was made and received Dr. Blackwell's categorical assurance that there would not.

The grim mood of the court was interrupted for a while by the testimony of Michael Kidney, a dock labourer with the doleful expression of a bloodhound, with whom Stride had been cohabiting intermittently for the previous three years. After giving evidence that supported the identification of the victim, Kidney launched into an attack on the police who, he claimed, could have caught the culprit if they had accepted his offer of help. He had presented himself at Leman Street police station on the previous Monday in, even by his own admission, an intoxicated state and asked to be given the services of 'a strange young detective'. This prompted a certain amount of merriment in court which turned to outright laughter when, in answer to a further question from a juror as to whether he had any specific information, he replied, 'I am a great lover of discipline, Sir.'

When it became apparent that Kidney had no more useful information to give, the coroner dismissed him and soon it was the turn of George Bagster Phillips, the doyen of the various police surgeons associated with the Ripper murders. He gave evidence of having been called to Dutfield's Yard at 1.20am on the morning of Sunday 30th October and arriving at the scene some time after Dr. Blackwell. He confirmed all the details concerning the position and state of the body and also referred to the small packet of cachous that had been found clutched in Elizabeth's left hand. Later in his evidence a juror asked whether it might not have been expected that a victim of such a violent assault would have dropped the packet at once. The reply that he received, 'That is an inference that the jury would be perfectly entitled to draw', is absolutely typical of such a considered and meticulous witness as Phillips.

A detailed account of the post-mortem examination then commenced. Phillips, who as the senior police surgeon to H Division was in charge, reported with his customary manners that, 'Dr. Blackwell and I made a post-mortem examination, Dr. Blackwell kindly consenting to make the dissection, and I took the following note:

> "Rigor mortis still firmly marked. Mud on face and left side of the head. Matted on the hair and left side. We removed the clothes. We found the body fairly nourished. Over both shoulders, especially the right, from the front aspect under collar bones and in front of chest there is a bluish discolouration which I have watched and seen on two occasions since. On neck, from left to right, there is a clean cut incision six inches in length; incision commencing two and a half inches in a straight line below the angle of the jaw. Three-quarters of an inch over undivided muscle, then becoming deeper, about an inch dividing sheath and the vessels, ascending a little, and then grazing the muscle outside the cartilages on the left side of the neck. The carotid artery on the left side and the other vessels contained in the sheath were all cut through, save the posterior portion of the carotid, to a line about 1/12 of an inch in extent, which prevented the separation of the upper and lower

135

portion of the artery. The cut through the tissues on the right
side of the cartilages is more superficial, and tails off to about
two inches below the right angle of the jaw. It is evident that the
haemorrhage which produced death was caused through the partial
severance of the left carotid artery."

He was making an important point but one which may have been lost on the
jurors. Arteries such as the carotid have a thick muscular wall. When they are
completely divided the muscle contracts and often closes the lumen of the vessel so tightly as to completely staunch the blood flow. If, however, as in this case,
there is even the smallest part of the vessel wall not divided, this contraction
cannot fully shut the vessel down and vigorous arterial haemorrhage continues.
This undoubtedly accounts for the massive blood loss observed in the case of
Elizabeth Stride compared with the other victims, where the carotid arteries
were completely divided and blood loss was surprisingly small as a consequence.
Whether any of the jurors or even the coroner appreciated this point is doubtful
but it is evident that this is what Phillips meant by saying that the haemorrhage
was due to *partial* severance of the left carotid artery.

The coroner asked whether there was any possibility that the wound could
have been self-inflicted. Apart from the obvious point that no weapon had been
found anywhere near the body, the question elicited another important observation from Phillips: 'I have seen several self-inflicted wounds more extensive
than this one, but then they have not usually involved the carotid artery. In this
case, as in some others, there seems to have been some knowledge where to
cut the throat to cause a fatal result.' It is another important pointer to the fact
that the most experienced of all the police surgeons believed that the murderer,
assuming it to be the same man in each case, possessed anatomical knowledge.

The rest of Phillips's testimony, although meticulous and detailed, was unremarkable until he was asked by a juror whether any part of the roof of the
mouth was missing since Michael Kidney had said that Elizabeth had suffered
from such a deformity. This obviously took both doctors by surprise and Phillips
replied that such a thing had not been noticed. The coroner asked them to make
a further examination of the body with particular emphasis on this point and

the inquest was adjourned until the following week. When it resumed Phillips confirmed that the hard and soft palates of the victim were perfectly sound. He also confirmed that stains found on one of the two handkerchiefs that Elizabeth had been carrying were probably fruit stains but apart from that no trace of grapes or their stalks were found anywhere near the body. He gave his opinion with an authority that put the matter beyond doubt. 'I am,' he said, 'convinced that the deceased had not swallowed either the skin or seed of a grape within many hours of her death.'

This was an important piece of evidence because Matthew Packer, a fruiterer with a shop in Berner Street, somewhat belatedly remembered selling a bunch of black grapes to a man accompanied by a woman resembling Elizabeth about two hours before the murder. These grapes have featured prominently in the mythology of the Ripper. They first surfaced in a report in *The Times* on the day after the murder when it was claimed that some grapes were found tightly clasped in the right hand of the dead woman, and subsequent writers have repeated this statement. None of the policemen or the three doctors that saw *Who* the body *in situ* mentioned anything about grapes although all had seen the small packet of cachous clutched in her left hand. Several witnesses, however – including Louis Diemschutz, Mrs. Mortimer and Isaacs Kozebrodsky – told various newspapers that they had seen grapes in Elizabeth's right hand. Dr. Phillips, when questioned by the coroner about the blood staining to the right hand, said that he could not account for it but, 'There were small oblong clots on the back of the hand.' Is it possible that in the poor light in the alleyway, these were mistaken for black grapes by the witnesses?

Stephen Knight, in *Jack the Ripper: The Final Solution*, confidently put forward the theory that Dr. Gull and his Masonic accomplices, including the artist Walter Sickert, while riding around the East End in a coach on the lookout for Mary Kelly and her co-conspirators, spent the time injecting grapes with cyanide or some other noxious substance in order to drug the victims and more easily carry out the mutilations before dumping the bodies at pre-arranged locations. The fact that Gull was on public record in writing saying that he preferred raisins or grapes to alcohol as a restorative no doubt added fuel to this hypothesis. A late self-portrait of Walter Sickert, *Lazarus Breaks his Fast*, shows the artist eating a bowl of what appear to be prunes with a spoon. Since Sickert is known to have been fond of prunes for breakfast this seems a much more reasonable proposition than supposing them to be grapes, as Knight does in order to suggest that the picture was the artist's way of alluding to his part in the murder of Stride. Even a man as notably eccentric as Sickert is unlikely to have eaten grapes with a spoon unless they formed part of a fruit salad.

Despite the alleged finding of a grape stalk in the drain of Dutfield's Yard by a pair of dubious private detectives who apparently never showed it to anyone else, it is likely that Packer – having read the account in *The Times* of the grapes in Stride's right hand, which was also repeated by some other newspapers – conveniently remembered selling grapes to an unknown woman. He had a brief few days of glory, including being interviewed at Scotland Yard by the Assistant Commissioner, Alexander Carmichael Bruce, as well as by the *Daily Telegraph* and the *Evening News* – for which, no doubt, he received some recompense. In the end, however, his story was so full of inconsistencies and changes that everyone, including the police, decided that he was not a reliable witness and he was not asked to give evidence at the inquest. On the balance of probabilities it seems that grapes played no significant part in the death of Elizabeth Stride.

Another small mystery concerning Elizabeth Stride was that she told various people, including Michael Kidney, that she had nine children, two of whom drowned with her English husband in the *Princess Alice* disaster on 3rd September 1878. The *Princess Alice* was a paddle steamer returning from an excursion to Gravesend loaded with holidaymakers when it was in collision with a collier going downstream on a following tide. Six hundred and fifty people, including many children, were lost, the tragedy being compounded by the fact that it took place close to one of the main outfalls of the London sewers which was at the time in the process of discharging effluent into the river.

Elizabeth, who had arrived in England in 1866, married John Thomas Stride, a ship's carpenter, in 1869 at St. Giles in the Fields. The couple feature in both the 1871 and 1881 census and in neither is there any sign of children. John Stride actually died in the Poplar and Stepney Sick Asylum in 1884 from heart failure. It seems likely that the couple never had children and that Elizabeth's story was an attempt to gain sympathy and, possibly, compensation although there is no record that she ever officially claimed relief from the *Princess Alice* Fund.

Wynne Baxter commenced his summing up on Tuesday 23rd October and it took several hours. He spent some time on the initial problems of identification which had been greatly exacerbated by Mary Malcolm's insistence that the victim was her sister. It had been at times, he said, reminiscent of *The Comedy of Errors* since there were actually many similarities between Elizabeth Stride and Mrs. Malcolm's sister. He accepted that the woman seen by Marshall, Brown and PC Smith were one and the same and that she was Elizabeth Stride, otherwise known as Long Liz. He left the matter of whether the man seen with her was the same on each occasion open although he suggested that honest differences in recollection of the same person seen briefly by three different witnesses could account for the apparent disparities in the descriptions. One puzzling thing was the parcel wrapped in newspaper, 18in long by 6 to 8in wide, which Smith was certain that the suspect had been carrying but which was not seen by either of the others. Baxter conceded that it was of course perfectly probable that a woman of Stride's occupation might have been in the company of more than one man in the space of an hour. On balance though it seemed to be his opinion that it was the same man and that that man was the murderer. It took the jury no more than a few minutes to return the only verdict possible under the circumstances: Wilful Murder by Person or Persons Unknown.

CHAPTER FOURTEEN

The Pressure Mounts

Catherine Eddowes was identified within a few hours. Like all unfortunates she was well known around the pubs and doss houses of Spitalfields and the pawn ticket found in an old Colman's mustard tin proved to be for a pair of good new boots that had been bought by her paramour John Kelly – a casual market labourer – in Canterbury, before they returned from hop picking a few days before. On their arrival penniless back in the capital he had allowed her to pawn them in order that they could pay for breakfast and then, it appears, a good deal of alcohol in addition, because there was nothing left of the half-crown that they had obtained for the boots by the time that Catherine ended up in Bishopsgate police station.

Kelly quickly came forward and identified the body in the Golden Lane mortuary as that of his partner. John and Catherine had shared not only their bed, when they had one, but much hardship and doubtless some good times during the seven years they had been together. It cannot have been a pleasant task for him to identify her. Catherine was the first victim in which facial mutilation had taken place. The tip of her small snub nose was missing as was the lobe of her right ear and there were a series of stab wounds to her face, some taking the form of apparent glyphs such as the letter V, that have caused some historians of the Ripper murders to ascribe mystical or Masonic significance to them. Others maintain that they were accidental, caused by the wild flailing of her assailant's knife in the darkness as he went about his work lower down the body. Most likely some of them at least were deliberate, a rehearsal for what was to follow, possibly to steel the murderer's nerves for what he knew he had to do next, as well as a way of providing more of a link between the different killings.

Catherine Eddowes had been born in Wolverhampton 46 years before but had moved with her family to London as a baby. After the death of her father the family was split up and Catherine spent much of her early life in the workhouse or being looked after by relatives in the Black Country. At about the age of 20 she took up with Thomas Conway, an army pensioner, and bore him three children although she and Conway were probably never formally married. The couple scratched a living by hawking cheap trinkets and pamphlets written by Conway in the streets of the East End, before eventually splitting up due to Catherine's drinking and Conway's periodic violence. Not long afterwards she met John Kelly and moved into his lodgings in the notorious Flower and Dean Street.

The inquest was opened by Mr. S.F. Langham, coroner for the City of London, at the Golden Lane mortuary on Thursday 4th October. It seems to have been conducted with a good deal more courtesy and goodwill than was the case with some of Coroner Baxter's confrontational hearings. Mr. Crawford, the solicitor representing the City Police, addressed the coroner at the start of the proceedings by stating that he was there to render the coroner and the jury 'every possible assistance'. He added, 'If, when the witnesses are giving evidence, I think it desirable to put any question, probably I will have the coroner's permission to do so?'

'By all means,' replied Mr. Langham affably.

The first witness who gave evidence of identification was Catherine's sister Eliza Gould, a widow who also lived in the stews of Spitalfields. She seems not to have been on particularly close terms with Catherine and was unsure about how long ago it was since she had last seen her. John Kelly then gave evidence of having lived with Catherine for the past seven years. Under questioning by Mr. Crawford and one of the jurors he painted a picture typical of the chaotic, dysfunctional lives lived by the unfortunates of Spitalfields and their indigent partners. There was an initial insistence that Catherine was a woman of sober habits who never behaved in an immoral way, but he later admitted that she occasionally 'walked the streets' when they were short of money, which appears to have been most of the time. The fact that she had spent the night in Bishopsgate police station sleeping off the effects of drink was apparently of such little surprise to him when he heard of it on the Saturday night that he didn't bother to inquire further but waited for her to turn up the next day, as she usually did. It was a world in which a man pawned the only pair of decent boots that he had in order to raise two shillings and sixpence – almost all of which was promptly spent on drink – and appeared totally unmoved by his partner having to sell herself to other men in the mean back alleys of Spitalfields in order to survive. Yet despite – or maybe because of – the unpromising milieu in which such people lived, they still managed to form bonds of real affection that bound couples like John and Catherine together for years at a time. It is striking that two other Ripper victims also had longstanding relationships with men to whom they were not married, Elizabeth Stride with Michael Kidney and Mary Jane Kelly with Joe Barnett.

Such couples frequently fell out, usually when 'in drink' to use the parlance of the time. On these occasions injuries were not uncommon. Walter Sickert, wondering at the relationship between the street prostitutes that he used as models and their consorts, wrote: 'Extraordinary lives. Men who live on them, now & again hitting them with 'ammers, putting poisonous powders on cakes, trying to cut their throats, drugging their whisky &c.' Whilst obviously greatly exaggerated for effect, he had a point. Bruises and the occasional black eye were a part of life for unfortunates but time and again they returned to their men for the companionship and protection that they afforded.

After John Kelly had finished his testimony, Frederick Wilkinson – the deputy of the lodging house in Flower and Dean Street which had been home to the couple for most of the previous seven years – gave evidence. He was particularly questioned about whether any strange man had taken a bed there between 1am and 2am in the morning on which the body had been found in Mitre Square. For some reason the police seemed convinced that when the killer left

Mitre Square he had headed north-east and taken a room in the very same doss house in which John Kelly was then asleep. Either that, or they suspected Kelly himself, although Wilkinson was convinced that he had not left the building after retiring to bed at about 10pm. After repeated questioning about who could have taken a bed in the early hours of the morning, he said that he could not remember but he might have made a note in his notebook, which he was duly sent back to the lodging house to fetch.

Frederick William Foster, the architect and surveyor who had produced accurate and highly detailed plans of Mitre Square and the surrounding area for the inquest, showed the jury the likely route taken by the murderer from Dutfield's Yard in Berner Street to Mitre Square, a distance of about three quarters of a mile. It would, said Mr. Foster, have taken from 12 to 15 minutes to walk it. He was then asked whether a man travelling on foot from Mitre Square to Flower and Dean Street would have passed through Goulston Street and replied that, although there was more than one possible route, that one would have been the most direct. In this he was correct but in fact a man taking that route would only have passed through the extreme northerly end of Goulston Street and the entry where the blood-stained piece of apron had been found was more towards the southern end. A man walking south down Goulston Street would have been heading back towards the Whitechapel Road.

When Wilkinson returned with his notebook he was unable to shed much light on who might have booked in between 1am and 2am and admitted that a doss house such as the one of which he was deputy housed upwards of a hundred people every night and his records did not include the names of any of them. He remembered that at emptying out time the next morning there were at least six men he did not recognise, but at what time any of them had arrived he could not say. With at least 50 doss houses in Flower and Dean Street alone and a similar density in the surrounding streets, the floating population of Spitalfields ran into many thousands every night, crammed into an area of less than half a square mile. It is little wonder that the police found the job of tracking individuals and identifying strangers completely beyond their capabilities.

It was now time for the medical evidence to be given, the part that most of the pressmen and, no doubt, their readers had been waiting for. This time there was no opposition by any of the police surgeons involved to making all the details known. Like Polly Nichols and Annie Chapman she too had been disembowelled through a long midline incision.

Dr. Brown gravely gave his evidence about the condition of the body when he first saw it on the pavement in Mitre Square: 'The abdomen was all exposed; the intestines were drawn out to a large extent and placed over the right shoulder; a piece of the intestines was quite detached from the body and placed between the left arm and the body.'

Mr. Crawford, the city solicitor, then intervened. 'By "placed", do you mean put there by design?'

'Yes,' said Dr. Brown.

'Would that also apply to the intestines that were over the right shoulder?' asked Crawford and again he received the affirmative. The section of intestine that had been cut out was almost certainly the descending colon, although it was not described as such at the time. In life it lies directly in front of the left kidney and the operator's intention in removing it was no doubt to give him better access to the organ which, it was later found, had been 'expertly removed by division of the renal artery'.

It would require very precise knowledge of human anatomy to know that and when the coroner subsequently asked Brown if anatomical knowledge had been shown in removing the kidney, he replied, 'It would require a great deal of knowledge as to its position to remove it. It is easily overlooked. It is covered by a membrane.' This is true, the membrane in question being the posterior peritoneum, and Dr. Brown's comment that it could be easily overlooked was meant to apply to the well-lit surroundings of the post-mortem room. A pavement in a dark corner of Mitre Square was quite another proposition.

The first doctor actually to arrive on the scene had been Dr. George Sequeira who, although not a police surgeon, was known by the police to be the nearest resident doctor. He was not called to give evidence until the second day of the inquest but when he did so it was in marked contrast to Dr. Brown's. He had not fully examined the body but pronounced life to be extinct and gave it as his opinion that Catherine had been dead for no more than 15 minutes. He then told the jury, 'I think that the murderer had no design on any particular organ of the body. He was not possessed of any great anatomical skill.' Some historians have used this statement to support their arguments that the Ripper was not a doctor or medical student. Dr. Sequeira however was 30 years old and had qualified with the LSA diploma, the lowest qualification that allowed a man to practise medicine, less than two years before. By contrast Dr. Brown was 45 and had at least 15 years' more experience than Dr. Sequeira. George Bagster Phillips, who conducted the post-mortem on Annie Chapman and oversaw those on Elizabeth Stride and Catherine Eddowes, was by far the most experienced surgeon involved in the Ripper murders. He was never in any doubt that they were dealing with someone with an excellent knowledge of anatomy if not an actual practising surgeon. Most surgeons and anatomists today would agree with him.

Brown continued his testimony. Having completed his examination of the body in Mitre Square and having found, once again, surprisingly little blood on the front of Catherine's clothing but a large quantity draining away along the pavement suggesting that she had been lying on the ground, presumably unconscious, before having her throat cut, he decided that it would be prudent to call Dr. George Bagster Phillips before having the body removed to the mortuary. This shows how much store his colleagues placed in Phillips and, since he now had more experience than anyone else in dealing with the results of the Ripper's activities, it was probably a wise decision.

The two doctors conducted the post-mortem at 2.30pm that afternoon. They noted the sun bronzing of her arms caused by her recent hop-picking expedition to Kent with John Kelly. Brown then described in remorseless detail the mutilations to Catherine's face which had brought a new level of horror to the killings, before moving on to describe the wounds to the neck.

> 'The throat was cut across to the extent of about 6 or 7 inches. The
> sterno-cleido-mastoid muscle was divided; the cricoid cartilage
> below the vocal chords was severed through the middle; the large
> vessels on the left side of the neck were severed to the bone, the
> knife marking the intervertebral cartilage. The sheath of the vessels
> on the right side was just open; the carotid artery had a pin-hole

opening; the internal jugular vein was open to the extent of an inch and a half – not divided. All the injuries were caused by some very sharp instrument, like a knife, and pointed. The cause of death was haemorrhage from the left common carotid artery. The death was immediate. The mutilations were inflicted after death.'

Once again it seemed that the weapon used had an extremely sharp, narrow, long blade with a pointed tip like a typical amputation knife. And again, revolting as the mutilations were, none of them were perpetrated before the victim *was* was dead. A sadistic, woman-hating killer is much more likely to inflict injuries whilst the object of his hatred is still conscious, but the Ripper apparently never did so. By the same token, a frenzied schizophrenic – his mind disintegrating into turmoil and confusion – would not have been capable of going about the killings and the subsequent dissections in the methodical, ordered way in which the Whitechapel murderer did. Inevitably it was the mutilations that captured the attention of the police rather than the killings themselves and perhaps that caused them not to look for a pattern or a motive but to assume, as they so often stated, that they were 'the work of a madman'.

The police surgeon then turned his attention to the abdominal wounds:

'The walls of the abdomen were laid open, from the breast downwards. The cut commenced opposite the ensiform cartilage, in the centre of the body. The incision went upwards, not penetrating the skin that was over the sternum; it then divided the ensiform cartilage, and being gristle we could tell how the knife had made the cut. It was held so that the point was towards the left side and the handle towards the right. The cut was made obliquely. The liver was stabbed as if by the point of a sharp knife. There was another incision in the liver, about two and a half inches, and below, the left lobe of the liver was slit through by a vertical cut. Two cuts were shown by a jag of the skin on the left side. The abdominal walls were divided vertically in the middle line to within a quarter of an inch of the navel; the cut then took a horizontal course for two and a half inches to the right side; it then divided the navel on the left side – round it – and then made an incision parallel to the former horizontal incision, leaving the navel on a tongue of skin. Attached to the navel was two and a half inches of the lower part of the rectus muscle of the left side of the abdomen. The incision then took an oblique course to the right. There was a stab of about an inch in the left groin, penetrating the skin in superficial fashion. Below that was a cut of 3in, going through all tissues, wounding the peritoneum to about the same extent.'

Two important points emerge from this part of Brown's evidence. Once again the Ripper had used a typical surgeon or pathologist's method of opening the abdomen, avoiding the umbilicus by directing the incision to the right of it and leaving it on a small flap of tissue. This is done because the umbilicus, or navel, is composed of very tough fibrous tissue which is exceedingly difficult to penetrate with a needle, making the job of sewing up the abdomen at the end of the operation or post-mortem difficult. By avoiding it – and for reasons lost in the mists of time it is always bypassed to the right – the operator saves himself this difficulty. There is no logic to this if the killer intended, as he obviously did, to leave the wound open. It would have been much easier, and quicker, simply to have continued the incision down the midline in a single sweep that bisected the navel. In taking a few extra seconds to bypass it, he was revealing the fact that he had either dissected the human body himself or had observed others doing so. It was not a manoeuvre that, for instance, a butcher or a slaughter man would have made.

The other point concerned the observation that Brown made regarding the position of the knife when the ensiform cartilage (which is an old-fashioned name for the structure that is now known to surgeons as the xiphisternum, or the lower end of the breastbone) was divided. It shows that the operator was positioned on the right side of the body. This is the side from which doctors worldwide are taught to examine the human body and from which the vast majority of open surgical operations on the abdomen are carried out. It may be a small point but again it seems to indicate that the Ripper was familiar with medical procedures.

As well as the missing left kidney, the womb had again been excised, although this time less expertly as it had been divided through its lower third, leaving the cervix behind. However, given that the entire operation was carried out between PC Watkins's first passing the spot on his beat at 1.30am and his return 15 minutes later, in the darkest corner of Mitre Square whilst kneeling on the paving stones, it was an astonishing feat. Few medical students or even surgeons, then or now, could emulate it, even if so inclined. Brown was asked if he thought that the murderer had been disturbed during the act and replied that he thought he had had adequate time to complete his task, the reason being, he said, was that the lower eyelids had been nicked. He clearly thought that this was deliberate and would not have been done if the operator had been under particular pressure of time. He was then asked why he thought the facial mutilations had taken place to which he replied, 'Simply to disfigure the corpse, I should think.'

At the end of the first day of the inquest the coroner announced that the Lord Mayor had put up a £500 reward for the discovery of the murderer. It was a sum worth the equivalent of £25,000 today and was widely welcomed, the more so because the Home Secretary and the civil authorities had steadfastly resisted offering any reward for the Ripper's capture until then, despite enormous pressure to do so from the press and the general public.

The inquest was then adjourned until Thursday of the following week. When it re-convened, Catherine's daughter Mrs. Annie Phillips was questioned about the possible whereabouts of her father and two brothers, whom the police had been unable to trace. Her father was supposedly Thomas Conway, the army pensioner with whom Catherine had taken up in her early life and whose initials 'T.C.' were tattooed on her forearm. Despite extensive police investigations, the police had been unable to trace him. Annie, who seemed to be indifferent to the fate of her family and did not even appear to be particularly put out by her mother's awful death, was of no further assistance to the proceedings and was soon dismissed.

The police and other residents of Mitre Square gave further evidence of the finding of the body; Lawende and his friends, who had encountered the mysterious pair at the entrance to Mitre Square, gave their evidence before the attention of the court was turned towards the vexed question of the Goulston Street graffito.

Constable Alfred Long of the Metropolitan Police took the brunt of it. He could not remember – under questioning by Mr. Crawford, the solicitor representing the City Police – whether he had written the word 'Jews' or 'Juwes' in his notebook, nor was he certain whether he had placed the word 'not' in the correct position. When he revealed that he had not even brought his notebook to court with him, Crawford asked the coroner to direct that he be sent back to his police station in Westminster to fetch it.

Whilst he was gone, Detective Constable Daniel Halse of the City Police gave his evidence of the finding of the Goulston Street graffito. Compared to Long's evidence it was a model of clarity and precision. He had no doubt whatever about the order of the words or the spelling of the word 'Juwes'. He described the height of the letters, the fact that they were written in a 'good schoolboy's round hand' and made the observation that the writing appeared to be fresh otherwise, as he pointed out, there would have been signs of rubbing caused by people passing by in the narrow passageway. In the absence of the writing itself, DC Halse's version is likely to be the most accurate to have come down to us.

He was questioned about the decision to erase the writing and said that he and others of his City Police colleagues that were present protested against it and asked that it should at least be left long enough for their commander – Acting City Commissioner Major Smith, who was already on his way from Mitre Square about five minutes' walk away – to see it. Even this request was refused and because Goulston Street was Metropolitan territory there was nothing that Halse could do about it other than to make as accurate a copy of the graffito as he could in his notebook. When his colleague Detective Hunt arrived the two men did something that the Metropolitan Police had failed to do. They visited every apartment in the Wentworth Model Dwellings and interviewed the inhabitants.

It was a point not lost on the jury. At the time that Halse and Hunt started their interviews, nearly two hours had elapsed since Long had first discovered the piece of apron and the chalk message on the wall. If they had been left by the murderer returning to his lodgings in the building, he would have had adequate time to clean himself up and conceal the weapon. At this point PC Long reappeared at the inquest with his notebook and was given an extremely hard drubbing by the coroner, the City solicitor and members of the jury. They repeatedly asked him why he had not searched the buildings and questioned the residents whilst the trail was still hot but Long, who it seems was allowed to be a scapegoat by his Metropolitan Police superiors, was able to do little more than mumble unhappily, 'I did what I thought was right under the circumstances.'

Crawford in particular praised the diligence of the City Police who were operating off their own territory and therefore under something of a handicap and, by implication, heaped opprobrium on the Mets who, it became increasingly obvious, had blundered at every step of the way. By the time the reports of the inquest were published in the next day's papers, the pressure on the Metropolitan Commissioner, Sir Charles Warren, was becoming nearly intolerable.

A curiosity of the Eddowes inquest was the verdict. The coroner, Samuel Langham, addressed the jury just before they withdrew to consider the verdict. Having first presumed that they would return a verdict of 'wilful murder by person or persons unknown', he then had a second thought and said that on reflection, perhaps it would be sufficient to return a verdict of wilful murder against some person unknown, inasmuch as the medical evidence conclusively demonstrated that only one person could be implicated[114]. The jury duly returned that verdict. It was the only one of the five Ripper verdicts in which the crime was positively ascribed to a single person. It is difficult to see how Langham reached that conclusion since, if the murderer had had an accomplice acting as a lookout for instance, it would have made it persons rather than person.

CHAPTER FIFTEEN

Hue and Cry

The day following the 'Double Event', the headless, limbless torso of a woman was found in a cellar of the very building in Whitehall that the Metropolitan police were themselves in the process of refurbishing as part of their new head-quarters. Shortly afterwards one of the missing arms was found floating in the Thames. The woman had been dead for a matter of weeks and the police moved quickly to distance the killing from the Whitechapel murders, but it did nothing to improve public confidence and it joined the growing catalogue of murders in 1888 that remain unsolved to the present day.

The newspapers were in uproar over the following days. There was a clamour for the resignation of Warren and Henry Matthews, the Home Secretary. Publication of the mocking 'Dear Boss' letter received by the Central News agency a few days preceding the 'Double Event' and the 'Saucy Jack' postcard on the following day did nothing to dampen the furore.

It was at about this time that the use of bloodhounds to track the murderer was suggested. Sir Charles Warren, desperate to try anything that would rescue his rapidly plummeting reputation, accordingly engaged Edwin Brough, a Yorkshire breeder of bloodhounds, to bring a couple to London for trials.

The news, when it hit the papers, provoked gales of ridicule. As many people rushed to point out, the chances of a dog being able to pick out and follow an individual scent in the teeming, crowded streets of East London was ludicrous. To be fair it was never Warren's intention to use them *in* under those circumstances but to reserve them in the event that another body was found in an isolated spot during the hours of darkness and to give them their head only if the streets were relatively deserted. To that end he gave orders that in future no body should be removed from the site of the crime until after he personally had been summoned and the dogs were present.

'Burgho' and 'Barnaby' duly arrived by train from Scarborough together with their owner and were quickly put through their paces in Regent's Park and Hyde Park under various weather conditions and at different times of day. Sir Charles himself insisted on being tracked and declared himself satisfied with the result. It was concluded that they worked well at night, particularly in frosty conditions. Overall their performance was judged satisfactory and Warren personally authorised their use in the event of another Ripper murder. Unfortunately the Home Office neglected to pay Brough or to settle the matter of insuring the valuable pedigree dogs whilst they were in police hands, and so after a few days he sent Burgho to Brighton to take part in a dog show and entrusted Barnaby to a friend whilst he returned home to Scarborough.

By this time there were many theories about the possible identity of the Ripper. The police had questioned hundreds of witnesses and innumerable theories were advanced in letters to the authorities and to newspapers by armchair detectives, medical men, ministers of religion and retired generals. Most assumed that it could only be the work of a madman, a devil incarnate, a criminal lunatic and this equated in many peoples' minds to a foreigner – amongst whom, although generally unspoken, the large immigrant Jewish population counted.

There were many alleged sightings of men seen with the four victims within minutes of their murders. The trouble was that no two really matched any one description. Ages ranged from the 20s to about 40, height from 5ft 3in to 5ft 9in. Some were described as of foreign appearance, some wore peaked sailors' hats, some were drunk, some were sober; there was no consensus. Possibly the three independent sightings of PC Smith, William Marshall and James

Brown before the murder of Elizabeth Stride were the most consistent but even they differed in several essentials.

There was however one other good sighting. On the morning of 8th September, when Annie Chapman was murdered in the backyard of 29 Hanbury Street, a Mrs. Long (some newspaper reports also seem to refer to her as Mrs. Darrell or Durrell although that may be a different person) was passing the house on her way to Spitalfields market. The time of the murder could be fixed with almost total certainty as having taken place between 5.30am and 5.45am when the body was found. Albert Cadosch, the Frenchman lodging next door, had heard something heavy fall against the board fence that separated the two yards a little after 5.30am and that something was almost certainly Annie's body.

Elizabeth Long was certain about the time because she remembered hearing the clock on Truman's brewery in Brick Lane strike the half hour as she turned into Hanbury Street[115]. She saw a man and a woman standing near the door of number 29 and she afterwards visited the mortuary and positively identified the body as being that of the woman she had seen. She also saw the man but did not get a good view of his face as he was turned away from her. 'I did not see the man's face,' she said, 'but I noticed that he was dark. He was wearing a brown low-crowned felt hat. I think he had on a dark coat, though I am not certain. By the look of him he seemed to me a man over forty years of age.' She went on to say that he looked 'foreign' but what she meant by that is not clear since, by her own admission, she did not see his face. 'Shabby-genteel' was her final summing up.

What she had described was a typical lower middle-class man in a clerical or non-manual occupation; in that part of London there were thousands who could have answered the description. The billycock hat, either black or brown, of the sort that would later generally be called a bowler, was described as a low-crowned hat to distinguish it from a high crowned or 'top hat' that was worn by men slightly higher up the social scale. In cold weather it was often worn with either an Inverness cape or an Ulster overcoat. It was Francis's usual get up[116].

The problem was it could also have been a perfect description of practically every middle-aged detective working on the case, as the many contemporary who photographs and drawings show. Perhaps that was part of the problem; the man that Mrs. Long described was too ordinary, too much like one of them. It was altogether too close to home and maybe that is why they preferred to concentrate on young 'foreign looking' men in sailors' garb. The idea that the Ripper might be a middle-aged man with a wife at home and a pair of carpet slippers warming in front of the fire was just too unbelievable.

Nevertheless, this remains perhaps the best description of the Ripper that exists. Mrs. Long gave her evidence firmly and confidently. She was a sober, respectable woman – not a man whose memory was blurred by alcohol as many of the other witnesses were – and she had been at precisely the right place at the right time. Most importantly it puts the age of the murderer perhaps ten years or more higher than other descriptions. Many other people writing about the events of that night have reported her as saying 'a man about forty years of age'. There is no doubt at all from the many newspaper reports of her evidence that what she actually said was 'a man over forty years of age'. It is a very important observation. What the detectives should have been looking for was a lower middle class, 50-year-old man living in Stepney, not a foreign-looking sailor in his 20s.

Indeed, in that respect, the police could have done worse than heed the advice of Queen Victoria herself, who was taking a very keen interest in affairs. She dictated a letter to the Home Secretary following the resignation of Sir Charles Warren on 9th November in which she advised a greater number of detectives in the streets at night, better street lighting and that special attention should be given to single men living alone[117]. The police had in fact already carried out an investigation of men living alone in lodgings in the immediate area with no positive result, one problem being that, without warrants to search individual premises, if permission was refused which was frequently the case, they had no option but to leave empty-handed. There is no evidence that the rest of her advice was acted upon and even her private secretary, Sir Henry Ponsonby, to whom she dictated the letter, wrote in a footnote: 'Perhaps these details might be omitted.'

On 5th October, three days after the unidentified woman's torso was found at Scotland Yard, a further letter was sent to the Metropolitan Police by

Tom Bulling at Central News. This time, curiously, he sent only the envelope and a transcript of the letter and the original, if indeed there was an original, has never surfaced.

Bulling's transcript read:

> 5th October 1888
> Dear Friend
> In the name of God hear me I swear I did not kill the female
> whose body was found at Whitehall. If she was an honest woman
> I will hunt down and destroy her murderer. If she was a whore
> God will bless the hand that slew her, for the women of Moab
> and Midian shall die and their blood shall mingle with the dust. I
> never harm any others or the Divine power that protects and helps
> me in my grand work would quit for ever. Do as I do and the light
> of glory shall shine upon you. I must get to work tomorrow treble
> event this time yes yes three must be ripped. Will send you a bit of
> face by post I promise this dear old Boss. The police now reckon
> my work a practical joke well well Jacky's a very practical joker ha
> ha ha keep this back till three are wiped out and you can show the
> cold meat.
> Yours truly
> Jack the Ripper

Although much less well known than its predecessors it is recognised as the third 'Dear Boss' letter even though, significantly, the author used a different salutation in this one and one that, importantly, is unique in the entire canon of Ripper letters. Bulling's reason for not sending the original to Chief Constable 'Dolly' Williamson can now only be guessed at. Some people, including apparently the police themselves, believe that there was no letter and, like the previous missives, the entire business was a put up job by Bulling himself. This theory was reinforced in their minds when, shortly afterwards, Bulling took to drink and was later fired by the managing director of Central News for sending a telegram announcing the death of Bismarck which stated bluntly

'Bloody Bismarck is dead.' Possibly he meant the epithet literally but Bulling was sacked nonetheless[118].

It is difficult to see why Bulling would have written the letters. The fact that the first one was held by Central News for two days before being handed to the police robbed it of its immediacy. No attempt was apparently made by the agency to pass any of the three communications to their clients, the world's press; that was done by the police themselves although undoubtedly Central News gained some publicity in the process.

The wording of the final letter connects it firmly to its predecessors. There is the same use of Americanisms such as 'quit', 'wiped out' and 'reckon'; the same slightly laboured attempts at humour and the use of 'ha ha' to emphasise that the author had made a joke in case the reader was in any doubt. One thing, however, marks the letter out as different – the desperate attempt to distance the writer from the Whitehall murder. If it had been written by Bulling or another journalist as a joke, or by someone else who falsely wanted to claim responsibility for the Ripper murders, surely claiming yet another victim would have added to the story. Denying any responsibility for it does not make sense. Only if the actual Ripper had written it and he wanted to ensure that only a particular group of murders and no others were ascribed to him does it add up. The pseudo-religious rant about the daughters of Moab and Midian was no doubt included to reinforce the connection between the killings and give them a shared motive. It also gave a common flavour to the crimes and, because of the Old Testament references, another link to the Jews.

So why did Bulling not pass the actual letter to the police? We do not know for certain that he did not. He may have passed on a transcript as a temporary measure whilst the original was being photographed, and it could later have been lost from the police files as so many of the other Ripper letters were. Maybe, realising that the police had no great interest in it and thought that it was a fake, he decided to keep it as a souvenir or for sale if it later turned out to be genuine. In any event it attracted much less attention from the police, the press and from subsequent historians of the Ripper murders than the earlier letter and postcard and yet, in some ways, if it is genuine, it is the nearest we get to the actual writer. It marks him out as a scholar and a literate man since

there is little artificial attempt to disguise this as there was in the previous communications. Whether the author was Bulling or Francis, the letters are almost
certainly by the same person that wrote the earlier 'Dear Boss' missives.   *who*

It is regrettable that the police did not take it seriously for several reasons.
The salutation 'Dear Friend' does not seem to have been used in any of the other
600 or more letters sent to the authorities or the world's press. It was a personal
idiosyncrasy of the writer and, since none of the others used it, it must be assumed, unusual at the time. It was, however, one that Francis is known to have
used on at least one other occasion as he addressed one of his three suicide notes
to 'Dear Friends'. Then there was the chillingly prophetic reference to sending 'a
bit of face' with his next letter. Surely at that point only Mary Jane's killer knew
the details of what lay ahead.

Finally there is the point that this was the last letter that this particular writer
sent to Central News. With, what only he knew to be, the last killing the letters
ceased. Bulling, his colleagues and the general public could only assume that
the murders would continue and, in fact, the vast majority of the hoax Ripper
letters were received after the murder of Mary Jane Kelly. Only the actual killer
knew that with her death the job was done; any further letters were pointless
and could only add to the risk of discovery. On balance it seems a fair assumption that one man was responsible for the 'Dear Boss' letters and that they were
written for a very definite purpose, that of reinforcing the link between the five
murders and making them appear to be the work of a maniac with no particular
animus against any one of the victims.

As the inquests on Stride and Eddowes drew to their close the population of
London, particularly those living in the East End, waited in anticipation. No-
one seemed in any doubt that the Ripper would strike again and the possibility
of the police apprehending him before he did so seemed to be diminishing by
the minute. They did not have long to wait. On the night of 8th November, the
eve of the Lord Mayor's Show, the drama reached its gruesome finale.

CHAPTER SIXTEEN

Oh Murder!

As the world held its breath and the damp October days gave way to an even wetter November, Francis prepared for the final act. He knew, although no-one else did, that to fit the established pattern of them being carried out a few days before or after a new moon, it had to take place between 30th October and 9thNovember[119]. The night of 8th and 9th November was the most propitious. It was the eve of the Lord Mayor's Show and from 4am onwards most of the City Police and their Metropolitan colleagues from the surrounding divisions – including H, the one in which Spitalfields lay – would be engaged in lining the route and controlling the crowds which some newspapers estimated (almost certainly overestimated) as numbering 3 million. The year of 1888 was the height of the Fenian troubles and the authorities in London were fearful that the terrorists would use the occasion to perpetrate a bomb outrage, perhaps even an assassination attempt on the Lord Mayor himself as an embodiment of the hated British occupation of their native land. He knew that only a bare minimum of officers would be left in Spitalfields in the early hours of that Friday morning[120].

By now Francis knew exactly where Elizabeth was living. He had kept watch and had seen her comings and goings. He knew her friends and her habits.

He knew that Joe Barnett had moved out of the room in Miller's Court and that had been an unexpected bonus. Even though, when he was working, Joe was usually in the markets in the early hours of the morning, there was always the chance that he might not be working on that particular night or might chance to pop back during his meal break. With him off the premises a major risk had been removed.

He was confident that Elizabeth did not know he had her under observation. If she had suspected as much she would certainly have disappeared again. There were probably a few anxious moments when he thought she may have caught a glimpse of him, passing on the other side of the street or across a crowded bar in the Ten Bells or the Britannia. Possibly she did feel a faint uneasiness, a premonition that she was being watched, and she apparently said as much to her friend Julia Venturney. But it was not enough to make her move out of her room in Miller's Court. She probably felt safe there. Although it was on the ground floor, the windows could be secured with catches and the door had a lock. Only she and Joe knew that it could be unlocked easily by slipping a hand through the broken pane of glass, moving the coat that served as a curtain aside and turning the knob on the inside. There were dozens of other people living in rooms within a few feet of hers and any attempt to break in would give her plenty of time to scream for help. The only way an unwelcome visitor could gain access to her bolt hole was if she let him in.

Much is known about the night of 8th November. At about 7.45pm Joe Barnett called in on Mary Jane and found her in the company of another woman. There is some doubt about who this was because both Maria Harvey, a washer-woman who gave evidence at the inquest, and Lizzie Allbrook, a 20-year-old friend of Mary Jane's, claimed to have been there when Joe arrived and to have left shortly afterwards. Maria Harvey said that she had left some dirty shirts, a child's petticoat, a man's overcoat and a woman's bonnet with Mary Jane; the shirts possibly for washing for which Mary Jane might have expected to make a few pennies.

Joe left soon after 8pm. Despite having split up with Mary Jane only eight days before on account of her habit of taking in other unfortunates for whom she felt pity, they were still on friendly terms and Joe was genuinely sorry that, as he was out of work again, he had no money to leave her.

Mary Ann Cox was another of the unfortunates who lived in Miller's Court. At about 11.45pm she was returning along Dorset Street to dry out and get a little warmth back into her bones as the night was wet and raw. She spotted Mary Jane 'very much intoxicated' a few steps in front of her as she turned into the passageway leading to the court. She was in the company of a short, stout man with a blotchy face and a full carroty moustache. He was dressed in a shabby overcoat and a billycock hat and carried a quart can of beer. He was presumably Mary Jane's next client of the night, although as she closed her door and said goodnight to Mary Cox she announced that she was going to sing. A few minutes later several people in the rooms off the court heard her sweet voice singing 'A Violet Plucked from Mother's Grave' and she continued singing for at least an hour until Mary Ann returned for a second time at 1am. It is doubtful that the man with the carroty moustache remained to hear her entire performance although no-one saw or heard him leave.

Mary Ann, who appears to have been having a busy night herself, went out a third time returning at 3am. This time there was no sound from Mary Jane's room and it was in darkness. For whatever reason, Mary Ann Cox was unable to sleep that night. She didn't even bother to undress but lay in a restless slumber listening to the few sounds in the court until daybreak.

She was not the only resident of Miller's Court who had a disturbed night's sleep. It was as if a foreboding hung over the squalid dwellings and their wretchedly poor residents that night. Elizabeth Prater, who lived in the room above Mary Jane, came back at about 1.20am that morning after an unsuccessful night's soliciting. The staircase to her room was separated from Mary Jane's room by a partition so flimsy that even the faintest light, had there been one at that time, would readily have penetrated the chinks. She could, she said later, easily hear Mary Jane moving about in the room when she was up and about. Privacy was not a commodity that your few pennies rent could purchase in Miller's Court. At 1.20am that morning there was no light in Mary Jane's room and it was as silent as the grave.

Perhaps because of the presentiment that hung in the air like a miasma that night, Elizabeth barricaded herself into her room by moving two tables up against the door. She slept only fitfully and at about 3.40am she was awakened by her kitten Diddles brushing against her face. Something, it seems, had disturbed her pet because a moment later Elizabeth heard a woman's voice – she described it as a suppressed cry – calling, 'Oh, Murder.' It seemed to come from outside in the court but as it was muffled and it was not repeated she had difficulty in placing it. Elizabeth later said that because such cries were common around Dorset Street she took no notice of it and went back to sleep. The truth almost certainly was that she was too petrified to move until the grey light of dawn penetrated her grimy curtains. Then, at 5am, she hurried out to the Ten Bells, fortified herself with a glass of rum and hot water and retreated to bed again to catch up with her lost sleep. Later that day she watched the body being taken out of the court in a shell covered with a dirty tarpaulin before giving her interview to the reporter from *The Star*[121].

The social life of the unfortunates and destitutes of Spitalfields seems to have paid scant regard to the hours that ruled the lives of the ordinary men and women of Britain. Sarah Lewis, who described herself as a laundress but in reality was probably another unfortunate, decided to pay a call on her friend Mrs. Keyler at 2 Miller's Court at 2.30am. After talking for a while, Sarah decided to pass the rest of the night in a chair whilst her friend presumably returned to her bed. Sarah too could not sleep. The clock of All Saints in Spital Square striking 3.30am woke her and she remained awake until shortly before 4am when she too heard a cry of 'Murder'. It seemed to her to be outside the door of number 2, which was almost opposite Mary Jane's room. Like Elizabeth Prater, she also decided that discretion was the better part of valour and did nothing about it.

It was not until 10.45am the next morning – when Mary Jane's landlord, John McCarthy, decided to have one last despairing attempt to get the twenty-nine shillings due in back rent from her – that the dreadful truth was discovered. He sent his assistant Thomas Bowyer to number 13 with instructions to wake her up and not to take no for an answer. Bowyer knocked repeatedly on the door that opened onto the passageway, then tried it and found it locked. He went into the court and crouched down at the smaller of the two windows to peer in through the broken pane, having pushed aside the coat that served as a curtain.

As his eyes became accustomed to the dim light in the room, a scene of such dreadfulness gradually materialised as has never been equalled in the history of crime.

CHAPTER SEVENTEEN

The Horror in Room 13

By the time John McCarthy and Thomas Bowyer recovered sufficiently to make their way to Commercial Street police station, the procession for the Lord Mayor's Show had reached Leadenhall Street and was snaking its way down Fenchurch Street just a few hundred yards from Mitre Square, where Catherine Eddowes's body had been found less than a month before. The sound of the marching bands and the roar of the crowds that packed the narrow streets could easily be heard on the moisture-laden air.

Inspector Beck quickly returned to the court with the two shaken men. He too peered through the broken window and was no less shocked by what he saw. Although McCarthy and Bowyer had been careful not to say a word to anyone else, it was obvious now that something was up and a small group of people started to gather in Dorset Street and peer down the narrow passageway. At 11.15am Dr. George Bagster Phillips, the senior police surgeon to H Division, arrived. As he later told the inquest with masterly understatement, 'I looked through the lower of the broken panes and satisfied myself that the mutilated corpse lying on the bed was not in need of any immediate attention from me, and I also came to the conclusion that there was nobody else upon the bed, or within view, to whom I could render any professional assistance.'

A few minutes later, Detective Inspector Abberline arrived and took charge of the crime scene. Beck told him that the bloodhounds had been sent for and were on their way and, after consulting with Dr. Phillips, he decided to defer forcing the door until such time as they arrived in order to give the dogs the best chance of picking up the Ripper's scent before anyone else entered the room. They did not know that at that moment one hound was in Brighton and the other in Scarborough. Nor did they know that Sir Charles Warren, the commissioner, had tendered his resignation a little over 12 hours before and that this time it had been accepted by the Home Secretary.

It was now 11.30am and Inspector Beck had secured the court, giving orders that no-one other than the police and others on official business were to be allowed to enter or leave. Word was beginning to spread throughout the area that another Ripper murder had taken place and the small knot of people in Dorset Street had now grown to a crowd of several hundred. Abberline ordered that the street be sealed at both ends allowing no-one to pass except *bona fide* residents. Uniformed constables were posted and the street was cordoned off with ropes.

Then the waiting began.

For two long hours the group of men in the court waited, tense, white-faced, each with his own private thoughts. They had all peered through the broken window and none of them would forget what they had seen for the rest of their lives. Inside lay the remains of a young woman who a few hours before had been alive and singing, brimming over with life by all accounts even if her particular way of life was not one that most people would have condoned. Abberline must have been wondering how much longer this could all go on before his own job was in jeopardy.

Eventually Superintendent Arnold arrived bringing word that neither the bloodhounds nor Sir Charles Warren would be coming, and at 1.30pm he gave the order to break open the door. No doubt because it was his property, John McCarthy was allowed the job of forcing the lock. Had they known it, all that was required was for an arm to be inserted through the broken window and the knob on the spring lock could have been turned with ease, as Mary Jane and Joe had been using this method for some weeks. As it was McCarthy forced the end of a pickaxe between the door and the frame and leaned against the shaft.

With a splintering of wood, the door flew open only to strike the bedside table that was just to the right of the entrance.

It was a small room, no more than 12ft square. On the wall to the left of the door two windows looked out onto the yard. The wooden-framed bed was to the right of the door, hard against the flimsy partition that divided the room from the rest of the house. A couple of wooden chairs and two small tables comprised the rest of the sparse furniture, one table near the far window and the other between the bed and the door. The men entered, Abberline and Phillips leading.

A fire had been burning in the grate and despite the time of year the room was still warm. The offal-like smell of flesh that was already starting the process of decomposition hit them like a foetid blanket. Even Phillips, who had seen thousands of bodies in the course of his work, must have recoiled at the sight that confronted them. The official accounts given in the reports of the inquest are simply inadequate to convey the sheer awfulness of the scene.

The bed was sodden with blood and liquid faeces. Lying towards the near edge were the remains of what had once been a human being. The few small recognisable details served to emphasise the horrific unreality of the rest. Mary Jane's left arm lay crooked at the elbow, the hand hanging languidly into the cavity that once contained her internal organs but which was now as empty as a carcass on a butcher's hook. The smooth white skin of her forearm was savagely disfigured by a series of parallel knife wounds. The puffed sleeve of her cotton shift, still recognisable, covered her shoulder but the rest of the garment had disappeared into the reeking mess on the bed. Her legs were splayed apart and flexed at the knees in an obscene parody of sexual accessibility but where her external genitalia had once been was now a gaping, bloody cavity. The flesh and muscle of the right leg had been carved from the bone and an unsuccessful attempt had been made to hack through it with the little hatchet that normally stood by the fireplace to chop kindling for the fire. The doctors would later catalogue the position of the various viscera that had been arranged around the corpse like bouquets of flowers at a wake, but they all noticed her amputated breasts, one of which lay like a cushion beneath her head while the other had been placed by her right foot.

Most hideous of all was her head. Mary Jane's features had been systematically sliced away taking with them the nose, cheeks and eyebrows, leaving behind only her vivid blue eyes to stare sightlessly up from the putrid remains. Her once beautiful thick dark hair lay in a matted, blood-soaked halo framing the remains of her face. It was a sight the like of which none of them had seen before or would ever see again.

Silently the men turned their attention to the rest of the room. At the foot of the bed, eloquent in its orderliness, was a neatly folded pile of day garments. The training imparted by her mother and her time as a lady's maid had left their imprint on Elizabeth. In terrible contrast, lying on the surface of the table beside the bed was a mass of almost unrecognisable flesh that later turned out to be the front wall of the abdomen, which had been removed in three large flaps. The partition wall beside the bed had been sprayed with arterial blood and the pillow and sheets on that side were also drenched in it. Abberline found a clay pipe that later turned out to belong to Joe Barnett, and a stub of candle stuck in a broken wine glass on the table by the window, and that was about it. Apart from the charred remains in the fire no other item remained that gave any clue as to the identity of either the killer or the victim.

Following the 'Double Event', Robert Anderson, Assistant Commissioner of the Metropolitan Police, had decided that in the event of any further Ripper murders Mr. Thomas Bond should be called upon to conduct the medical enquiries. Bond was a surgeon at the Westminster Hospital and one of the first lecturers in forensic medicine to be appointed in Britain. Although he was a man of significant medico-legal experience and had already been involved in the Whitehall torso case, as his obituary in 1901 made clear, despite his title he was not actually an operating surgeon but more of a high-class general practitioner[122]. This may well help to explain the contrary view he took later regarding the degree of anatomical and surgical skill displayed by the Ripper.

He arrived at 2;pm, about half an hour after the room had been broken into. He had already read all the notes pertaining to the previous four murders and was in the process of writing a report to which he would now be able to add his first-hand experience of the death of Mary Jane.

It had also been decided that, in the event of another Ripper crime, the body would be photographed *in situ* before being examined or removed to the mortuary for further examination to take place. A local photographer, no doubt badly shaken and more used to taking portraits of civic worthies and wedding groups, recorded the scene in the room from two different angles. In order to get as wide an angle for the first picture as possible, he set up his tripod in the yard and took the photograph through the open window. The second of the two surviving pictures was taken from the other side of the bed after apparently pulling it away from the partition wall. Curiously the photographer was apparently working for the City Police rather than the Mets, and after copies in Scotland Yard's files disappeared – probably having been purloined as souvenirs by an official – copies were found in the City Police archives by Donald Rumbelow in 1968. However, by that time they had already been published in other places, notably by the French forensic pathologist Alexandre Lacassagne in his 1899 book, *Vacher l'éventreur et les crimes sadiques*.

By this time news of the discovery of yet another Ripper crime had become common knowledge and people began drifting away from the Lord Mayor's Show in their thousands and streaming towards Spitalfields, where the police were already struggling to keep them out of Dorset Street. It was clear that they needed to get the body away from Miller's Court as soon as possible. Bond, assisted by Phillips, conducted an examination of the body on the bed and made a series of gruesome discoveries.

They soon established that, unlike the other victims, Mary Jane had briefly realised the danger she was in and had managed to fight off her attacker for a few seconds, since her right hand had a defensive wound on the thumb where she had attempted to grab the knife blade and a series of abrasions on the back where it may have been forced against the wall. Who can imagine what she must have felt in that last moment as she recognised her assailant and it suddenly blazed in on her that it was he who had been responsible for the terror of the past three months? She had been lying towards the right side of the bed, nearest to the wall, when her neck had been cut severing the windpipe, the muscles and all the major vessels right down to the spinal column. It had been all over in a few seconds, allowing just enough time for a single muffled cry of 'Murder' before merciful death enveloped her.

The killer almost certainly started by amputating both breasts before slitting open her abdomen and systematically emptying it of its contents. The organs were distributed about the bed in a way that mocked any shred of dignity that her death might otherwise have had. The uterus, genitalia, both kidneys and one breast formed a macabre pillow beneath her head, the other breast was by her right foot, the liver between her legs, the intestines – which had been totally excised – were between her body and the wall, and her spleen lay to the left of the body. Within the stomach and abdominal cavity were the partially digested remains of fish and potatoes. It seems that Mary Jane had made enough from one of her clients that night to buy herself a fish and chip supper[123].

The final discovery was the most chilling of all. Mary Jane's heart had been extracted from within the chest by opening the pericardial sac from beneath the diaphragm. Despite a thorough search of the room and its human debris it was not found, although attempts were later made by the authorities to suppress that fact. The symbolic nature of the act is inescapable although it was lost on people at the time. She had once stolen someone's heart and he was now taking hers.

A horse-drawn cart carrying a temporary coffin or 'shell' arrived and, as soon as the two doctors had completed the initial examination, the cadaver and the other remains were scooped up and removed, covered by an old tarpaulin and taken to the Shoreditch mortuary. This was the first hint of official interference in the conduct of the investigation. Dorset Street was in Spitalfields and the official mortuary for that district was the Whitechapel one attached to the Old Montague Street workhouse to which the bodies of Polly Nichols and Annie Chapman had been taken. It was to lead to trouble once the inquest opened.

CHAPTER EIGHTEEN

The Aftermath

Mr. Bond conducted a full post-mortem examination at the mortuary later that day, although most of the work had already been performed by the Ripper. Almost all that remained to be done was to open the chest cavity and ascertain the condition of the lungs on which he found some pleural adhesions and some nodular consolidation. Both are signs of previous mild tuberculosis, although the condition was so common in 19th-century Britain as to be nothing more than incidental[124]. He did not apparently open her skull and examine the brain as Phillips had done on previous occasions and in many respects his examination report was much more perfunctory than those undertaken by the H Division police surgeon. In fact, as a police surgeon seven years older than Bond, it is likely that Phillips had carried out many more post-mortems in the course of his career than Bond, whose main job was treating the living.

In addition to the *in situ* and mortuary post-mortem reports, Bond gave his opinion on the murders and wrote a detailed profile of the man likely to be responsible for the atrocities. He made two important points: firstly he was certain that the five murders were committed by the same man (although he had not been asked to comment on the murder of Martha Tabram).

Secondly, he was sure that all of the victims were lying supine at the time that the necks were cut. In fact both of these points had previously been made by Phillips in his evidence to the various inquests but Bond, as a surgeon at a prestigious teaching hospital and forensic consultant to Scotland Yard, inevitably carried more weight.

He expressed some views on the times that had elapsed between death and the finding of the bodies and in some of these he was well wide of the mark. He believed that three or four hours might have elapsed in the cases of Polly Nichols, Annie Chapman and Catherine Eddowes, despite all of the facts arguing against this. In each case not only was there definite evidence from policemen and others that there had been no body at the spot 15 minutes before the discovery of the corpse, but there had been clear medical evidence that the bodies were still warm, rigor mortis having not set in and, in two cases, liquid blood still flowing from the wounds. Bond was in direct opposition in these assertions to the police surgeons who were actually present within minutes of each of the crimes. In the Miller's Court case he deduced that death had occurred between 1am and 2am whereas, judging by the evidence of Mary Ann Cox, ElizabethPrater and Sarah Lewis, it is much more likely that it took place at around 3.45am.

He also differed from Phillips and Brown, the most experienced of the City and East End police surgeons, in stating quite categorically that no surgical skill or anatomical knowledge had been displayed in any of the murders. He went further and said, 'In my opinion he does not even possess the technical knowledge of a butcher or horse slaughterer or any person accustomed to cut up dead animals.' This was completely contrary to the views of both Dr. Phillips and Dr. Brown, but then it must be remembered that Bond had only actually seen the last body where an unprecedented degree of savagery had been used with absolutely no attempt to employ any surgical or dissecting skill. Mary Jane's body had been literally hacked to pieces in a way that suggested that the murderer was in a completely different frame of mind at the time.

In addressing the type of person who could have perpetrated such deeds, Bond wrote:

The murderer must have been a man of physical strength and of great coolness and daring. There is no evidence that he had an accomplice. He must in my opinion be a man subject to periodical attacks of Homicidal and erotic mania. The character of the mutilations indicate that the man may be in a condition sexually, that may be called satyriasis. It is of course possible that the Homicidal impulse may have developed from a revengeful or brooding condition of the mind, or that Religious Mania may have been the original disease, but I do not think either hypothesis is likely. The murderer in external appearance is quite likely to be a quiet inoffensive looking man probably middle aged and neatly and respectably dressed. I think he must be in the habit of wearing a cloak or overcoat or he could hardly have escaped notice in the streets if the blood on his hands or clothes were visible[125].

Assuming the murderer to be such a person as I have just described he would probably be solitary and eccentric in his habits, also he is most likely to be a man without regular occupation, but with some small income or pension. He is possibly living among respectable persons who have some knowledge of his character and habits and who may have grounds for suspicion that he is not quite right in his mind at times.

This is regarded as perhaps the first true attempt at criminal profiling in history and in some areas, as it will be seen, Bond could hardly have been closer to the truth in his description. His speculation that the murderer may have been suffering from a 'revengeful or brooding condition of the mind' was also, as it turned out, right on target and pathognomonic of a person with STPD, but he opted instead for the alternative explanation of satyriasis, the male equivalent of nymphomania. In this he completely ignored the fact that in none of the five cases was any evidence of sexual connection or masturbatory activity found even though the police surgeons were highly attuned to looking for them.

He made another observation that might be highly significant. He commented that the corner of the sheet to the right of Mary Jane's head was 'much cut and saturated with blood' which to him suggested that it may have been placed over her face whilst the facial mutilation was in progress. Was Francis so overcome by the face of the woman he had once loved that he could not bear to look at it as he cut it to ribbons? Was that why he spared her deep blue eyes[126]?

Bond himself was a curious character. The son of a wealthy Somerset farmer, he qualified in medicine at King's College Hospital, London, and then signed on as a medical officer in the Prussian Army during the brief Austro-Prussian War of 1866. After gaining his FRCS he was appointed Assistant Surgeon at the Westminster Hospital in 1873, but in effect he saw only Out Patients for the next 20 years and had no practical operating experience during this time. He became a police surgeon to A Division and built up a large medico-legal practice, giving evidence in many celebrated murder trials. However, as his obituary in *The British Medical Journal* made clear: 'It might be said that he was too dogmatic, but it was part of his nature to see one side of the case, and having expressed an opinion he was not to be shaken.' In 1901 he suffered a painful stricture of the urethra and after some weeks of suffering he committed suicide by throwing himself out of his bedroom window. It is possible that Bond, who expressed very forthright views on the evils of venereal diseases, might in fact have been suffering from a gonorrhoeal stricture and this may have contributed to his state of mind at the time.

The inquest on the body from Miller's Court was held by Dr. Roderick Macdonald, coroner for North-East Middlesex at Shoreditch town hall on Monday 12th November, four days after its discovery. Macdonald was the son of a crofter from the Isle of Skye and by dint of intelligence and sheer hard work had qualified in medicine and become Member of Parliament for Ross and Cromarty, representing the Crofters' Party. He was a doughty Highlander who did not defer to anyone. In 1886 he had competed with Wynne Baxter for the post of coroner for East Middlesex. It was, apparently, an acrimonious contest which Baxter won. A year later, however, it was decided to divide East Middlesex into North and South coronial divisions and Macdonald – who had only narrowly been beaten by his rival – was allocated the Northern one, something that could not have endeared him to Baxter.

Francis Spurzheim Craig's signature and the address on the first 'Dear Boss' letter. Are they by the same hand? (*Envelope:* © *The National Archives*)

The plaque that marks the spot in the corner of Mitre Square where Catherine Eddowes was murdered in the early hours of 30th September. (© *Wynne Weston-Davies*)

Sketch of Catherine Eddowes's body, said to have been made by Frederick Foster, the City Surveyor. (© *Evans Skinner Crime Archive*)

Postmortem City of London police photograph of Catherine Eddowes after the autopsy. The long midline scar is a continuation upwards of the one made in her abdomen by the Ripper. (© *Evans Skinner Crime Archive*)

28 Collingham Place. Probably the site of the 'gay house near Knightsbridge' which Joe Barnet spoke of in his inquest testimony and in which Elizabeth worked for the Frenchwoman after leaving service as the Marchioness of Londonderry's lady's maid. (© *Wynne Weston-Davies*)

McCarthy and Bowyer trying to gain entry to Room 13, Miller's Court on the morning of 9th November. (© *Jane Coram*)

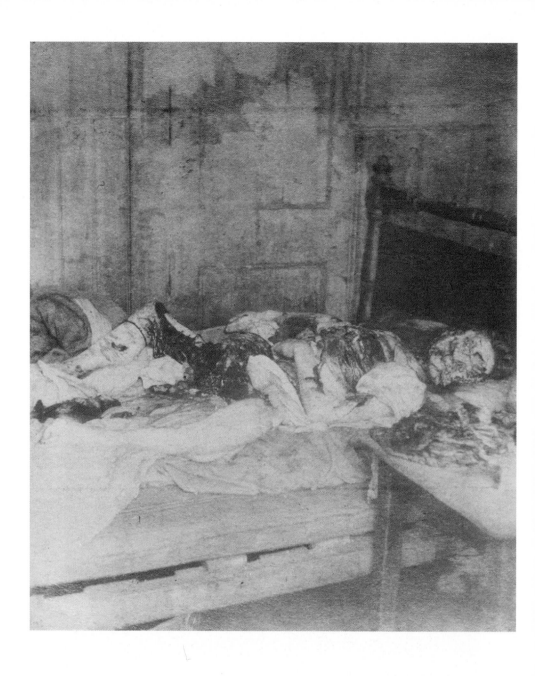

The police photograph of the body in Room 13, Miller's Court. This was the scene which confronted Inspector Abberline and the others when they entered the room. (© *Evans Skinner Crime Archive*)

161 Drummond Street. In 1888 this was the Monmouth Hotel and Coffee House, a cover for one of the brothels operated by Ellen Macleod. Elizabeth stayed here for part of 1886 after parting from Francis. (© *Wynne Weston-Davies*)

The unmarked grave in Hammersmith Old Burial Ground, Margravine Road in which Francis Craig and his parents are buried. (© *Wynne Weston-Davies*)

It seems likely that there was interference at a high level in Mary Jane's inquest. Her body had been taken to the Shoreditch mortuary which placed her remains under the jurisdiction of Macdonald. It should, by rights, have stayed within Baxter's territory but it seems that the powers that be had become frustrated by his management of the inquests, his implied criticism of the police and his intimidation of witnesses. Almost certainly someone at a high level, probably the Home Secretary himself, had issued orders that the body be taken out of Baxter's jurisdiction even before it was removed from Miller's Court.

Macdonald seems to have been only too well aware of the role he was being asked to play and was probably party to the manipulation. When the inquest opened after the jury had been sworn in, one of the jurors addressed the coroner: 'I do not see why we should have the inquest thrown upon our shoulders, when the murder did not happen in our district, but in Whitechapel[127].'

Macdonald was obviously prepared for this challenge and his reply was swift and severe. 'Do you think that we do not know what we are doing here, and that we do not know our own district? The jury are summoned in the ordinary way, and they have no business to object. If they persist in their objection I shall know how to deal with them. Does any juror persist in objecting?'

They did. The juryman stubbornly continued, 'We are summoned for the Shoreditch district. This affair happened in Spitalfields.'

'It happened within my district,' snapped Macdonald.

This was not true and everyone present in the court knew it. Another juryman then laid down a challenge: 'This is not my district. I come from Whitechapel, and Mr. Baxter is my coroner.'

It is clear that the old enmity between the two coroners was at least partly behind this extraordinary mutiny and Macdonald moved swiftly to quash it once and for all. 'I am not going to discuss the subject with jurymen at all. If any juryman says he distinctly objects, let him say so.' He allowed a suitable pause for further challengers to his authority to make themselves known but when none did he continued, 'I may tell the jurymen that jurisdiction lies where the body lies, not where it was found, if there was doubt as to the district where the body was found.' There was of course no doubt whatever as to where the body had been found. Miller's Court and Dorset Street lay very definitely within

Whitechapel and the coronial jurisdiction of Wynne Baxter, who may well have been behind the jurors' revolt. In the course of a long and busy professional life in which he held innumerable public offices and made many contributions to the fields of science, horticulture and literature, he never once received any national honour or recognition, and this episode may have been one of the reasons why that was so.

Before the courtroom proceedings commenced, the jurymen were taken by Inspector Abberline to see the body in the Shoreditch mortuary and the room in Miller's Court where it had been found. During their absence Dr. Macdonald took the opportunity to address the reporters assembled at the press bench on the subject of jurisdiction, taking great care to say that he had not received any communication on the subject from his counterpart in Whitechapel. The *Telegraph* the next day reported him as saying that, 'The body was in his jurisdiction; it had been taken to his mortuary; and there was an end of it. There was no foundation for the reports that had appeared. In a previous case of murder which occurred in his district the body was carried to the nearest mortuary, which was in another district. The inquest was held by Mr. Baxter, and he made no objection. The jurisdiction was where the body lay.' It is clear that there was considerable public unease over what was seen as political interference in the judicial process and Macdonald was taking every opportunity to quell it but with little success.

When the court reconvened, the first person to testify was Joe Barnett. It can have been anything but easy for him; he seems to have been genuinely fond of Marie Jeanette as he knew her, and to have had to look at her hideously mutilated face for purposes of identification must have been a terrible experience. 'I have seen the body,' he said, 'and I identify it by the ear and eyes, which are all that I can recognise; but I am positive it is the same woman I knew. I lived with her in number 13 room, at Miller's court for eight months. I separated from her on October 30th.' The coroner asked him why he had done so and he replied, 'Because she had a woman of bad character there, whom she took in out of compassion, and I objected to it. That was the only reason.' It was one of several references to Mary Jane's generous nature by those who knew her and which may ultimately have led to her downfall.

Joe then continued to give evidence that contained almost all the known details about Mary Jane's background and existence until the time they had first met on Good Friday 1887. It was during this that details of her having worked from a high-class brothel in the West End emerged, as well as her trip to France with someone she apparently did not get on with and about her liaisons with the mysterious Morganstone and Joseph Flemming after her arrival in the East End.

Finally the coroner asked him if Mary Jane had seemed fearful of anybody during her last weeks. 'Yes,' Joe replied, 'Several times. I bought newspapers, and I read to her everything about the murders, which she asked me about.' The coroner then asked whether she had expressed fear of any particular individual. Joe does not appear to have fully understood the question and took it to mean was Mary Jane afraid of him. He replied, 'No, Sir. Our own quarrels were very soon over.'

At the end of his evidence the coroner thanked him and congratulated him on having given his evidence very well indeed, which was probably recognition of the fact that Joe – who had a speech impediment – must have found the whole experience a considerable ordeal.

At that point Macdonald told the jury that he proposed that Dr. Phillips should come to court briefly that afternoon to state 'roughly what the cause of death was' in order that the body could be buried. He added that it would not be necessary for all the medical details to be given in court. It was clearly going to be a very different sort of inquest to the previous ones. *from*

After that, John McCarthy, Thomas Bowyer, Mary Ann Cox, Elizabeth Prater and Sarah Lewis gave their evidence about the movements of Mary Jane on the evening before her death and the discovery of the body. A discordant note was struck when Caroline Maxwell, wife of another of the Dorset Street lodging house deputies, gave her evidence. She was cautioned by the coroner before doing so since, as he presumably already knew, her account of the last hours of Mary Jane differed markedly from all the others. She swore that she had seen and spoken to Mary Jane in the street outside Miller's Court between 8am and 8.30am in the morning, three hours before Bowyer had peered through the broken window and seen the body on the bed. She gave a vivid account of a severely hungover Mary Jane telling her that she had been to the Britannia on the corner of Dorset Street and Commercial Street for a glass of beer, before having brought it up again – Maxwell even adding that she had seen the vomit in the gutter. She hurried off to Bishopsgate to purchase her husband's breakfast and when she returned about half an hour later Mary Jane was talking to a man outside the Britannia.

Although several later commentators have attempted to reconcile this sighting with the facts, even going as far as to suggest that the body on the bed was not that of Mary Jane but a substitute lured there as part of some undefined conspiracy, it seems that Caroline Maxwell must have been mistaken as to the identity of the woman she had seen. Both Dr. Bond and Dr. Phillips stated in their reports that Mary Jane's stomach contained the partly digested remains of a meal of fish and potatoes and if she had consumed a glass of beer and then vomited, then that would have been brought up at the same time.

Dr. George Bagster Phillips was then called and gave the most perfunctory medical evidence of any of the five Ripper murders, no doubt relieved that he would not again have to go through the ordeal he had endured at the hands of Baxter at the inquest on Annie Chapman. Death, he said emphatically, was caused by severance of the right carotid artery whilst the deceased was lying towards the right side of the bed with her head in the top right-hand corner, after which she was moved towards the left side of the bed. No other injuries or mutilations were mentioned and the coroner allowed him leave. It is curious that Phillips was called at all since it was not him but Thomas Bond who had carried out both the *in situ* and mortuary post-mortem examinations. It was another small example of interference by the legislature in the affairs of the judiciary.

There was then a short adjournment and when the jury returned Macdonald addressed them again: 'It has come to my ears that somebody has been making a statement to some of the jury as to their right and duty of being here. Has anyone during the interval spoken to the jury, saying that they should not be here to-day?' On receiving a negative response he gave one last admonition: 'Then I must have been misinformed. I should have taken good care that he would have had a quiet life for the rest of the week if anybody had interfered with my jury.'

The final witnesses included Julia Venturney, Mary Jane's friend from across the passageway, who confirmed that she had last seen her alive at 10pm the previous evening and that she had not heard anything during the course of the night[128]. She was followed by Mrs. Harvey who verified that she had been with Mary Jane when Joe Barnett had called at a 7.45pm. Then Inspector Beck and Inspector Abberline described the actions they had taken after arriving at Miller's Court. Abberline gave an account of the fire set in the grate that had been fierce enough to melt the spout off the kettle and that it appeared to consist mainly of a large quantity of women's clothing. When asked by the coroner why he thought it had been done, he replied that he presumed that it was to give more light for the murderer to work to.

Finally the coroner addressed the jury as to whether they felt that they had heard enough on which to base a verdict. He said that he personally did not think that anything more would be gained by hearing more medical evidence. Dr. Phillips had already given the cause of death as having been severance of the right carotid artery and in his view that was enough. Anything more should be placed in the hands of the police and, hopefully, left to another court to hear.

The jury did not demur and within a few minutes brought in a verdict of Murder by Person or Persons Unknown. Macdonald gave permission for the body to be released for burial and that was it; the shortest inquest of any of the Ripper victims was over in a matter of a few hours. Many people at the time and since have found it strange that the most complex, the most dramatic of all the crimes, the one that appeared to stand out from all the others, should have been treated in so cursory a way. The suspicion that Dr. Roderick Macdonald MP had colluded with the authorities has not diminished with the passage of time.

There has been considerable speculation over the ensuing years as to how the murderer gained access to Room 13. The door was clearly locked at the time the body was found and most people, including the police of the day, have assumed that Mary Jane unwittingly took her killer back to her room herself as a client. If Francis was the killer and Mary Jane was his wife Elizabeth, that would have been unthinkable, assuming that she recognised him. The evidence, including that of Mary Jane singing in the early hours of the morning, suggests that her last client, possibly the man with the blotchy face and the carroty moustache that Mary Ann Cox had reported as having accompanied her back to her room at a 11.45pm, had left a short time later and that she had then decided to call it a day. She had announced her intention of going to the Lord Mayor's Show the next morning and possibly she thought she would have what for her was an early night.

She was dressed in a shift with her day clothes neatly folded at the foot of the bed when her mangled corpse was found, adding to the likelihood that she had retired for the night. It seems more probable that her killer had managed to waken her and then gain admission by tricking his way in. Elizabeth would certainly not have let Francis in if she had realised that that was who it was. There is only one sort of person that Mary Jane is known to have had no hesitation in letting in to her room on raw cold nights such as that November evening. Another woman, especially an unfortunate.

When the police searched the room the next day they very carefully sifted through the remains of the fire that had burned so fiercely that it had melted the spout off the kettle. They were looking for human remains, particularly the missing heart. They reported that none had been identified but that a large quantity of woman's clothing had been burnt, including a bonnet. Abberline assumed that the purpose had been to provide more light despite the fact that there was at least half a candle remaining unused.

If Francis had put a woman's shawl and long skirt over his own clothes and shielded his face under a bonnet before tapping on Mary Jane's window it would have been a woman's silhouette that she saw outlined against the dim light from the Court. Already befuddled by sleep and drink she may briefly have slipped out of bed, opened the catch on the door and let the stranger in. From the blood stains on the wall and the bed itself, Bond concluded that Mary Jane had been lying on the far side of the bed when she was killed and that her body had then been moved to the side nearest to the door to give her dissector better access. If so, had she lain on the far side of the bed to make room for someone she had taken pity on to lie down next to her? It may have been that fatal kindly gesture that cost her her life.

There was another purpose to the fire. After the butchery was over, Francis is certain to have searched the room minutely. Elizabeth had received letters whilst she was in Miller's Court, possibly from Johnto or other members of her family, forwarded by Ellen Macleod. Such links with her former life would have been precious to her and are likely to have been kept to be read again when homesickness overtook her. There may have been photographs and other mementos of her past, possibly even a wedding ring engraved with their joint initials, although that is more likely to have been sold or pawned long since as it bore no sentimental value to her. Anything that Francis found that could possibly connect him to the mutilated remains lying on the bed or could identify her had to be destroyed along with his blood-soaked disguise[129].

CHAPTER NINETEEN

The Last Act

The funeral of Elizabeth's *alter ego* took place on the morning of Monday 19th November. Her body had been lying in the Shoreditch mortuary attached to St. Leonard's church since her gruesome death. As it was impossible for Joe Barnett or any of her friends to defray the costs of a proper burial, Mr. Henry Wilton – who had been sexton of St. Leonard's for more than 50 years – bore the cost of it himself as a gesture to the poor of East London.

In the time between the murder and her funeral the police in London, Wales and Ireland had been engaged in an enormous effort to identify the dead woman whose name few now believed to be Mary Jane Kelly. The case had received massive coverage in newspapers throughout Britain and around the world. With, by her account, two living parents, seven brothers and a sister – not to mention a cousin living in Cardiff who, according to Joe, had lured her into prostitution in the first place – it was inconceivable that, had her story been genuine, one of them would not have recognised her and come forward.

The major problem was that, unlike the other victims, it was not possible to publish a post-mortem photograph of her face since it had been mutilated beyond all recognition. Various periodicals attempted to show artists' reconstructions of her but they were so far from reality as to be absurd. The *Penny Illustrated Paper* carried a supposed drawing of her outside her room in Miller's Court which portrayed a statuesque blonde woman in middle age wearing a stylish full-length coat of the kind that certainly had not formed part of her wardrobe for at least three years and a hat, a garment that Mary Jane is known seldom to have worn. Despite her various nicknames – which included 'Fair Emma' and 'Ginger'– it is almost certain that the woman who called herself Marie Jeanette Kelly had thick dark hair and this seems to be borne out by the picture taken by the police photographer, although it may have been so saturated with blood that it was difficult to tell.

The polished oak and elm coffin was carried out of the mortuary on the shoulders of four pall-bearers at 12.30pm whilst the bells of St. Leonard's tolled a funeral knell. The same bells would have been familiar in name to the occupant of the coffin, through the words of the old nursery rhyme, 'When I grow rich say the bells of Shoreditch'. Elizabeth had once briefly known prosperity, if not actual wealth, when she worked at Ellen Macleod's establishment in the West End, but she was never to be rich and her life had been cut brutally short. Despite the circumstances it appears to have been a surprisingly cheerful and compassionate one and the people of the East End responded accordingly. By the time the coffin was placed in the glass-sided, horse-drawn hearse the street outside the church was packed with hundreds of people and the police were having a hard time keeping them back from the funeral procession.

The coffin bore a brass plate inscribed 'Marie Jeanette Kelly. Died 9th November 1888 aged 25 years.' Two wreathes of artificial flowers and one of heartsease or wild pansy, the nearest available relative of the violet that she had sung about on the night of her death that would have been available in November, were placed on the coffin and numerous other floral tributes were heaped alongside, many bearing cards from the public houses that she had frequented in life.

Joe Barnett and some of the other mourners who had been fortifying themselves for the coming ordeal in a nearby public house emerged and took their places in the two open carriages behind the hearse. Joe, John McCarthy and, probably, his wife occupied the leading one and four of Mary Jane's women friends who had given evidence at the inquest, the other. The police struggled to open a passage through the crowd in order that the cortege could move off[130]. Men removed their hats and women threw flowers and shouted 'God forgive her', as, under a leaden sky, the carriages started the five-mile journey to Leytonstone Catholic cemetery. Although there was not the slightest evidence that she was Catholic, the authorities seem to have presumed that a girl who used the name Kelly and claimed to have been born in Limerick was likely to be of that faith.

The route was densely lined with spectators all the way to the cemetery although many of those following on foot had dropped back after the first mile or so. Nevertheless there was sufficiently large a crowd at the cemetery that the authorities decided to close and lock the gates after the carriages had pulled up outside the Chapel of St. Patrick. The cemetery and its surroundings have hardly changed in the years since the funeral. The chapel, which is only used for funerals, is austere and devoid of ornament inside and out. As the hearse drew up, Father Columban OSF came out of the building accompanied by a cross bearer and two acolytes and escorted the coffin and the small group of mourners to the freshly dug grave.

Most people have assumed that the OSF means that Father Columban was a Roman Catholic Franciscan priest, but he was not. The Order of St. Francis is an Anglican order of Franciscans, the Catholic equivalent being the Order of Friars Minor, so, although Mary Jane was buried in a consecrated Catholic cemetery, the funeral was actually conducted by an Anglican[131].

When it was finished the mourners made their way back to the cemetery gates. A persistent story says that as they did so a man who had been standing some distance away stepped forward and either spat or urinated into the grave. There seems to be no substance in the report as it does not seem to have been mentioned in any newspaper account at the time and it may have been invented by children keen to cash in on the generous amounts of money that were being handed out by reporters anxious for good copy. Were it to be true it would be interesting to know if he was a middle-aged man wearing an Inverness coat and a billycock hat.

Once outside, Joe and some of the women made for the Birkbeck Tavern, a pub that still stands on the corner of Langthorne Road a few hundred yards from the cemetery gates, in order to drown their sorrows while the remainder returned in the carriages to Whitechapel.

At this stage of course no-one could know that the terror was finally over. Only 12 weeks had elapsed since Polly Nichols's body had been discovered in Bucks Row but to many, especially perhaps the senior policemen and the unfortunates of Whitechapel, it must have seemed a lifetime. To the general public the last horrific murder in Miller's Court seemed to herald a new and even more terrible phase in the killings, and the trickle of letters from would-be Rippers, some motivated by a perverted sense of humour, others by genuinely troubled minds, increased to a deluge. No more however were sent by the scribe who had sent the two letters and a postcard to Central News – or not, at least, for another eight years.

Over the next days, as the police continued investigations that looked increasingly desperate and equally futile, the efforts to identify Mary Jane were stepped up. To many of the senior officers working on the crimes, the Miller's Court murder looked different. The degree of savagery alone marked it out from the others. If they could only find out the true identity of the victim it might lead them to the killer. As perhaps the most likely suspect they took Joe Barnett in for questioning, but he had been at his new lodgings – 24 and 25 New Street, Bishopsgate, another doss house – and the deputy was able to confirm that he was there at the time of the murder.

Joe was only one of many men arrested in the days following Mary Jane's death. They included a man, apparently French, with a pointed moustache, who was found to be carrying a pocket medical case containing bottles of chloroform; a man called Compton who had already been arrested once in Shadwell for wandering around in a blood-stained coat and shirt; and a man with a blacked-up face who proclaimed himself in a loud voice to be Jack the Ripper as he walked the streets of Whitechapel. When the police discovered that he was a young doctor from St. George's Hospital he was released with a warning. It seems that any number of young men were quite prepared to run the very real risk of being lynched for the thrill of a few minutes of notoriety.

Another suspect was introduced into the confused picture when, belatedly, on 12th November – after Mary Jane's inquest had closed – George Hutchinson presented himself at Commercial Street police station with another, apparent, sighting. He gave a highly detailed account of Mary Jane, who he knew, having approached him in Commercial Street in the company of another man at 2am on the morning of her murder. She wanted to borrow six pence, which he was unable to lend her. For some reason George decided to follow the couple as they turned into Dorset Street and headed for Miller's Court. He said that the man had scowled at him and turned his head away as if not wishing to be recognised. Hutchinson decided to keep watch from across the street. He would have had a perfect view of the door to her room which opened off the right side of the short alleyway and he stayed there for at least an hour, according to his account, but the man did not emerge.

He gave a vivid description of the man, so vivid indeed that many people at the time and since believed that it owed more to George's imagination and desire for reward than it did to reality. He described him as being about 34 or 35 years of age, dark and of 'Jewish appearance' with a black moustache curled at the ends and wearing a full-length dark overcoat trimmed with astrakhan fur. His shoes were partly covered by grey spats with white buttons. He wore a black Homburg type hat, white collar and black silk tie held in place with a gold horseshoe pin, and across the front of his waistcoat he wore a 'huge' gold watch chain from which hung a gold seal fob with a red stone. It was an amazingly detailed description of the sort of man rarely seen in Dorset Street but which closely matched the public and police image of the killer. The newspapers were full of artists' reconstructions of the man over the next few days and a more villainous-looking character it would be hard to imagine. Just to complete a portrait that would exactly fit the public perception of the Ripper he was, according to George, carrying an elongated parcel bound up in American cloth and carried from a small strap.

It was just too perfect and most people now believe that Hutchinson was yet another publicity seeker trying to take advantage of the large sums being offered by the reporters for good, lurid copy. If not, why had he not come forward at the time of the murder rather than waiting until after the inquest was closed? Hutchinson, or a man answering his description, was spotted hanging around across the street from the entrance to Miller's Court at about the right time but leaning against lamp posts was a favoured occupation for penniless men in the

East End and maybe it gave him time to dream up a perfect picture of the Ripper.

It was a measure of the growing desperation of the police that on the day of the inquest Scotland Yard issued a statement that read:

> Murder.-Pardon.-Whereas on November 8th or 9th, in Miller-court, Dorset-street, Spitalfields, Mary Janet [sic] Kelly was murdered by some person or persons unknown, the Secretary of State will advise the grant of her Majesty's gracious pardon to any accomplice not being a person who contrived or actually committed the murder, who shall give such information and evidence as shall lead to the discovery of the person or persons who committed the murder.
>
> (Signed) "CHARLES WARREN,
> "The Commissioner of Police of the Metropolis,
> "Metropolitan Police Office, 4, Whitehall-place, S.W.
> 10th November, 1888.

This almost unprecedented action resulted from a Cabinet meeting that had taken place in the Foreign Office on Saturday 10th November, one of the very few times that the Cabinet has ever met at a weekend when the country was not at war. It bore the signature of Charles Warren who, by 10th November, had in fact resigned from the post of Commissioner. As a new one had not been appointed by the 12th, it was clearly felt best if it went out under Warren's signature.

In due course the police in Limerick, Dublin and Cardiff reported that no trace of any of Mary Jane Kelly's family or relations could be found in any of those cities nor was there anyone serving in the 2nd Battalion of the Scots Guards who admitted to being the brother of the murdered girl. It was becoming more and more clear that Mary Jane was not who she had said she was. In fact the official certificate of death issued by Coroner Macdonald gave her name as 'Marie Jeanette Kelly otherwise Davies[132]'. On 17th November, when it was signed, there was sufficient doubt about her true identity to issue an ambiguous certificate but one that probably came closer than anyone knew to the truth.

As the police hunt for the murderer continued the interest of the international press reached a climax and then, as no further killings ensued, began to diminish. There were many false alarms and arrests. Large numbers of these were precipitated by the foolish behaviour of the men concerned, either inadvertent or, in many cases, intentional. Many people sought to profit out of their experiences. An anonymous would-be reporter contrived to get himself arrested twice on 23rd and 24th November at Leman Street police station and then published an account in a penny pamphlet entitled '*The Whitechapel Atrocities. Arrest of a Newspaper Reporter*' that he hawked around the city[133]. He described having spent four nights in Spitalfields and Whitechapel 'in order to obtain, for journalistic purposes, information not so much in regard to the murders as to the life, habits and customs of the denizens of these dark and dismal localities'. He apparently spent some time in a public house 'hard by Spitalfields Church' where he encountered 'a black-visaged, thick set, desperate fellow, with a savage look in his dark eyes'. Whether or not such a person was a regular customer of the Ten Bells – and almost certainly he was not – it fitted most people's perception of the Ripper perfectly.

The unknown reporter himself was questioned closely as to his whereabouts on the night of 8th and 9th November. Only when things began to look serious did he finally tell the police that he had been at home with his parents on the night in question. When asked what he was doing at home he chose to reply, 'I was doing indoors what the police of Spitalfields seemed to be doing on their beats – sleeping.' It was not perhaps the most judicious of answers and he could count himself lucky that he was released with only a caution at 4am on Sunday 25th November.

Gradually, with no further killings over the next six months, public anxiety lessened. The police kept up their investigations and every lead was assiduously followed up, but as the days passed the leads became fewer. There were other killings in the Whitechapel area; the body of an unknown woman was found under a railway arch in Pinchin Street on 10th September 1889 and that of Alice McKenzie in Castle Alley in July of that year, both with their throats cut, but it was obvious to Dr. Phillips and the police that they did not carry the full signature of the Ripper. A boy of 8 had his throat cut and was eviscerated in

Bradford in December 1888 and Phillips was dispatched north to examine the body. In his opinion it was a copycat killing but not by the Ripper. A man was arrested for it and later acquitted.

Perhaps because the killer who called himself by the almost pantomime name of Jack the Ripper whilst carrying out such savage killings and mutilations was never caught, public interest has remained high and, if anything, even increased with the passage of time. On average, two new books about the events of three months in 1888 appear every year. Inevitably there have been conspiracy theories, most of them preposterous and based on absolutely no evidence. Prince Albert Victor, Eddie to his family, may have been a louche, promiscuous man like his father but he was not Jack the Ripper. Nor were Sir William Withey Gull, Queen Victoria's elderly physician, or Walter Sickert, the first of the English Impressionist artists. It was not a depressed and probably paedophile barrister called Montague John Druitt whose corpse was fished out of the Thames a month after the last killing, nor was it a mad American doctor called Tumblety. Neither the Masons nor the Fenians were involved in a conspiracy to kill East End prostitutes. If the latter had been, it would not have been in their nature to keep quiet about it.

That is not to say that there was not a conspiracy. There was, but it was a conspiracy of silence by a few people – including Elizabeth's brother John – who felt themselves in some way responsible for what had happened and guilty that they had not intervened sooner.

In some ways John might be considered to be the sixth victim of Jack the Ripper. He was close to his elder sister and initially kept in touch with her when she disappeared from Argyle Square, which was close to his own lodgings with the family of a Welsh dairyman in Leigh Street. He was a talented young man – apprenticed as a cabinet maker to Maples, he gained his Master's qualification at the remarkably young age of 24. His skill at producing the marquetry and decorative cabinet work that made Maples famous throughout the world ensured that his name is recorded to this day by the Victoria and Albert Museum. When he became engaged to the daughter of a prosperous Caernarvonshire owner of a chain of chemists shops his future must have seemed assured.

Although he visited Elizabeth whilst she was in Breezer's Hill, she may have considered it too risky to remain in touch with her brother once she decamped for Spitalfields. Joe Barnett was not aware of him having been in evidence during this period although he knew that Johnto had visited her at Breezer's Hill. When the massacred remains were found in Miller's Court, John had no immediate reason to connect the blue-eyed girl who called herself Marie Jeanette Kelly with his sister but gradually – as the months passed, and Elizabeth failed to make any contact with the family she had once been so close to – the nagging possibility took root and grew until it became a certainty. By that time he was married with a young family of his own. His wife and her family were strict North Welsh Calvinistic Methodists and it is doubtful if he ever told them about Elizabeth. Instead, as the guilt for not having done more to protect his vulnerable sister grew to become an intolerable burden, he took solace in the bottle and suddenly, around 1892, he gave notice to Maples. The V&A record him as having 'left of his own accord' and to this day there is still mystification about why one of the leading craftsmen of the late Victorian era should suddenly have vanished into oblivion.

After that for Johnto and his young family it was downhill all the way. In a restless urge to distance himself from London he took a succession of ever more menial jobs all over Britain, in Canterbury, Portsea, Gloucester, Margate, Chester and Wigan, before finally taking his wife and his younger children on an assisted passage to Australia in 1913. By that time, his hands shaking and skills ruined by drink, he could only describe himself as a carpenter. He was no more successful there and eventually he deserted his family and returned to England where on New Year's Day 1932 he left the workhouse which had been his home for many months and walked out into the grey waters of Christchurch harbour. His jacket containing a suicide note was found neatly folded in a shelter on the quayside but his body washed in and out with the tide for three weeks before being spotted by a fisherman.

Johnto had been a hard-working, ambitious and talented young man. Like his sister he was warm-hearted and popular with his family and friends but something happened around 1890 to change him into a depressed, alcoholic wreck. Almost certainly it was the growing suspicion of who the woman in

Room 13 really was. He seems to have told no-one else until shortly before his own death, when he blurted out in an emotional outburst to his own youngest son John that his sister, John's aunt, had been an upmarket London prostitute and that she had come to a bad end. No more than that and it was a secret that his son in turn did not pass on until shortly before his own death in 1996. The legacy of Miller's Court had lived on for nearly 50 years before it claimed the last victim of Jack the Ripper.

CHAPTER TWENTY

Where's Jack?

Some time after the murder in Miller's Court, Francis left his lodgings in the East End and returned to live, yet again, with his elderly parents in Hammersmith. Exactly how soon after is not known but to have left abruptly and too soon afterwards would have risked drawing attention to himself. If he had been writing for the *East London Advertiser* during the period of the murders he may have considerably advanced his journalistic career, for the accounts that paper carried are full and vivid and were syndicated to other newspapers. With his inside knowledge, a cynic might say, it would not have been difficult to write pieces of such conviction and immediacy. Whichever paper he was contributing to, it seems to have done him some good for early the following year he was appointed editor of the *Indicator and West London News*, a prestigious local newspaper serving Paddington, Kilburn, Marylebone, Shepherds Bush and a large segment of West London.

Although he probably started the job in about April of 1889, the first recognisable piece carrying his initials F.C. at its foot was an article in the edition of Tuesday 18th June 1889 entitled 'Sketches in Pen and Pencil'. It was an account of a journey by canal from Paddington to Perivale and included an accomplished sketch of the lepers' window in the local church by a Mr. W.G. Kemp. This suggests that not only was Francis on the editorial staff of the *Indicator* by this date – just seven months after the final Ripper murder – but that he was probably well established, since he would hardly have been entrusted with the writing of such an important piece with an expensive illustration if he was not already well thought of.

He probably moved in person from the East End in April or May of 1889, since the Mile End Road address was still on the divorce petition when he appointed Thomas Webster of 3 Howard Street, Strand, as his solicitor on 29th March[134]. His motive for appointing a new solicitor to continue a divorce action against a woman he already knew to be dead, for the very good reason that he himself had killed her, might at first sight seem odd. In fact it was probably a clever move. It would have cost nothing to simply appoint Webster and in doing so it would keep the divorce action alive and indicate to anyone sniffing around that Francis believed his wife to be still living. The fact that there are no further entries of any sort in the notes indicate that neither he nor his new lawyer did anything actively to try to trace Elizabeth. By the time of the census of 1891 Francis was definitely living once more with his elderly parents at 10 Andover Road, Hammersmith, which his father had somewhat pretentiously re-named 'Ralahine Cottage'. In that census he described himself as married although, ten years later in 1901, he had reverted to the status of single[135].

For almost the whole of his life until he started to write editorial material for the *Indicator*, Francis had been mute to history with few exceptions such as the piece he had contributed on the subject of a local centenarian to *The Times* under his own name in 1875. He certainly wrote many thousands of words of copy for other newspapers during his lifetime but, as a penny-a-liner they did not carry his signature and so it is impossible to identify them as his work so many years later. It is not even certain which newspapers he worked for during this period. Now, having achieved the position of editor, suddenly Francis has a voice which is still audible today.

The paper was published twice a week, on Tuesdays and Fridays. On page 2, below the banner, there was always a weighty leading article on a subject of national or local importance. Following that was a column entitled 'Notes and Comments' signed by 'Citizen' who is certainly – at least in part – Francis, although others on the staff of the paper may also have contributed occasional material. There are contextual and stylistic features that link the copy with many other articles and poems that he contributed over the initials F.C.. He was almost certainly contracted to write the leader and Notes and Comments, and paid an additional fee for anything he wrote over and above that, possibly to fill space when news and advertisements were not sufficient to occupy all the available space.

He was an excellent editor. The quality of material, both editorial and news copy, in the *Indicator* during his tenure stands out as far superior to that of the majority of local newspapers at the time. He introduced many innovative features such as a children's section and a women's correspondent writing not about the usual domestic matters but about controversial issues to do with women's rights. He attracted more advertising since the paper had to add extra pages to accommodate it and this must have meant that he had increased its circulation. His meticulous, obsessional attention to detail fitted him ideally for an editorial role and it is no wonder that the proprietor regretted losing him when he resigned in 1896.

Once it becomes possible to identify his work, Francis emerges as a different person. In print he was educated, articulate, witty, funny, decidedly eccentric in places and obviously highly intelligent. Some surprising things emerge. He was a keen sportsman and had obviously participated in sports like football and rowing. He held liberal Conservative political views, being an avid supporter of the Member of Parliament for South Paddington, Lord Randolph Churchill, father of Winston. How that went down with his left-wing, socialist father can only be guessed at. His support for Churchill was not unconditional, however. On one occasion something that Lord Randolph had done or said caused this mild rebuke:

> Oh! Randy, please to moderate
> The rancour of your tongue;
> I do admire you very much,
> But yet, 'not quite so strong.'

Like many 19th-century journalists he was fond of inserting such little pieces of poetry into his copy. They are hardly more than doggerel, brief jingles to make a political point or to inject some humour. It was an art form that George Robert Sims perfected and from which he made a fortune from his annual compilation *The Dagonet Ballads*. There was this example of Francis's quirky style from Tuesday 8th October 1889:

The Gospel Fowl Convention
[Mr. and Mrs. Wiggin invited contributions of fowls for their gospel-bazaar at Queens Park]

Our own 'Pote' Cackles
Now, cackle, cackle, strut and fray
But first we'll sing a hymn and pray
Walk up! Walk within!

Come buy us up ye Christian folk
Come buy fine eggs with luscious yolk
Cluck, black Spanish, do!

A Brahma Pootra, big as goose
Has run its head into a noose
Buy it, neck and crop!

A chick is in the milk afloat!
A cock just clearing out his throat!
Cock-a-doodle-do!

This barn door fowl is best of all,
Come 'buy, buy, buy,' both great and small,
Buy our sitting hens!
FC

It is a curiously written piece. The rhyming couplets are straightforward enough but the third line of each verse is oddly worded and seems to be disconnected from the rest of the poem. Each contains five syllables and possibly they are meant to be onomatopoeic attempts to convey the crowing of a cock, but unless they are read aloud it is easy to miss that.

The verse provoked a letter in the next issue of the *Indicator* from 'One of your regular readers' in which the author expressed puzzlement as to why it featured in a piece about the Temperance movement. Craig replied below the letter:

> Mr and Mrs Wiggin – God bless them! – invited contributions of fowls, ie they called a convention of fowls, for their festival to aid the Gospel work of the Queens Park Tabernacle. I was not there, but I take the idea to be :- Come all ye good people willing to aid us in our great labours in this vineyard, bring your fruits, flowers, provisions, potatoes, coals and FOWLS, old fowls, young fowls, crowing cocks, interesting promising cockerels, sitting hens: hence 'The Gospel Fowl Convention.' – THE WRITER OF THE VERSE

Henry Wiggin wrote a good-humoured letter to the newspaper the following week pointing out that the editor had been levelling 'harmless fun' at himself and Mrs. Wiggin for some time but proposing the newspaper might consider lending its support for their plan to raise money to provide a Christmas Dinner for a thousand aged people at Queens Park. In the event the plan came to nothing because the local clergy considered that they had more than enough to do for their own parishioners than to be able to assist in the venture.

Other themes that illuminate Francis's character emerge in the items in Notes and Comments, or 'leaderettes' as he called them. He was extremely concerned about cruelty to children and wrote many pieces in support of the recently founded National Society for the Prevention of Cruelty to Children. He wrote a vivid account of a blind girl having a red hot poker drawn close to her sightless eyes, of a terminally ill boy being immersed in a tub of icy water by his mother 'to hasten his dying' and of an adolescent girl being pummelled in the breasts and kicked in the groin and abdomen when she collapsed to the ground.

Further matters close to his heart were the Polytechnic movement, free libraries and free access to public spaces – all of which his father would certainly have endorsed – and the welfare of survivors of the Charge of the Light Brigade, which would have been less popular with Craig Senior who, having witnessed the Peterloo Massacre as a young man, had no warm feelings for the cavalry[136].

He had decidedly, and maybe significantly, strong views on funerals. Like Charles Dickens he supported the National Funeral Reform Society. This body campaigned for less money to be spent on funerals and all the trappings of death including overpriced coffins and monumental masonry. By the end of the 19th century simple headstones had given way to elaborate monuments with sculpted angels, Celtic crosses and wrought iron grave surrounds, and the NFRS was concerned that the poorer members of society were being pressurised into paying money they could ill afford for the funerals of their loved ones and urged the middle classes to set a good example by moderating the ostentation of their own funerals. Francis was eventually interred in the same grave as his parents and, to this day, although the plot is identifiable, it has no headstone or surrounds.

In April 1894 he forwarded a letter from an outraged reader to the Superintendent of the Hammersmith Old Burial Ground concerning an incident that had occurred at the funeral of 'Madame des Roches' (in fact, although the French socialist feminist Jeanne Deroin was married to Antoine Desroches, she never used her married name). This had taken place in the cemetery a few days before and William Morris attempted to deliver a funeral oration over the grave. He was prevented from doing so by cemetery staff who insisted, wrongly, that it was illegal for anyone except an ordained minister of the church to speak at a burial. When Morris persisted the gravediggers were ordered to start filling in the grave. It was perhaps this incident that caused Morris not to attempt to deliver the ode that he wrote for his old friend E.T. Craig, Francis's father, when he died and was buried in the same cemetery.

An example of Francis's sense of humour, or at least of his interest in the quirks of mankind, is this piece published in Notes and Comments on 11th April 1890:

> A rather curious case came before Mr Cooke at Marylebone the other day. One Giovanni Cura – a name of itself redolent of art – was charged with 'exhibiting an indecent picture' whilst with his ice cream barrow in High Road, Kilburn. When the matter was gone into it appeared that Giovanni 'with an eye to business,' had painted, or caused to be painted on one panel of his barrow no less an interesting a scene than that of 'The Flood.' The artist, in order to give a realistic aspect to the picture had exhibited ladies and gentlemen, or men and women (as the case may be) in *puris naturabilis* or, in the simple vernacular, without any clothes on, running about to escape the Deluge. Of course, what the Italian Masters, or our own Etty might do in the way of cabinet studies or pictures for national galleries, cathedrals &c. could not be tolerated for *al fresco* exhibition[137]. Mr Policeman comes by and speedily marches Giovanni off to the lock up as a violator of the proprieties, in fact as an obscene and filthy fellow. A solicitor was procured and, such are the vagaries of fashion, even the man of law blushed and he himself (says the police reporter) objected to the picture and ordered his client to paint it out. The Magistrate, being a highly proper man, blandly coincided. Thereupon the picture was painted out.

Another incident, when Francis observed a woman sitting on the top deck of an omnibus losing not only her hat but her wig too when passing beneath a tree branch in Kensington Church Street, prompted this ditty:

> 'Those boughs are far too great a check,
> I swear they want some lopping;
> They catch me in the nape of neck
> And they spoil the ladies' 'topping.'

Francis's sporting interests included rowing. The reference in the 1871 census to Cambridge, apparently in the mistaken belief that the census enumerator was asking where he had been educated, has been exhaustively researched. Despite the strong suspicion that he may once have been a medical student, there is no sign of his name in the registers of admissions to the university. In 1890 he wrote a long and detailed account of the annual Oxford and Cambridge Boat Race and from the expert knowledge it displays it seems likely that he himself had once been an oarsman. A few years before, at the personal invitation of the famous oarsman Dashwood Goldie – who was Cambridge President from 1870 to 1872 – he had watched the race from one of the steam launches that followed it. On that occasion he was in the company of a number of distinguished journalists who he obviously counted as friends, including Robert Wormald – editor of 'Bell's London Life', who he described as an old 'Varsity' man – George Powell of *The Times* and Mr. (later Sir) Thomas Wemyss Reid, then editor of the *Leeds Mercury* and later of *Cassells* and *The Speaker*. Despite his unpromising journalistic beginnings Francis had obviously made his mark by 1890 and seems to have been well-regarded. In that year he made what must have been a bold decision and watched the race from a balloon hundreds of feet above the course, giving a vivid account of it in the *Indicator* on 28th March. His allegiance was made quite clear by his references to the sky, glimpsed between the clouds, being a 'pure Cambridge blue'.

It is of interest that in the same year Harry Dam, an American journalist living in London and who in 1888 had been working on T.P. O'Connor's popular newspaper *The Star*, was injured in a balloon accident. Dam was widely suspected, at the time and since, of being the author of the 'Dear Boss' letters, although he vehemently denied it until his death in 1906. He was also credited with being the person who put forward the theory that a man known as 'Leather Apron' was the author of the Ripper murders, a story that enjoyed popular support until the appearance and vindication of John Pizer at the inquest of Annie Chapman. Francis and Dam almost certainly knew each other through both having worked as reporters in Whitechapel at the time of the murders. It is interesting to speculate that they may also have had a connection through the use of balloons as a platform for journalism and indeed whether they shared the basket suspended above the Thames on this occasion.

There are frequent references to sport – including horse racing – throughout Francis's years as editor and, given the circumstances, this startling statement: 'I have no time for brutal pastimes. I class the Rugby game of football as brutal …' Presumably, though, he did not class murder as a pastime.

A short editorial piece that he wrote in 1896, a few months before he resigned, has an intensely personal flavour. A recent Act of Parliament gave women vastly improved rights to seek judicial separation from brutal or indolent husbands and at the same time to claim the right to continue to enjoy his financial support. Francis clearly felt that it was weighted much too far in favour of the woman. He wrote, with more than a touch of irony:

> Miserable disheartened wives be of good cheer! The New Year brings
> into force an Act that we believe will not infrequently be heard in
> our Police Courts. Women who have brutal and lazy husbands have
> now a remedy for that ill – a much more effective one than they have
> had in the past. Last week for the first time a Magistrate granted a
> decree of judicial separation between a couple on the sole grounds of
> her husband's desertion. As far as we can judge this 'lord of creation'
> had not been actually cruel and with the exception of occasional
> visits he had merely stayed away from his wife for a period of two
> years – not providing her with sufficient means. This new Act for the
> benefit of unhappy married females, for such it is, gives a magistrate
> the power to break the tie of wedlock between man and wife if the
> former has been found guilty of cruelty or wilful neglect to provide
> for her and her infant children. Besides declaring the couple judi-
> cially separated the magistrate can order the husband to contribute
> to maintenance of his 'better half' to the amount of £2 per week,
> which has to be paid to an officer of the court. In the case we refer to
> the husband was ordered to pay an allowance of 30s weekly. Women
> who have bad husbands reaps [sic] untold benefits from the new Act
> but the unfortunate man who possesses a drunken, bad wife is left
> out in the cold. He must live on in misery, at least as far as this Act is
> concerned. Why should it not apply to both sexes alike?

The reference to drunken, bad wives and to living on in misery were obviously deeply and personally felt but it is doubtful if any of his readers except perhaps the proprietor Arthur Lane would have been aware of it. Is Francis trying to plead that had such an Act been available in 1885 he would not have had to go to the lengths he did to avenge himself on a drunken, bad wife? If so it is casuistry on a breath-taking scale.

It becomes clear from the pages of the *Indicator* that Francis was an excellent, if at times eccentric, communicator in print. What he found difficulty with was verbal communication. Arthur Lane, the proprietor of the newspaper, who knew him well for more than 20 years, described him as a nervous, sensitive man – although that is certainly not the impression that comes across in print. On the pages of his own newspaper he appears as a bold, forthright, often humorous man, a colossus of the printed word expressing trenchant views on everything from the British colonisation of South Africa to the importance of retaining ancient public rights of way. This ambiguity of his character goes a long way to explaining his actions in the three years between 1885 and 1888. The pen and, seemingly, the knife gave him the confidence that he lacked in his face-to-face dealings with other people.

E.T. Craig was growing old. Although he still kept up a steady output of pamphlets, letters and articles, he no longer held the influence he once had. He finally wrote the story of Ralahine that he had neglected to do for more than 50 years, but by now few people remembered it or were interested. The great days of co-operation and living in communes had passed. It is a good book but diminished by the passage of time and memories that had become blurred. He was anything but modest in retelling his part in the story but probably that is with a good deal of justification.

What is not contained in the book or in anything else he ever wrote is a direct reference to his son. There are numerous mentions of his wife Mary in the book and in various of his papers, but nowhere was Francis ever recorded. It was mutual. Both Arthur Lane and Francis's friend Edward Warren, stated categorically at his inquest that Francis had no relatives. Admittedly, by 1903 both his parents were dead, but Warren said that he had never known anything of his relatives in all of the 30 years that he had known him and yet, for almost the whole of that time, Francis was living under their roof in the same borough in which Warren collected the rates. It seems that despite living together, neither father nor son publicly acknowledged the existence of the other throughout their lives and that speaks volumes for their relationship.

E.T. supplemented whatever small income he still received from writing articles – mostly for socialist organs like the *Cooperative Weekly* which did not pay generously – by continuing to sell health improving medicaments and devices by mail order. He advertised in local newspapers and in some of the political journals for which he wrote, and the stock was stored at the Craigs' house in Andover Road. No doubt in the years after he left the East End Francis helped his father to pack the parcels before taking them to the post office in Hammersmith Broadway for dispatch. When he was not at the *Indicator*'s office in Harrow Road, Paddington, it was probably his only occupation.

Possibly the piece that gives the best insight into Francis's state of mind in the months immediately after he left the East End is the poem of his that has been quoted earlier, which was published in the *Indicator* on 27th December 1889:

AN EDITOR'S CHRISTMAS

The last page was finished and he yawned in his chair
While the ink on his pen he wiped off on his hair
He mused for some time, then laid down the pen
And, donning his coat, he locked up the den.[138]

Then home to his lodgings, in a dingy back street,
He walked in thin shoes, through the down-falling sleet;
And opening the door, to the fifth storey climbed,
As the bells of St Nicholas merrily chimed.

His coat and his hat he hung on a nail,
And then tried to read by his candle-light pale;
A feeling of drowsiness soon o'er him came,
And tired out, he slumbered and dreamed him of fame.

The Real Mary Kelly

He seemed to be sitting in a sumptuous room
Where bright chandeliers made the walls to illume;
Where tables were loaded with all they could hold
Of presents and gifts as in good days of old.

A Christmas tree standing upright in a block!
The sight gave his brain a most terrible shock;
Subscriptions and contracts were there by the score,
And bank notes as well – some thousands or more.

What could it all mean? His head must be wrong;
His eyes must deceive or surely weren't strong;
The lamp of Aladdin ne'er could have done more
To add to the table's most bounteous store.

Kind providence truly had come to his aid,
And brought the success for which he had prayed;
No more would he wander around for the news,
While his feet met the paves through the soles of his shoes.

The bank-bills would buy him a new suit of clothes,
And next year he'd hang up a whole set of hose;
His faith in the public again he'd renew
And give them a paper both novel and new.

Alas! His air-castles were bubbles that broke,
When he turned in his chair, and in turning, awoke;
The room and the table all vanished in air –
Gone, gone to the dickens – he never knew where.

The bell of St Nicholas pealed forth its chime,
As oft it had done before in its time;
And gray [sic] streaks of dawn shone in his cold lair,
Proclaiming that Christmas in earnest was there.

The fire was all out, o'er the table were strewed
The bills and the notes for which he was sued;
With a sock in his hand, he had fallen asleep,
While mice through its holes played 'hide and go peep.'

But people that morn who laughed in high glee
O'er jokes from his pen till they scarcely could see,
Knew little the hardships the writer went through,
Who gave them on Christmas good stories and new.

As poetry it leaves much to be desired but the whole tone of the piece chimes, like the bells of St. Nicholas, with his probable mood at the time. It is that of a lonely man immersed in self-pity, beset with feelings of failure and being under-appreciated. The description of a man with holes in his shoes creeping in to dingy lodgings at the end of a long day is probably an accurate enough picture of the three years he had spent in his digs in the Mile End Road, and the table piled with 'the bills and the notes for which he was sued' reflects his constant anxiety about money.

The line, 'The sight gave his head a most terrible shock' and the phrase 'his head must be wrong' need to be viewed with caution and are probably there more to provide suitable rhymes than because Francis at that time considered himself to be in any way mentally disturbed.

More interesting, in view of the 'Dear Boss' letters, are the Americanisms that have crept in. As well as the word 'den' he spells the colour 'gray' at a time when the usual spelling in England was 'grey' and, although this could conceiv-ably be a typographical error, the name of the game could not be. 'Hide and go peep' is the American name for the game which in Britain is, and was, more commonly known as 'hide and seek'. The construction 'dreamed him of fame' is also more commonly encountered in American vernacular than in English. It seems that Francis's two years in the USA had a profound and lasting effect on him.

The references to the bells of St. Nicholas is interesting. The nearest church of that name to his lodgings in the Mile End Road was the Wren church of

St. Nicholas Cole Abbey in the City of London. In 1883 the Rev. Henry Shuttleworth, a cleric of progressive and socialist views, became the rector. Surprising though it sounds, he installed a bar and instituted political debates and musical concerts. As a result his congregation grew to several hundred and it seems that Francis might well have been amongst it. It was possibly his only source of solace and comfort during the time he spent in the East End.

After his return to the family home in 1889 Francis would accompany his father to evenings at William Morris's house in Hammersmith and political discussions at Hammersmith town hall. E.T. was a well-known figure locally, usually wrapped in a plaid shepherd's cloak and wielding a long ear trumpet. His temper did not improve with the passage of time and Francis must have found the task of looking after his parents, in addition to editing a successful newspaper, increasingly burdensome. E.T. must have been an exceptionally hard man to live with. There is abundant evidence of his irascibility. One day in the 1880s he was in the garden of Kelmscott House when George Bernard Shaw asked to have his head read – presumably as a joke since for most people other than Craig phrenology was well and truly discredited by then. E.T., who certainly did not consider it a laughing matter, duly complied and during the process Shaw mischievously asked, 'Do I have a bump of veneration?' E.T. is recorded as having shrieked, 'Bump! It's a 'ole there!' and to have savagely thrust his walking stick into Morris's lawn. Morris's daughter May said that at that period E.T. would, 'make speeches in a fife-like voice which sometimes recovered its old chest register in a sort of bellow that beat upon one's ear drums'.

On 15th December 1894 E.T. Craig died. The death certificate gives bronchitis and heart failure as the cause of his demise. He was 91 years old, a very good age in the 19th century, so maybe his years of abstemiousness and physical exercise paid off. His funeral took place on 22nd December, no doubt organised by Francis. He was buried in plot A15 on the north side of the Avenue in the Old Hammersmith Burial Ground off Margravine Road. There was a choice of burial in consecrated or unconsecrated ground and Francis – or maybe his father – chose the former, curiously for a family that was probably atheist.

The plot is next to the main path, not far from the cemetery gates, and would therefore have been one of the more expensive ones. The burial service was read by Thomas Gage Gardiner, Rector of St. George the Martyr, Southwark, rather than by the cemetery chaplain who usually conducted the services in the Old Burial Ground. E.T. Craig had been a figure of national importance in his time and there were fulsome tributes in *The Manchester Guardian* and the *Cooperative News* and, in due course, an entry in the *Dictionary of National Biography*. William Morris, who would himself be dead within two years, wrote a funeral ode but he did not attend the ceremony.

Francis resigned prematurely from being editor of the *Indicator* in 1896 at the age of 58. It seems to have taken the proprietors by surprise and, judging by his evidence at the inquest, it seems that Arthur Lane, the managing director, would have been more than happy to let him continue in the role. During his seven- or eight-year editorship the circulation of the newspaper had grown and, because it was attracting a greater volume of advertising, its size had been increased from four pages to six. Francis did, however, continue to contribute articles and to report inquests and court proceedings.

Possibly because Lane had tried his best to persuade Francis not to resign, he became paranoid and formed the delusion that the owners of the *Indicator* were going to pursue him through the courts for breach of contract, something that they had no intention of doing. Money appeared to be a major issue for him. He seemed to have an embedded horror of becoming insolvent, maybe as a result of the small fortune he had spent in the pursuit of Elizabeth which may have taken him to the brink of bankruptcy. In the period after the death of his parents he gave large sums of money to both Arthur Lane and his friend Edward Warren for safekeeping and in order for them to issue it back to him in regular, small, manageable amounts like a child's pocket money.

It seems that by 1896 Francis's health, both physical and mental, was beginning to give way and his recognition of this may have contributed to his decision to resign from the *Indicator*. He had also suffered a prolonged and painful attack of writer's cramp the previous year; the condition, now known as repetitive strain injury, would have been a serious handicap for a professional writer. There was an additional reason.

After the death of her husband, the health of Francis's mother Mary also started to decline. She became progressively senile and suffered from respiratory difficulties. Towards the end of her life she became bedridden and no doubt Francis struggled to look after her as he carried on with his job at the *Indicator*. It was probably the strain of coping with this situation that finally led him to resign although, typically, he would not have told Arthur Lane the reason. In the Craig household family matters were strictly hidden from public scrutiny.

In October 1896, a few months before his mother died, a letter, written in the familiar red ink, was received at Commercial Street police station, Spitalfields. It read:

14 October 1896

Dear Boss

You will be surprised that this comes from yours as of old Jack the Ripper. Ha. Ha. If my old friend Mr Warren is dead you can read it[139]. You might remember me if you try to think a little Ha Ha. The last job was a bad one and no mistake nearly buckled, and meant it to be best of the lot curse it. Ha Ha. Im alive yet you'll soon find it out. I mean to go on again when I get the chance wont it be nice dear old Boss to have the good old times once again. You never caught me and you never will. Ha Ha. You police are a smart lot, the lot of you couldnt catch one man. Where have I been Dear Boss youd like to know. Abroad, if you would like to know, and just come back. Ready to go on with my work and stop when you catch me. Well good bye Boss wish me luck. Winters coming 'The Jewes are people that are blamed for nothing' Ha Ha have you heard this before

Yours truly

Jack the Ripper

The letter was immediately forwarded to Scotland Yard where it underwent careful scrutiny. A Metropolitan Police memorandum dated 18th October 1896 reads:

> With reference to the attached anonymous letter signed 'Jack the Ripper' wherein the writer states that he has returned from abroad and is now ready to commence work again, *vide* Chief Constable's memo re same.
>
> I beg to report having carefully perused all the old 'Jack the Ripper' letters and fail to find any similarity of handwriting on any of them, with the exception of the two well remembered communications which were sent to the 'Central News' Office, one a letter dated 25th September 1888 and the other a post card bearing the post mark 1st October 1888, *vide* copies herewith.
>
> On comparing the handwriting of the present letter with handwriting of [word illegible] document I find many similarities in the form of the letter. For instance the ys, ts and ws are very much the same. Then there are several words which appear in both documents viz dear Boss, ha ha (although in the present the capital H is used instead of the small one.

The writer of this memorandum was Chief Inspector Henry Moore, Abberline's immediate subordinate at the time of the Whitechapel murders and, because he continued to work on the crimes for months after Abberline had been moved on to other matters, probably the most experienced of the remaining detectives that had worked on the Ripper case. He went on to say *Who* that the phrase 'The Jewes are the people that are blamed for nothing' was almost identical with the Goulston Street graffito which was 'undoubtedly by the murderer'.

Despite noting all of these points of similarity, Moore finally concluded that this letter was not written by the same person as the original 'Dear Boss' letters, basing his belief solely on the fact that it was sent to Commercial Street police station, not Central News. Superintendent Donald Swanson – Moore's superior and another of the senior officers that had been engaged on the Ripper murders – agreed with him, writing on the bottom of the memorandum:

> In my opinion the handwritings are not the same. I agree as at
> A. Agree that the letter may be put with other similar letters. Its
> circulation is to be regretted.
> Donald E [sic] Swanson
> Supt.

It is worth noting that Tom Bulling, the journalist who had forwarded the three previous Ripper missives to Scotland Yard and who himself was believed by some to have been their author, had been sacked by Central News earlier that year. Francis would almost certainly have known this and may have felt that, with Bulling's departure, a letter stood more chance of reaching the right quarters if it was sent via the police station most nearly connected with the crimes.

The letter, like the original 'Dear Boss' letters of 1888, may or may not have been written by Francis. The handwriting is similar but looks rather laboured as if written very slowly. At his inquest in 1903 Arthur Lane said that Francis had had a 'stroke of paralysis' and suffered from writer's cramp as a consequence, although he did not say when this was. If it was before this letter was written it might explain the difference in character from the previous letters.

The linguistic style and the chilling humour it contains are almost identical with its predecessors. There is also the same deliberate attempt to make it appear to be the work of an uneducated man that suggests that, even if Francis himself was not the author, it was written by the same person that had been responsible for the others. The reference to the 'good old times' is reminiscent of a similar reference in *An Editor's Christmas*. The letter was written within months of Francis's resignation from the *Indicator* at a time when he was under great strain caring for his invalid mother. It could have been his way of letting off steam, of relieving the stress he was under. Could the reference to having the good times once again have been nostalgia for a brief period in his life when Francis had felt in control of the situation, unlike his present predicament,

212

jobless and having to shoulder the burden and embarrassment of nursing his senile mother and caring for her every bodily requirement?

Francis stayed on at 10 Andover Road until the death of his mother in April the following year. Probably because he was largely incapable of looking after himself from a domestic standpoint or maybe because the house held too many painful memories, he moved into lodgings with John and Phoebe Reading in Carthew Road, a few streets away. As the only lodger, paying a good rent, he would probably have had the larger of the two bedrooms at the front of the house and been provided with breakfast and an evening meal. He was apparently a good tenant, paying his rent promptly and causing a minimum of inconvenience to the Readings.

In due course Lane, Warren and his landlord John Reading gave evidence at his inquest that painted a picture of Francis's behaviour and state of mind in those last years. Arthur Lane said that he was a nervous, sensitive man but Warren disagreed saying that, in his experience, he was self-confident – but he had known Francis for longer than Lane and may have been thinking of him in earlier days. All agreed that his behaviour had become increasingly erratic. Warren and Reading both described being in conversation with him, sometimes even in the course of a meal, when he would abruptly break off and flee from the room. This is typical of schizotypal personality disorder with a psychotic overlay; Francis's mind was beginning to crumble.

His physical health also began to deteriorate although most of his symptoms were psychosomatic. He slept badly and suffered from constant dyspepsia. He complained about his nerves. After a restless night's sleep his day started with a glass of warm milk brought up to his room by Phoebe Warren, no doubt to sooth his raging indigestion. Who knows what nightmares of that room in Miller's Court haunted his sleep?

CHAPTER TWENTY ONE

Encore?

At some time in either 1901 or 1902 Francis took a trip to France, apparently with some friends. The date is not clear since Edward Warren said at the inquest in early 1903 that it was 'a year ago' but both he and Arthur Lane were extremely imprecise in their recollection of the dates of events such as Francis's marriage – in Lane's case by more than five years. Whenever it was, it seems to have coincided with a crisis in Francis's mental state.

According to Edward Warren he visited Paris in the company of two men. One, whom Warren believed was called Hunter, disappeared and when Francis returned he told his friend that he feared that he was suspected of his murder and was being followed by both the French and English police. Research has failed to find any reports of an Englishman of this name dying in France during the years 1900 to 1903 other than a George Hunter who died in Menton in the South of France in 1900 and who does not seem to be relevant.

However, in March 1901, the body of a man was found floating in the river Liane near Boulogne. He was reported to have been strangled before being dumped in the river. Investigations by the French police and their English counterparts established that the body was that of Sergeant David Pool of the

Metropolitan Police. He did not seem to have been robbed and the motive for the murder was unclear[140].

Pool's presence in France was a mystery. He had reported sick with influenza a few days before and had been given leave to return to the Covent Garden section house where, as a bachelor, he was living. As a constable in 1888 he was attached to H Division and had been involved in the Ripper investigations. Pool was not a run-of-the-mill policeman. He was the son of Superintendent David Pool, Deputy Chief Constable of Dumfriesshire, and was an educated man, having been a schoolmaster before joining the Metropolitan Police. A Pool family story has it that he claimed to know the identity of Jack the Ripper but then so did hundreds of people in the last ten years of the 19th century.

Nevertheless he was just the sort of person that *whom* Francis might have known. Newspaper reporters at Thames Magistrates court would have been familiar to most of the local constables, who supplied them with titbits of news, usually in return for a small financial reward. Being an educated man and older than most of his contemporaries, Pool might have been a man who could easily have formed a lasting friendship with Francis and thus be someone who might well have accompanied him on a trip to France. The annual police leave at this time was ten days per year and Pool, whose father had died a few weeks before, may have used up his entitlement in attending the funeral and decided to take a few days extra as 'sick leave'.

Boulogne was the main terminal for the Channel packets and, not infrequently, tourists on their way back from the Continent would break their journey to have a last lunch in one of the many excellent restaurants along the banks of the Liane. Could it have been that Francis, in his disturbed state, was already suspicious as to what David Pool knew or suspected, and perhaps there was a jocular remark as they took a post-lunch stroll down the riverside along the lines of, 'You know, Francis Old Man, even you could have been the Ripper. You lived in the area at the time, knew it like the back of your hand – and didn't they say that the man who sent those letters to Central News was a reporter?' With Francis already suffering extreme paranoia it might just have been sufficient to seal Pool's fate.

Whatever happened on that trip, Francis came back a changed man. His eccentricity seems suddenly to have escalated to delusional, schizoid behaviour. Edward Warren spotted him one rainless day in August hurrying along Hammersmith Broadway dressed in his heavy Inverness coat and crouched under an umbrella as if to shield himself from identification by invisible pursuers. John Reading recounted how on some evenings Francis would come down from his room and sit talking to him before suddenly and without warning jumping up and rushing upstairs.

In early November 1902 Francis asked Edward Warren to look after £50 for him. It was a sum that would be worth perhaps a hundred times that now and it is easy to appreciate Warren's reluctance to be responsible for it. Since Francis is known to have had a bank account it is hard to understand why he might have wanted his friend to look after it. Shortly afterwards Francis instructed Warren to hand it over to anyone he might send for it but Warren refused, saying that he would only hand it over to Francis himself. It looks as if Francis was leaving the money as an insurance against his having to go on the run at a time when the authorities might have put a stop on his bank account. He may even have had a bolt hole already identified and a trusted courier who would collect it from Warren at the critical moment. In any event Warren wanted nothing more to do with it and handed it all back. Francis paid £45 back into his account on 7th November and £5 the following month.

It is apparent from the inquest testimony that Francis's mental state was in a downward spiral by late 1902. Fifteen years after the horror of Miller's Court, the strain of what he had been living with had finally taken its toll. On 2nd March 1903 the scene was set for the finale. It is clear that something odd happened on that last day for, as his landlord John Reading said, Francis was out all day in the pouring rain and came home in the evening drenched to the skin. What took place on that final day we can now only conjecture.

CHAPTER TWENTY TWO

The Last Day

The 2nd March is a day of almost unceasing rain. The grey skies above London remain sullen and static as a steady drizzle soaks the pavements and sends rivulets of sooty water down grimy walls. Francis is awake and has been pacing his room long before Mrs. Reading taps on his door and, in response to his reply, has entered and placed his regular glass of warm milk on the bedside table. She asks if he is ready for his shaving water yet and, receiving an answer in the affirmative, she has returned with a bowl and a jug of steaming water. He lathers his neck and face in the small mirror above the washstand and gives the razor a few swipes across the leather strop to set the edge before starting the familiar routine that he has performed every day for nearly 50 years.

As he tilts his head back and taughtens the skin of his neck, he feels temptation creeping over him. The smooth white sheet of foam looks like virgin snow. It would be easy to let the blade slide down through it like a ploughshare and effortlessly follow the familiar contour from one angle of the jaw to the other.

He resists. It is not time yet. There is work to be done.

He rinses the razor and dries it on the rough white towel before replacing it in its case. He dresses automatically. There is no need for thought. He has only two suits and one is with the tailors in the Broadway for repair. He puts on a clean shirt, a new collar and the black silk tie that is shiny with dirt where the knot has been tied so many times.

Downstairs Mrs. Reading offers him bacon, bread and dripping for breakfast but he declines and takes his Inverness coat and his brown hat from the hall-stand before venturing out. Instead of turning right when he leaves the house he turns left and takes the long way round by way of Dalling Road in order to include Andover Road in his route. He walks slowly the length of the street, looking at the familiar houses. Outside number 10 he pauses and looks hard at the cottage. The fanlight above the front door still bears the word Ralahine picked out in gold letters, faded now by 20 years of sunlight. The rain drips off the brim of his hat and soaks into the thick tweed of his coat.

Were there any happy times there? He can't remember. Were there ever any happy times? What does it matter now? They are all in the past, in another century.

He glances across at number 3 but the rain stings his eyes and he walks on.

When he reaches the Broadway he buys a return ticket on the District Railway to West Ham. He does not need to look at the map. The line from Hammersmith to Whitechapel has been open since 1884 and the eastward extension beyond that has been open a year now. The journey takes 40 minutes and, since it is rush hour, he has to stand most of the way, steam rising from his sodden coat.

It is still raining, if anything even more heavily, when he leaves the station at West Ham. He has about two miles to walk in a northwards direction but the streets are no problem to him. He knows them well. He buys a large bunch of tulips and daffodils from a barrow in Leyton High Road but before he has gone far the rain has caused the brown paper they are wrapped in to dissolve and he is forced to cradle them in his arms. One or two slip from his embrace and fall to the brimming gutter.

He reaches the cemetery and turns in through the gate. There is no-one in sight, just ranks of dripping Madonnas and rain-soaked angels. It is a long time since he was last here but he knows the spot exactly. Nothing marks the grave. It is just a muddy patch of grass. He stands in front of it for a moment and then opens his arms and lets the flowers tumble out to form an untidy heap on the ground. He is not very good at this sort of thing and doesn't know what to do next. He just stares down at the ground as if trying to see through it to what lies beyond his sight. There is absolute silence except for the patter of rain on the trees.

He loses track of time as he stands there thinking of what might have been. Eventually he turns away and walks quickly back towards the cemetery gates through which her funeral procession had wheeled all those years ago. He hardly glances at the Birkbeck Tavern where all her friends had gathered after the funeral to be plied with drink by reporters keen to wring out one last story, some anecdote or other that would satisfy their readers' *schadenfreude*. He could have told them a thing or two if he'd had a mind to.

On the way back he gets off at Stepney Green and crosses the road to look at the house they had lodged in at Lemon's Terrace. Their first home together. He had had such hopes at the beginning but it was there that it had started to go wrong. Within days she had wanted to return to her familiar haunts in the West End. He should have been stronger. He should have stood up to her threats and entreaties. But it was not a skill that his father had taught him. He had only ever been taught to yield, to comply with what others demanded of him. Possibly if he had known how to resist they would still be there, children nearly grown up, a son waiting to go to medical school perhaps, daughters as pretty as their mother.

As he makes his way back towards the station he is accosted by a man who has recognised him. 'Craig, isn't it? My word! I haven't seen you in these parts for years. What have you been doing with yourself? Keeping well I hope? Well, mustn't keep you hanging about in this rain …' He can't remember who it was. A court official perhaps or another reporter. It doesn't matter now.

When he reaches Hammersmith he walks down Fulham Palace Road to the cemetery. The moisture from his coat has now penetrated through to his suit and he can feel the dampness beginning to seep through even that. He walks up the central avenue of the burial ground until he reaches the spot where his parents lie. There is nothing to mark this grave either, no headstone, just a narrow strip of grass between two other graves. He has no flowers to leave here.

It is starting to get dark by the time he reaches Carthew Road but the rain has finally tailed off as if every drop has been wrung from the grey, floor-cloth sky. Mr. Reading meets him in the hall and is surprised at how saturated he is. He gives him the Inverness and the coat of his suit and asks him if he could dry them in front of the kitchen range. He thanks his landlord kindly but, no, he is not hungry. He is going to have an early night.

Sleep doesn't come. He lies looking up at the slight flickering of the street light reflected on the ceiling of his room. He hears the Readings come up to bed and the murmur of their voices in the room next to his. Every time he closes his eyes he sees a muddy patch of grass strewn with flowers and he smells the wet asphalt of the paths.

He thinks of the next day. He does not think he is going to see her. He does not believe in an afterlife. He will not see her again. He does not *want* to see her. That is precisely the point. Once he is gone so she too will vanish. There will be no more memories, no laughing face to visit his dreams. He doubts if there is anyone else who remembers her now and within a few days he will also be forgotten. It will finally be over.

In the early hours he gets up, takes a fresh reporter's pad and pencil and sits at the table. The words won't come. Now the time is approaching he doesn't know what to say.

Sorry perhaps.

Yes, he is sorry for what the Readings will find when they enter his room. They do not deserve it; they have been good to him these last few years. He writes slowly: 'Very sorry; you have acted very kindly to me, I consider more than kindly whilst I have been with you. I have been severely tried physically.' It is hardly adequate, he knows that but he has no other words.

He must make some attempt at an explanation. Not an apology. There can be no apology or forgiveness for what he has done, no atonement. He takes another sheet from the pad. How can he explain it? If they had seen how he had treated those women no explanation would ever suffice. But he must try. He must explain that they were all dead before he carried out his work; that he had done no more to them than doctors and medical students did to the dead every day. But he knows it is no good – they are not doctors and they will never understand. He starts to write: 'It would only pain you to see the Doctor's treatment.' His hand is shaking and his normally clear handwriting is nearly illegible. It is no good, they won't understand. The best he can do is to try to tell them how he had been feeling. He starts again, 'I have suffered a deal of pain and agony, and was no doubt temporarily suffering from pressure of nerve complaints, including several …' But now his hand is shaking so much that he is unable to continue. It will have to do. The time has come.

He wipes his razor a couple of times on the strop and gets back in to bed. He pulls the sheets up close to his neck and raises his hand towards his throat.

CHAPTER TWENTY THREE

Swansong

Unlike his victims, death came slowly to Francis. He had tipped his head right back before he drew the razor across his throat, which is a common thing for people attempting to cut their own throats to do. In doing so his anatomical knowledge had momentarily deserted him because the action causes the sheaths containing the great blood vessels of the neck to be pulled back either side of the spinal column[141]. Instead of severing the carotid arteries as he had intended, Francis merely succeeded in cleanly dividing his windpipe, which instantly deprived him of the power of speech.

He was taken to the West London Hospital, probably by horse-drawn ambulance although, by the early 1900s, the first motor ambulances were beginning to be seen in the streets of London. The hospital was a fine new one just east of Hammersmith Broadway. The building stands today but is now the headquarters of an international electronics company.

Word soon reached the Warrens, and Louisa and her daughter visited him the next day. It is a measure of their kindness and of their affection for Francis that they should have done so. He was not a relative, he was hardly more than a casual acquaintance and visiting anyone under those particular circumstances cannot have been pleasant. He was fully conscious but only able to communicate in writing. This suggests that the wound in his trachea had been left open and a silver tracheostomy tube inserted for him to breathe through. His chief concern, as it had been for months past, was financial. He was convinced that somehow he had lost all his money. The Warrens' daughter tried to reassure him that he had not lost any money but Francis seized the pad again and wrote, 'Yes, I am sure I have.' Then, as if he didn't have other things to worry about he asked – 'instructed' Edward said at the inquest – Louisa to visit a tailors on the Broadway to pick up some clothes that he had left for alterations.

Four days passed before Francis died on Sunday 8th March 1903 at 9pm in the evening. The cause of death was septic pneumonia caused by infected debris entering the lungs through the severed trachea and, because the recurrent laryngeal nerves had also been cut through, aspiration of food and stomach contents into the lungs. In the days before antibiotics it would have been a lingering death with Francis increasingly fighting for breath and vainly trying to cough up the thick sticky secretions that were slowly filling his lungs. He would have developed a fever and probably 24 hours before he died he may have lapsed into unconsciousness. It was not the rapid death that his victims had experienced but, like them, after death his body was opened and his internal organs thoroughly examined in the hospital mortuary. Apart from the pneumonia he was found to be in perfect health.

An inquest was convened at Hammersmith coroner's court on Wednesday 11th March. The coroner was Dr. C. Luxmore Drew, coroner for West Middlesex. Six years previously he had presided over the inquest of Augusta Dawes, an unfortunate whose throat had been cut in Holland Park on 25th November 1894. It was an incident that had awakened memories of the Ripper and indeed a letter was received a few days later by Kensington police station signed Jack the Ripper and posted in Ireland. The culprit was quickly identified as Reginald Saunderson, the 21-year-old nephew of Colonel Edward Saunderson, MP for County Cavan, who had absconded earlier that day from a mental institution in Hampton Wick. He was brought to trial and found unfit to plead by reason of insanity.

At Francis's inquest, before the formal proceedings commenced, the coroner addressed the court to say how sorry he was to be presiding over the inquest of

Mr. Craig as he was well known to his court having been present in his professional capacity on so many occasions in the past. Evidence was taken from Edward Warren, the Readings and Arthur Lane, managing director of the *Indicator*. All agreed that Francis was an eccentric and socially awkward character but clearly likeable and well-regarded. Phoebe Reading gave evidence about having taken up their lodger's usual glass of warm milk and, receiving no answer to her tap on the door, had left it on the table outside. On returning to the kitchen she had not noticed anything on the hall floor but a few minutes later she found a scrap of paper folded into a small pellet which, when unfolded, read, 'Dear Friend, My throat is cut. I hope you will forgive me.'

Her husband John had gone up the stairs to Francis's room and had found him sitting up in bed with a muffler wound around his neck. His first impression was that he had a sore throat and the note was just his colourful journalist's way of expressing it but then, as he leaned across the bed, Francis had seized him by the throat. With his other hand he gestured wildly at his own throat and Reading, clearly shaken, asked, 'Can't you speak Mr. Craig?'

Francis had hastily scrawled on his reporter's pad with a pencil that Reading gave him, 'Fetch any doctor urgently' and then, to the other man's astonishment, had drawn a meticulous plan of the surrounding streets marking out the places where a medical man might be found. Whatever his original intention, Francis had plainly decided that he wanted to live.

When John Reading returned with Dr. Martin and PC Beck a few minutes later, Francis was still fully conscious and sitting up in bed. Beck gave evidence about searching the room and finding two more notes and, on his bedside table, the razor he had used. One note was clearly intended for the Readings and said: 'Very sorry; you have acted very kindly to me, I consider more than kindly whilst I have been with you. I have been severely tried physically.'

The other was an attempt at an explanation, written in a shaky hand, perhaps as Francis tried to screw up his courage for the final act. It read: 'It would only pain you to see the Doctor's treatment. I have suffered a great deal of pain and agony, and was no doubt temporarily suffering from pressure of nerve complaints including several …' There the note ended, the writer obviously too overcome with emotion to continue. Since the only record of the notes is contained in two local newspaper verbatim accounts of the inquest and the notes themselves have long been lost, it is impossible to say whether the word 'Doctor' was capitalised or not. The reporter from the *Fulham Chronicle* assumed that the second note was written after Francis cut his throat, but as it was apparently found in a different part of the room it seems more likely that it was written before the event and was his attempt to explain something that had happened a long time ago.

The Ripper had tried to masquerade as a doctor or a medical student. He joked about the police thinking that he was a doctor. Francis may even have been known, sarcastically, by his father as 'the Doctor' when he tried, unsuccessfully, to pursue life as a medical student many years before. It makes little sense otherwise – why should the Readings or anyone else have been pained to see the doctor's treatment? – indeed there would have been no doctor's treatment if Francis had succeeded in his attempt, only a brief confirmation of death. The note only makes sense if Francis himself is the doctor in question and it would, certainly, have pained them all very much if they had seen the treatment he had meted out to five unfortunate women in the streets of Whitechapel 15 years earlier.

Dr. W. Kenneth Breton, who had looked after Francis while he was in the West London Hospital, gave the cause of death and added that Francis had behaved 'funnily' whilst in hospital. It is tempting to think that an elderly man who desperately wanted to convey to others that he was Jack the Ripper, whilst confined to bed and deprived of the power of speech, might indeed have seemed to be behaving funnily, but that is mere speculation. The verdict was, 'Suicide whilst of unsound mind and when irresponsible for his actions'.

He was buried in the same grave as his parents on 14th March 1903. The ceremony both in the small chapel and at the graveside was performed by Rev. F.W. Northmore, chaplain to the cemetery. The *Indicator*, the paper of which he had been the editor, published a brief account of it on the back page of the edition of Monday 16th March. Amongst the mourners mentioned by name was Arthur Lane, the managing director of the *Indicator*, and three others from the staff of the newspaper, as well as Mrs. Phoebe Reading, Francis's landlady. Almost certainly the Warrens were also present but probably few others.

The funeral arrangements were made by an undertaker near the *Indicator*'s office in Harrow Road, Paddington, so it seems likely that the newspaper arranged and paid for the funeral. He did not, as far as is known, leave a will as there is no record of probate. What happened to his possessions which, it is safe to assume, included a large number of books, is not known. Was there a creased photograph of Elizabeth? Was there even a gold wedding ring? We will never know. As his coffin was lowered into that unmarked grave, Francis Spurzheim Craig effectively passed from history leaving only a *nom de guerre* that has become more infamous and long-lasting than he could ever have imagined.

Epilogue

The Ninth of November, the painting by William Logsdail of Sir James Whitehead's Lord Mayor's Show in 1888, is in the Guildhall Art Gallery. It is a magnificent painting, one of the finest narrative pictures of the late 19th century, and it is pervaded by a feeling of optimism. The streets still glisten with the torrential rain that had fallen during the night but overhead the sky is lightening as the last of the clouds are driven away to reveal patches of blue sky. Remarkably the Lord Mayor himself hardly features. His gilt coach is seen in the background as it rounds the bend in front of the Royal Exchange and the Bank of England, but it is the common people of London who take centre stage. Three liveried footmen fill the centre foreground of the picture, strutting towards the viewer with their beadles' staves as if to herald a new dawn, but they are framed on either side by ordinary Londoners: old women in bonnets and shawls, top-hatted City gents, policemen and children perched on their parents' shoulders to get a better view. It is a depiction of hope, of a new beginning. Whether Logsdail was influenced when he painted it later from his sketches by the knowledge that within a couple of hours and less than a mile from the scene he presents, the body of Mary Jane Kelly would be discovered and the brief era of Jack the Ripper would be over, is unlikely, but it is impossible to escape the sense of a fresh start that it conveys.

The tragic saga of Jack the Ripper is actually a love story. It is the tale of a lonely, dysfunctional man's obsession for a beautiful, lively young woman. Their introduction was possibly a prank that went wrong. Who could have forecast that Francis would fall headlong for a girl so much his opposite? Elizabeth had little education or intellect. She was what would today be called a party animal. What mattered to her was the company of friends, music, dancing, laughter. Francis was by contrast a solitary man. Any conversation longer than a few minutes became a burden from which he had to escape. The idea of singing or dancing would have horrified him. What he sought was love, tenderness, understanding, the very things that had been denied to him by doctrinaire parents fixated on their own cranky theories on the upbringing of children. Who knows that, given time, he might have learned to socialise, he might have fathered children to whom he could have shown affection such as he had never experienced. When the object of his desire deserted him it was more than he could take. He sought her out, beseeched her to come back to him, to give it another try, but Elizabeth had never been in it for anything other than a laugh. The idea of spending the rest of her life with this strange, reclusive man was unthinkable.

For his part the prospect of losing the only other human being for whom he had felt real emotion was unbearable. It brought back all the old bitterness, the sense of failure and disappointment, the inability to please his father. It festered within him and eventually came out like an abscess being lanced in the 12-week orgy of killing that finally drove him to destroy the only thing he loved. The rest of his life must have been passed in a kind of numbness where he did a mundane job automatically and tried to blot out of his mind the terrible thing that he had done.

In the end it was no good. He couldn't forget Elizabeth, the few times that they had been happy together, the sound of her laughter, the wonder on her face as she saw Paris for the first time. The remorse grew and grew until eventually it overwhelmed him. He may have made a final pilgrimage to see the places that they had known together, culminating in a visit to her grave. Then he returned to his room in a humble cottage in West London and attempted to atone with his own life.

And even that was a failure.

Bibliography

BOOKS

Ackroyd, Peter. *London, The Biography*. Chatto and Windus, London, 2001.

Acton, William. *Prostitution, considered in its moral, social and sanitary aspects, in London and other large cities*. John Churchill, London, 1862.

Anon. *The London Dissector or System of Dissection Practiced in the Hospitals and Lecture Rooms of the Metropolis*. Third Edition. John Murray, London, 1811.

Armytage, W.H.G. *Heavens Below: Utopian experiments in England, 1560–1960*. Routledge and Keegan Paul, London, 1961.

Baron, Wendy and Richard Shone. *Sickert Paintings. Catalogue of the exhibition at the Royal Academy of Arts, London and the Van Gough Museum, Amsterdam, Nov 1992–May 1993*. Yale University Press, New Haven and London, 1992.

Beeton, Isabella. *A Book of Household Management*. S O Beeton, London, 1861.

Begg, Paul, Martin Fido and Keith Skinner. *The Complete Jack the Ripper A to Z*. John Blake, London, 2010.

Begg, Paul and John Bennett. *Jack the Ripper. The Forgotten Victims*. Yale University Press, New Haven, CT, USA, 2013.

Birnes, W.J. & R.D. Keppel. *Serial violence: Analysis of modus operandi and signature characteristics of killers.* CRC Press, Boca Raton, FL USA, 2009.

Borrow, George. *Wild Wales.* Ed. J.B. Foreman. London, 1862.

Bowman, Francesca. *Shapely Ankle Preferr'd.* Chatto and Windus, London, 2011.

Browse, Lillian (Ed.), *Sickert.* Faber and Faber, London, 1943.

Clapham, Sir John Harold, Michael Roissey Poston, Edwin Ernest Rich (Eds) *The Cambridge Economic History of Europe, Vol 5, The Economic Organisation of Early Modern Europe.* Cambridge University Press, Cambridge, 1977.

Clarke, Steven. *Dirty Bertie, An English King Made in France.* Century, London, 2014.

Combe, George. *Lectures on Phrenology* (Ed. Andrew Boardman). Simkin, Marshall & Co., London, 1839.

Cornwell, Patricia. *Portrait of a Killer. Jack the Ripper. Case Closed.* Little, Brown, London, 2002.

Cowling, Mary. *The Artist as Anthropologist.* Cambridge University Press, 1989.

Craig, Edward Thomas. *An Irish Commune, the History of Ralahine.* Martin Lester Limited, Dublin, 1919.

Craig, Edward Thomas. *Memoirs of E T Craig, one of the originators of the Co-operative Movement and historian of Ralahine.* Privately printed, London, 1885.

Craig, Edward Thomas. *The Triangular Carriage for moving through the air … for the prevention of war …* Hammersmith 1892.

Craig, Edward Thomas. *Ralahine idealised, or Organised production, distribution, and consumption.* Hammersmith, 1892.

Craig, Edward Thomas. *History of a Great Discovery in the Prevention of Premature Death by the power to restore the fluidity of the vital current, in cases of inflammation of the blood, etc.* Hammersmith, 1892.

Craig, Edward Thomas. *The Portraits, Bust and Monument of Shakespeare.* Frederick Pitman, London, 1886.

Craig, Edward Thomas. *The science of prolonging human life through nervous energy, and the vitalising distribution of the blood, by methods accessible to all, etc.* Privately printed, London, 1885.

Dabhoiwala, Faramerz. *The Origins of Sex. A History of the First Sexual Revolution*. Allen Lane, London, 2012.

Davis, Tracy C. *Actresses as Working Women, Their Social Identity in Victorian Culture*. Routledge, Taylor and Francis, London, 1991.

The Dictionary of National Biography. Oxford University Press.

Evans, Stewart P. and Keith Skinner. *Jack the Ripper. Letters from Hell*. Sutton Publishing, Stroud, 2001.

Flanders, Judith. *The Invention of Murder*. Harper Press, London, 2011.

Henderson, Tony. *Disorderly Women in Eighteenth-Century London: Prostitution and Control in the Metropolis, 1730–1830*. Longman, London and New York, 1999.

Holmes, Ronald M.; Stephen T. Holmes. *Serial Murder* (3rd ed.). Sage, Thousand Oaks, California, USA, 2010.

Horn, Pamela. *The Rise and Fall of the Victorian Servant*. Gill and Macmillan, 1975.

Hutchinson, Phillip. *The Jack the Ripper Location Photographs. Dutfield's Yard and the Whitby Collection*. Amberly Publishing plc, Stroud, 2009.

Jakubowski, Maxim and Nathan Braund (Eds) *The Mammoth Book of Jack the Ripper*, Robinson, London, 1999.

King, David. *Death in the City of Light*. Random House, New York, 2011.

Knight, Calum Reuben. *Jack the Ripper. End of a Legend*. Athena Press, London, 2005.

Knight, Stephen. *Jack the Ripper: the Final Solution*. George G. Harrap, London, 1976.

Lewis, Henry (Ed.), *Collins-Spurrell Welsh Dictionary*, Collins, London, 1960.

Lilly, Marjorie. *Sickert: The Painter and his Circle*. Noyes Press, London, 1973.

MacCarthy Fiona. *William Morris A Life for Our Time*. Faber and Faber. London, 1994.

McCormick, Donald. *The Identity of Jack the Ripper*. John Long, London, 1959 (Second Edn– 1970).

Marriott, Trevor. *Jack the Ripper. The Twentieth Century Investigation*. John Blake, London, 2007.

Mason, Michael. *The Making of Victorian Sexuality*. Oxford University Press, Oxford, 1994.

Mayhew, Henry. *London Labour and the London Poor* (Originally published 1851–52). Ed. Victor Neuberg. Penguin Books, 1985.

Nead, Lynda. *Myths of Sexuality. Representations of Women in Victorian Britain*. Basil Blackwell, Oxford, 1988.

Odell, Robin. *Jack the Ripper in Fact and Fiction. New and Revised Edition*. Mandrake, Oxford 2008.

Overton Fuller, Jean. *Sickert and the Ripper Crimes*. Mandrake, Oxford, 1990.

Oxford Dictionary of National Biography. Oxford University Press.

Richards, Alun John. *The Slate Railways of Wales*. Gwasg Carreg Gwalch, Llanwrst, 2001.

Ritchie, J. Ewing. *The Night Side of London*. Wm. Tweedie, London, 1857.

Rule, Fiona. *The Worst Street in London*. Ian Allen, London, 2008.

Severn, J. Millott. *Popular Phrenology*. William Rider & Son. London, 1918.

Shone, Richard. *Walter Sickert*. Phaidon, Oxford, 1988.

Sickert, Walter Richard (Ed. Osbert Sitwell). *A Free House! Or the Artist as Craftsman*. Arcade Publishing, New York, 2012.

Simpson, Keith. *Forensic Medicine*. Edward Arnold, London, 1958.

Sims, George Robert. *My life; sixty years' recollections of Bohemian London*. Eveleigh Nash Company, London, 1917.

Sims, George Robert. *How the Poor Live*. 1883. Reprinted by Kessinger Publishing (Dodo Press), London, 2009.

Sims, George Robert. *Horrible London*. 1883. Reprinted by Kessinger Publishing (Dodo Press), London, 2009.

Sims, George Robert (Ed.) and others. *Living London: Its Work and its Play, Its Humour and its Pathos, its Sights and its Scenes*. Cassell and Company, London, 1859.

Sleman, Tom (with Keith Andrews). *Jack the Ripper. British Intelligence Agent?* Bluecoat Press, 2010.

Starr, Douglas. *The Killer of Little Shepherds*. Simon and Schuster, London, 2011.

Sturgis, Matthew. *Walter Sickert. A Life*. Harper Perennial. London, 2005.

Sugden, Philip. *The Complete History of Jack the Ripper*. Constable and Robinson, London, 1994.

Summerscale, Kate. *The Suspicions of Mr Whicher*. Bloomsbury Publishing, London, 2008.

Tooley's Dictionary of Map Makers, Map Collector Publications in association with Richard Arkway Ltd, Tring, Herts, 1999.

Turgeon, Laurier. *Codfish, Consumption and Colonization: the Creation of the French Atlantic World during the Sixteenth Century*, from *Bridging the Early Modern Atlantic World: People, Products, and Practices on the Move*. Caroline Williams (Ed.). Ashgate Publishing, Farnham, UK and Burlington, VT, USA, 2009.

Turnbull, Peter. *The Killer Who Never Was*. Clark and Lawrence, 1996.

Van Onselen, Charles. *The Fox and the Flies, The World of Joseph Silver, Racketeer and Psychopath*. Jonathan Cape, London, 2007.

Wearing, J. P. *The London Stage 1890–1959. A Calendar of Plays and Players* (7 Vols). The Scarecrow Press, Lanham MD, USA, 1976–1993 .

Williams, Richard. *Montgomeryshire Worthies*. Phillips and Son, Newtown, 1894.

Who Was Who in the Theatre, 1912–1976: A Biographical Dictionary of Actors, Actresses, Directors, Playwrights and Producers of the English-Speaking Theatre. Gale Group, London, 1976.

Woods, Paul and Gavin Baddely, *Saucy Jack. The Elusive Ripper.* Ian Allen, Hersham, 2009.

PAPERS

Evans, A. 'E T Craig: proto-socialist, phrenologist, and public health engineer'. *International Journal of Epidemiology* 2008;37:490–505.

Garnett. R.G. E T Craig: communitarian, educator, phrenologist, *J Vocational Education & Training* 1963;15:135–50.

Keppel. R.D. 'Signature murders: a report of several related cases'. *Journal of Forensic Sciences* 1995;40(4):670-4.

Luddy, Maria. 'Abandoned Women and Bad Characters': prostitution in nineteenth-century Ireland. *Women's History Review*, Volume 6, Number 4, 1997.

Malone C. 'Murder by Design? – George Bagster Phillips and the enigma of the medical evidence in the Whitechapel Murders'. *The New Independent Review.* Issue 4 July 2012: 1–56.

Morton L.T. *'London's Last Private Medical School'.* Journal of the Royal Society of Medicine, Vol. 84, 1991.

Taylor, Rosemary. "'The City of Dreadful Delight.'" William Morris in the East End of London'. *The Journal of William Morris Studies.* Winter 2009 (9–28)

Wolf, G. 'A kidney from hell? A nephrological view of the Whitechapel murders in 1888'. *Nephrol Dial Transplant* (2008) 23:3343-3349.

LIBRARIES AND COLLECTIONS
The National Archives, Kew
The British Library, London
The London Metropolitan Archives, London
The Bodleian Library, Oxford
Gloucestershire County Libraries
Tower Hamlets Archives
Hammersmith and Fulham Archives
Kensington Library
Suffolk County Records Office
Durham County Archives
Camden Local Studies and Archives Centre
Powys Archives
British National Newspaper Archives, Colindale
Buckinghamshire County Library, Aylesbury
Hampshire County Library, Winchester
Bournemouth Library and Local Studies Centre
Westminster Library

Websites
Innumerable but particularly:
www.wikipedia.org

www.casebook.org

www.ancestry.com

www.findmypast.co.uk

www.historyofphrenology.org.uk

www.museumwales.ac.uk

www.wales-underground.org.uk

www.archive.timesonline.co.uk

Endnotes

CHAPTER ONE

1   The exact date of Mary Jane Kelly's first appearance in the East End is unknown but the consensus of most contemporary sources is that it was late 1885 or early 1886.

2   Mrs Buki was first mentioned in a report in *The Star*, 12th November 1888. The informant may have been Mrs Mary McCarthy, her sister Mrs Elizabeth Phoenix or Joe Barnett. Why the reporter spelled her name in that way or whether that spelling was suggested to him by his informant(s) is not known.

3   Henry Mayhew gives many colourful accounts of the brothels, the music halls and the public houses of the Ratcliffe Highway and St. George's Street in *London Labour and the London Poor*.

4   *The Star*, 12th November 1888.

5   Ibid.

6   Ibid. There were also reports in the *Morning Advertiser* and the *Daily News* on 10th November 1888, apparently by the same reporter, which quoted a woman who had known her when she lodged in Thrall Street before she met Joe Barnett, that categorically stated that she was Welsh and spoke Welsh fluently.

7   In Georgian London most prostitutes were second-generation Irish and as a result the names Moll or Molly were usually applied to them (*Source*: Rictor Norton, *The Georgian Underworld – A Study of Criminal Subcultures in Eighteenth-Century England*, published online and updated 28th January 2012). By the 1880s the famines resulting from the potato blight had caused massive Irish immigration into London and other cities. The resulting poverty forced even more Irish girls into prostitution and the soubriquet Kelly supplanted Molly as a generic term for a prostitute.

8   *The Star*, 12th November 1888.

9   Evidence given by Joe Barnett at Kelly's inquest. Marie Jeanette Kelly Inquest Papers MJ/SPC/NE. London Metropolitan Archives.

10   Neal Shelden, *Mary Jane Kelly and the Victims of Jack the Ripper*, Revised 2013.

11   *The Star*, on 12th November, reported Joe Barnett as having said that while she was living at Pennington Street her father came looking for her but, tipped off by her friends, she kept out of his way. If it was Elizabeth, her actual father had been dead for ten years by 1885. Joe or her friends may have made the assumption that an older man looking for her must have been her father, or Elizabeth may have encouraged them to think that, but it is more probable that the older man was Francis who, at 49, was old enough to be her father.

12   The thorough research conducted by the Sheldens included the 1871,
       1881 and 1891 censuses, rates books and electoral registers for Fulham,
       Tower Hamlets and Bow and builds an unassailable case for the identity
       of Mrs Boekü and the Morganstern brothers, proving that it is possible
       to solve mysteries by the use of modern computing power that baffled
       the police and countless historians for nearly 130 years.

CHAPTER TWO

13   Stout has several meanings and in the 19th century it was often used as a
       synonym for fit or healthy. Given that most other accounts, for instance
       that of Mrs Prater, describe her as good looking it is possible that this is
       what Mrs Phoenix intended.

14   For a graphic account of Dorset Street and others in the 'wicked half
       mile' and the slum landlords that controlled the area see *The Worst Street
       in London* by Fiona Rule.

15   There were at least three popular sentimental paintings of this name
       from which prints were made in the late 19th century. The one by
       Charles James Lewis (1830–1892) was the most popular and therefore
       most likely to have been the one on the wall of Miller's Court.

16   Although this has been repeated by a number of previous authors it is
       not known what the evidence for this is. At the inquest Thomas Bowyer
       stated that it was the pane on the furthest side of the window that was
       broken and, if this is so, it appears that it would be impossible to reach
       the door catch by inserting an arm judging from contemporary illustra-
       tions. At least four people (Bowyer, McCarthy, Phillips and Abberline)
       looked through the broken pane and it seems extraordinary that none of
       them noticed that the lock on the door could be reached by inserting an
       arm if that had been possible.

The Real Mary Kelly

17 Statement made by Joe Barnett to the Metropolitan Police at
    Commercial Street police station, 9th November 1888: 'She had a
    brother called Henry who was in the 2nd Battalion Scots Guards,
    known amongst his comrades as Johnto.' Evidence given by Joe Barnett
    at Kelly's inquest. Marie Jeanette Kelly Inquest Papers MJ/SPC/NE.
    London Metropolitan Archives.

18 This statement by Joe Barnett at Mary Jane's inquest seems to be the
    only evidence that she had met the man with whom she went to France
    at the French woman's brothel near Knightsbridge (Joe Barnett did not
    say that it was actually *in* Knightsbridge as many others have done since,
    only 'near Knightsbridge'). He seems to have made the assumption that
    that was where she had met him but there is no other evidence for it.
    If Mary Jane and Elizabeth were the same person it seems unlikely
    that she met Francis as a customer. The divorce petition appears to
    show genuine surprise that she was working as a prostitute and she
    would not have needed to use the story of being a widow if he knew
    her to be a prostitute.

19 Many people have reported that Joe suffered from echolalia based on
    transcripts of the evidence he gave at the inquest. This is not so much
    an impediment as a mannerism in which the final words of the previous
    speaker are repeated at the start of the subject's response. It is particu-
    larly associated with the autism spectrum although there is no other
    evidence that Joe was autistic. His responses to the coroner's questions
    and his frequent misunderstandings suggest that he may have had what
    today would be called a learning disability. The fact that the coroner
    thanked him kindly at the end of his testimony and congratulated him
    on the way he had dealt with the ordeal of giving evidence suggests that
    this was recognised at the time. It might not therefore be surprising if
    much of his evidence was confused and not to be relied upon.

20 It is not clear where they got this name from although it raises the

intriguing possibility that she was sometimes addressed by her friends by her actual Christian name. No British newspapers seem to have picked up on it.

21   Yet again it seems as if the more painstaking American reporters came closer to the truth than their British counterparts. In part that might be explained by the fact that most US foreign correspondents were salaried whereas the British reporters were largely freelance and therefore more prone to take shortcuts in their rush to outcompete their colleagues.

CHAPTER THREE

22   Frederick Stewart, the fourth Marquess was George Vane-Tempest's elder half-brother and nephew of Lord Castlereagh, the British Foreign Secretary who committed suicide in 1822. Frederick had married Lady Elizabeth Jocelyn, daughter of the Third Earl of Roden, in 1846 but their marriage was childless and they separated later when she converted to Roman Catholicism. Frederick lived a dissolute life thereafter and became insane, almost certainly as a result of tertiary syphilis. He died a recluse, confined in his own rooms for many years and looked after day and night by a private surgeon and several burly attendants. Ironically he died in White Rock Villa, St Leonards-on-Sea, a house owned by his estranged wife's family.

23   The exact connection is not clear but both her father, Edward and a Gilder son, Charles, had been land surveyors in and around Aberangell, both probably employed by Sir John Edwards. It is also possible that Edward in his youth may have been a part-time member of the Montgomeryshire Militia of which his employer was colonel and William Gilder was Captain and Adjutant. Landowners who were also colonels of militia or yeomanry regiments expected their labourers and younger male house servants to be members of their unit and they were often given time off in order to fulfil their military obligations.

If Elizabeth had grown up knowing the Gilders it would be natural that she might seek out the family and their alter egos, the Maundrells, once she arrived in London.

24   Entries in 1851 and 1861 censuses, the Montgomeryshire Militia Rolls and *The London Gazette*. William Gilder's bankruptcy took place in 1838, the year of Queen Victoria's Coronation. It was a year of great celebrations, balls, *levées* and military parades. His colonel, Sir John Edwards, was foremost in making a lavish display which Gilder no doubt did his best to keep up with. With a wife and six daughters between the ages of 12 and 24 to provide ball gowns for, the price of his own ornate dress uniforms and entertaining, the cost must have placed a disastrous strain on his meagre military salary. He spent the rest of his long life paying off his creditors.

25   Even conservative estimates put the *per capita* number of prostitutes compared with the population of London as much higher in the 18th and 19th centuries than it is today. *Source*: Tony Henderson, *Disorderly Women in Eighteenth-Century London: Prostitution and Control in the Metropolis, 1730–1830*. Longman, London and New York, 1999.

26   Evidence for Ellen Macleod's love of all things French includes the entry in the 1851 census where as a precocious 7-year-old she has obviously dictated her place of birth to the English enumerator as 'France, Côtes du Nord, Barach près de Lannion,' even including the accents although the bemused enumerator has misplaced these. Her only daughter Helen Kathleen followed her on to the stage and had a very successful career, specialising in French productions and French language parts.

27   William Macleod had an exemplary service record, acting as secretary to several admirals and commanders of the Far East Fleet, where his considerable linguistic talents would have stood him in good stead. Suddenly and inexplicably, in 1895, he was sent home in disgrace having

suffered a breakdown attributed to strain and alcohol. This may have coincided with his discovery that his wife had been a prostitute and the Madam of many brothels. It is tempting to look at Walter Sickert's picture '*Jack Ashore*', in which a dejected older man sits slumped at the head of a bed from which is rising a large naked woman with pendulous breasts, and imagine that this represents the moment when William Macleod realised that his marriage was finally over. He was eventually passed fit for Home Service only and retired in the rank of Paymaster in Chief. He appears never to have returned to his wife and when he died in 1937 he left his entire estate of £2,289.13.11 (a tidy sum in those days) to their only child Helen Kathleen.

28   At various times the extended Maundrell/Gilder family lived in at least seven different London addresses and owned several more. After the death of Robert John Maundrell in 1883, Frederica's name appears as the ratepayer or Head of the Household of their principal residences. Francis Craig's divorce petition names her sister as the 'occupier' of at least three brothels in the Holloway district of London and mentions three others which may also have been part of her empire, so it seems as if the two sisters owned or leased an extensive property portfolio.

29   *Source*: Steven Clarke, *Dirty Bertie: An English King Made in France*. Century, London, 2014. The Prince of Wales had a *fauteuil d'amour* (love seat) specially made and kept in the Hindu room at *Le Chabanais*. Exquisitely made in the *Louis Quinze* style, it had a velvet upholstered platform to support his considerable bulk, gilded stirrups and curved uprights for added traction. It enabled the heir to the British throne and up to two women to engage in sexual activity in an almost infinite variety of positions. It has recently been re-discovered and is now being restored by the original makers. It is interesting to speculate what the majority of his future subjects would have made of it had they known of its existence at the time.

30   Today Collingham Place is definitely in the Royal Borough of
      Kensington and Chelsea but the boundary between Kensington and
      Knightsbridge is ill-defined on 19th-century maps. Joe Barnett said that
      Marie Jeanette had worked in a French brothel 'near Knightsbridge' and
      Collingham Place would certainly have fitted that description.

31   The Maundrells moved to Kensington after the death of Robert John in
      1883 but they appear to have retained their old house, 81 Camden Road.
      Walter Sickert rented it in 1917. In her book, *Sickert: The Artist and His
      Circle*, Marjorie Lilly wrote about an old Gladstone bag owned by
      Sickert on which he had painted 'The Shrubbery, 81 Camden Road.'
      This is also quoted by Patricia Cornwell in *Portrait of a Killer*. See also
      Matthew Sturgis, *Walter Sickert: A Life*. Harper Collins, London, 2005.
      Walter Sickert's connection with the Maundrell/Macleod family is
      enigmatic but there seem to be so many hints in paintings such as '*Jack
      Ashore*' and the coincidence of him living in one of their houses as to
      make it very likely that he knew them over a considerable period of time.
      Judging by Francis Craig's divorce petition Ellen Macleod must have
      been a very well-known Madam in the Camden, Holloway, St Pancras
      area of London and, with her many literary and artistic connections, just
      the sort of person that the younger Sickert would have known.
           Sickert certainly spent a lot of time at Kelmscott House, watching
      the boat race from there and playing rumbustious games in the garden
      (Sturgis).
           Although no direct evidence for a friendship between Sickert and
      Sims has yet been found, it seems inconceivable that the two men did
      not know each other. Both their families were of a politically radical
      persuasion and friendly with William Morris. Both men were intimately
      connected with the theatre; Sims was a prolific playwright and Sickert,
      who had himself started life as an actor, retained a lifelong fascination
      with the theatre and the music hall. Both men were devotees of the Old
      Bedford Music Hall in Camden Town. Both were journalists and wrote
      for the same magazines and, perhaps more importantly, both men had an

appetite for the low life of London including gambling, consorting with prostitutes and attending prize fights. They shared many of the same friends including William Morris, Oscar Wilde, Charles Bradlaugh, Frank Harris and Richard Cobden.

Sickert was fascinated by prostitutes, who were the subjects of many of his paintings. It is not impossible that some of his models were girls that he met through Ellen Macleod. He was also deeply interested in the Ripper murders to the extent that he has himself been implicated or named as a suspect by many authors, notably Patricia Cornwell. In his later life he was a close friend of the author's uncle, who said that on many occasions Sickert would hint darkly that he knew more about the affair than he was prepared to say.

32   *Memoirs of E.T. Craig, one of the originators of the Co-operative Movement and historian of Ralahine.* Privately printed, London, 1885.

33   Garnett, R.G., *E.T. Craig: communitarian, educator, phrenologist.* J Vocational Education & Training 1963;15:135–50.

34   The term 'professor' meant little more than teacher in the 19th century and did not imply that the bearer held a university post. E.T. Craig was largely self-educated but in his youth had attended the Manchester Mechanics' Institute, the forerunner of UMIST, the present-day University of Manchester Institute of Science and Technology. Evans A. 'E.T. Craig: proto-socialist, phrenologist and public health engineer'. *International Journal of Epidemiology* 2008;37:490–505.

35   Ibid.

36   Combe, George. *Lectures on Phrenology* (Ed. Andrew Boardman). Simkin, Marshall & Co., London, 1839. Page 118.

37   His friend Edward Warren and his landlord John Reading both gave accounts of Francis's curious inability to sustain a face-to-face conversation. Inquest reports in the *Fulham Chronicle* and the *West London Observer*, 13th March 1903.

38   Francis is known to have travelled to America in 1864 and he probably stayed there for two years. His friend Edward Warren described at his inquest Francis journeying to Paris in 1901 or 1902. Much of his journalism concerns journeys and travel including trips through the British countryside by canal boat and by tricycle.

39   Arrivals, New York, April 1864. A Francis Craig, aged 26, is shown amongst the passengers. There is no other information except that he had embarked at Liverpool. Francis was 26 at the time and examination of the England and Wales censuses from 1851 onwards show that there was no other Francis Craig of exactly his age resident in England or Wales.

40   Editorial, *Oxford Journal*, 5th January 1884.

CHAPTER FOUR

41   Seymour Street is actually in Marylebone rather than Euston but possibly Euston Square's proximity to the station made it sound more commercial.

42   Fiona MacCarthy. *William Morris: A Life For Our Time*. Faber and Faber, London, 1994.

43   Edward Thomas Craig. *Oxford Dictionary of National Biography*.

44   The petition was a document setting out the reasons that the petitioner (Francis) was seeking a divorce. It could be written by anyone although was usually drawn up by a solicitor. The affidavit was a legal document

that had to be signed in the presence of a commissioner for oaths in which the petitioner swore that the contents of the petition were true. In Francis's case the two documents were more or less identical.

45   53 Tonbridge Street was a matter of a few hundred yards from the house where Francis and Elizabeth had lodgings in Argyle Square. Elizabeth was being surprisingly reckless in carrying out her trade so close to home. It was even nearer to the lodgings that her brother Johnto occupied in Leigh Street at the time. Her total disregard for risk fits well with Mary Jane's reported character in Whitechapel later.

46   Mary Jane Kelly told Joe Barnett that she was a widow and that her married name had been Davies, and both names are recorded in the Deaths Indexes for the October–December quarter of 1888 and on her death certificate, showing that the authorities considered that either name was as likely as the other to be her true name.

47   Journalists, then as now, have their names appended to their copy, re-porters do not.

48   A flavour of the sort of easy-going informality that characterised Warren is that in the 1881 census he gave his wife's name as Louie and his children's names as Minnie, Florrie and Charlie.

49   Harry McBlain is the only one of Elizabeth's clients who is identified by name in the divorce petition and no doubt that – and the fact that they met repeatedly during July and August of 1885 – is why he is named as the co-respondent. He was a widower, living with his two sons and four daughters in some comfort in a villa in Camden Town.

50   No evidence that Elizabeth and Francis actually spent time in Paris together has been found. Mary Jane Kelly told several people including Joe Barnett that she had been to Paris in the company of a gentleman

shortly before moving to the East End and Francis is known to have liked the city and to have travelled there at least once in later life. If they had any sort of honeymoon, Paris seems a plausible destination. The person she went to Paris with could equally well have been Harry McBlain.

51   Elizabeth's brother John, known to his family as Johnto, was at the time lodging with the family of a Welsh dairyman in Leigh Street near to the Craigs' home in Argyle Square. It would be natural for Francis to contact John after Elizabeth disappeared to seek news of her. If Elizabeth had written the letter to her brother he may have handed it over to Francis in a well-intentioned but misguided effort to re-unite the couple.

CHAPTER FIVE

52   According to Malcolm Barr-Hamilton, the archivist for Tower Hamlets, 306 Mile End Road was at the time directly opposite the old Beth Din Jewish hospital which still exists.

53   Notes attached to the divorce petition of Francis Spurzheim Craig. National Archives. Divorce Court File: 692. Appellant: Francis Spurzheim Craig. Respondent: Elizabeth Weston Davies Craig. Co-respondent: Harry McBain. Type: Husband's petition for divorce [hd]. J 77/354/692

54   Johnto is a common Welsh diminutive form of John. Strictly speaking it should be Ianto since there is no letter J in the Welsh language. It would be most improbable that a Welshman called Henry (in itself an unlikely name for either a Welshman or an Irishman to have been given at that time because of its English royal connections) would have been called Johnto by Scottish army colleagues. Elizabeth's family habitually used the '–to' diminutive form of boys' names. John's own eldest son Wynne would later be known as Wynnto in the family.

55   The police at the time and many historians since have searched the army
     records for evidence of a man called Henry Kelly serving with the Scots
     Guards at around this period. None have been found.

56   Sir Frederick Treves performed the first successful operation in Britain
     to remove an inflamed appendix at the London Hospital, Whitechapel,
     the following year, 1889. Before that time appendicitis frequently led
     to peritonitis and death. Elizabeth's younger sister Margaret Maria had
     died of the condition in 1879.

CHAPTER SIX

57   The *East London Observer*, 8th September 1888, reporting the inquest
     of Mary Ann Nichols, said that it was opened by Baxter 'fresh from his
     Scandinavian tour'.

58   *East London Advertiser*, 8th September 1888. The recent use of this spell-
     ing by Bill Gates amongst others has been a matter of comment. It does
     seem fairly good evidence that the *Advertiser*'s reporter was familiar with
     American usage.

59   In death people often appear younger than their actual age. Philip
     Sugden noted in his book *The Complete History of Jack the Ripper* that the
     police estimates of the ages of the victims were all younger than they in
     fact turned out to be.

60   Notes attached to the divorce petition of Francis Spurzheim Craig.
     National Archives. Divorce Court File: 692. Appellant: Francis
     Spurzheim Craig. Respondent: Elizabeth Weston Davies Craig.
     Co-respondent: Harry McBain. Type: Husband's petition for divorce
     [hd]. J 77/354/692.

61 It is likely that at least two copies of the documents existed, the one lodged with the High Court and Francis's own one. Possibly his original solicitor Arthur Ivens kept another or that may have been handed over to Francis when he decided to act for himself in 1887. The one in The National Archives is undoubtedly the one from the High Court so Francis may have struck out paragraphs 5 to 9 on his own copy to satisfy Ellen Macleod.

CHAPTER SEVEN

62 *East London Advertiser*, 23rd August 1888.

63 When given leave to be out of barracks for the evening, soldiers had to wear Walking-out Dress and infantry sergeants and below had to carry their bayonets slung from a scabbard above the left hip.

64 The Church of England Series 3 Wedding Service authorised for use from November 1977 was the first to mention the exchanging of rings in the Anglican Liturgy. Before then, in England it was usual only for the bride to wear a wedding ring. The wearing of wedding rings by men became popular in the United States following an advertising campaign by the American jewellery industry in the late 19th century.

65 www.wikipedia.org.

66 Ibid.

67 www.murderpedia.org.

68 Report of the inquest on Francis Spurzheim Craig, the *Fulham Chronicle*, 13th March 1903.

69   The depth of his feelings came out years later in a bitterly ironic editorial that he wrote for the *Indicator* attacking a recent Act of Parliament that, he thought, gave unwarranted succour to married women deserted to their husbands but no corresponding help to men deserted by, in his words, 'bad, drunken wives'. *The Indicator*, January 22nd 1896.

70   Holmes, Ronald M. and Stephen T. Holmes. *Serial Murder* (3rd edn). Sage, Thousand Oaks, California, USA, 2010.

71   Morton, L.T. *London's Last Private Medical School.* Journal of the Royal Society of Medicine, Vol. 84, 1991.

72   There has been an enormous amount of discussion by historians and Ripperologists and indeed by journalists and the police at the time as to whether the Ripper had anatomical training or surgical skill. Many have said that the rather crude way in which the abdomen of Catherine Eddowes in particular was opened indicates that he was not a skilled anatomist or dissector. This ignores the fact that the entire operation, from rendering Catherine unconscious, slitting her throat, exposing and opening her abdomen and then not only mobilising her small intestines and removing the descending colon but also removing both the left kidney and the reproductive organs took place in less than five minutes, in very poor light on the pavement of Mitre Square. Dr George Bagster Phillips was right in saying that it might have taken a surgeon upwards of an hour to do the same. It is hardly surprising therefore that an amateur who may have watched a few dissections many years before might have made a less than perfect job of it.

73   Examples of E.T. Craig's artistic skill is evident from the engravings credited to him that accompany some of his books and pamphlets in the British Library collection. Francis was employed as a mapmaker by William Spalding in Cambridge from 1871 to 1875 and the resulting *Plan of Cambridge and its Environs* together with the map that he drew

on his deathbed are adequate proof of his draughtsman's skills. In addition it is known that E.T. Craig was strongly in favour of children being taught to draw before they could read, *vide*: Evans A. 'E.T. Craig: proto-socialist, phrenologist and public health engineer'. *International Journal of Epidemiology* 2008;37:490–505.

74 Many authors and Ripperologists have contended that the victims were first strangled by the Ripper before their throats were cut. Strangulation however produces very characteristic bruising which is centred on the midline over the larynx or voice box with counter-pressure marks at the back of the neck. The police surgeons would have been familiar with this and have looked for it but it was not present in any of the canonical five victims. Bruising over the carotid areas, the jaw and the upper chest was found in a number of cases and this is consistent with the use of the carotid pressure points to render the victims unconscious. See *Forensic Medicine* by Keith Simpson for a description of the bruising found in cases of manual strangulation. Unless they had studied anatomy few people would have been familiar with the carotid pressure points in 1888.

75 Illustrated Catalogue and Price List. John Weiss and Son. 1889. Compiled by J.F. Foveaux. Printed by M.S. Rickerby, London.

76 *Oxford Dictionary of National Biography.*

77 There is much confusion in the literature regarding witness descriptions of hats worn by various Ripper suspects. In particular the description 'wideawake' has often been taken by modern writers to mean a broad-brimmed hat of the type worn by Australian soldiers. In the 1880s a wideawake was any hat made from pressed felt, known by that name because it had no 'nap'. The most popular hat for lower middle-class men was a domed hat of the sort later known as a bowler. In the 1880s it was variously known as a Coke hat, a low crowned hat (to distinguish it from a top hat) or a billycock.

78   Letter from Thomas Bond comparing the murder of Marie Jeanette
      Kelly (Mary Jane Kelly) with four of the previous murders, and an as-
      sessment of the murderer (copy of same in MEPO 3/140, ff 220-223).

CHAPTER EIGHT

79   Many newspapers including *The Times*, Friday 31st August 1888, re-
      ported the fires at the docks. The one at the Ratcliffe dry dock broke out
      too late for the Friday editions of the morning papers however. It was
      reported in the *Morning Advertiser*, Saturday 1st September 1888.

80   The *East London Advertiser*, Saturday 1st September 1888.

81   *Firesetting and Mental Health: Theory, Research and Practice*. Edited by
      Geoffrey L. Dickens, Philip A. Sugarman and Theresa A. Gannon. RC-
      Psych Publications, 2012.

82   Report of the inquest on Mary Ann Nichols, *The Daily Telegraph*,
      Monday 3rd September 1888.

83   Ibid.

84   In the 1880s and earlier, inquests were held as soon as possible after the
      discovery in suspicious circumstances of a body for the very good reason
      that, in the absence of refrigeration, storage of corpses for long periods
      was impracticable. This meant that opportunities for anything but, by
      today's standards, rudimentary forensic examination was impossible.

85   *East London Observer*, Saturday 8th September 1888.

86   Casual wards were not wards in the hospital sense but places of refuge
      attached to workhouses where, *in extremis*, a person could receive shelter
      for a single night. They were so overcrowded, filthy and unpleasant that

most destitutes preferred to sleep in the street rather than have recourse to them. Only on the bitterest of nights would most unfortunates contemplate a night in a casual ward.

87 Flower and Dean Street actually had no horticultural associations. It was named after John Flower and Gowen Dean, the two speculative jerry builders who first laid it out in 1655. Together with Dorset Street, Thrawl Street and Fashion Street, it was regarded as almost a no-go area by the local police.

CHAPTER NINE

88 *East London Advertiser*, Saturday 15th September 1888.

89 *Pictorial News*, 15th September 1888.

90 *East London Advertiser*, Saturday 15th September 1888.

91 Begg, Paul, Fido, Martin and Skinner, Keith. *The Complete Jack the Ripper A to Z*. John Blake, London, 2010.

92 *Source*: Kate Summerscale, *The Suspicions of Mr Whicher*. Bloomsbury Publishing, London, 2008.

93 Baxter was also coroner for the county of Sussex and he meant by this when he was hearing inquests in the county town of Lewes.

94 Police surgeons were paid for each examination they conducted. Having carried out the initial examination at the scene, Phillips could not assume that he was automatically going to be engaged to complete the post-mortem at the mortuary; he had to wait to be instructed.

95 Phillips had noticed what Llewellyn had missed on the previous victim, that at least one ring had been removed from Annie's ring finger. The murderer seems to have had an obsession with removing any rings worn by his victims. Since small quantities of money were left with the bodies, robbery can probably be discounted as a motive.

96 This suggests that Phillips had conferred with Llewellyn and the coroner before Polly Nichols's inquest and they had decided not to reveal the full details of her injuries in open court. If so Baxter had obviously had a change of heart. Throughout the inquests Phillips seems to have been worried that revealing too much titillating detail might encourage other copycat murders, besides having a natural reluctance to discuss injuries to the sexual organs in front of a lay audience particularly when women were present.

97 Details of surgical mobilisation of the small intestine can be found in many surgical textbooks including *Atlas of Pelvic Surgery*, Online Edition: Small bowel resection with end-to-end anastomosis using the Gambee technique. Clifford R. Wheeless Jr. and Marcella L. Rosenberg. This also shows the traditional midline surgical incision by-passing the umbilicus to the right as used by the Ripper.

98 This is perhaps the most telling of all Phillips's testimony and often overlooked or discounted by historians of the Ripper murders, few of whom have actually operated on or dissected a human body. What he was saying is that he, with his considerable skill and experience, could not have opened a dead woman's body – even in the favourable sur-roundings of a well-lit post-mortem room – and removed her pelvic organs in less than 15 minutes. The Ripper had considerably less time than that in the backyard of 49 Hanbury Street.

99 Despite occasional lapses before inter-hospital rugby matches, medi-cal students today are much more restrained than they were in the 19th

century. The *Echo* published an account on the day after the murder in Miller's Court of what amounted to a drunken rampage by medical students during the Lord Mayor's Show entitled 'Medical Students at "Play"'.

CHAPTER TEN

100 The original letter, like so much else of the original archival material connected with the Ripper case, was stolen from the police files by a souvenir hunter but as it was photographed at the time it has been possible to make a facsimile of it which is today in the files of The National Archives.

101 The following report was carried by at least 18 papers across Britain, including *The Portsmouth Evening News* on Friday 1st November 1878. Whoever the original author was, he seems to have shared Francis's facility for getting his pieces widely syndicated. It is of course perfectly possible that it was Francis who was working at the time as a reporter in Hammersmith, itself a centre of the Spring-Heel Jack sightings. If so it might explain his choice of name.

'Spring-Heel Jack' at Colchester.

'With the removal of 3rd Battalion, 60th Rifles from Aldershot to Colchester, Spring-heel Jack, whose vagaries at the former place excited considerable attention, seems to have changed his quarters, and the garrison at Colchester is in a state of excitement over his escapades. The principal field of his operations is the Abbey field, where he has visited several lonely sentries, all of whom he has frightened, and two so seriously that they are now under treatment at the garrison hospital, it being feared that the mind of one is completely unhinged. It is said that the sentries are to be doubled.'

There was another outbreak of Spring-Heel Jack sightings in January 1888 which continued into the spring and no doubt that was still fresh in the mind of the author of the Dear Boss letters.

CHAPTER ELEVEN

102 Taylor, Rosemary. 'The City of Dreadful Delight.' William Morris in the East End of London. *The Journal of William Morris Studies*. Winter 2009 (9–28).

103 The following year, 1889, another unfortunate, Alice McKenzie, was found murdered in Angel Alley, Whitechapel. At first she was thought to have been a Ripper victim but this was quickly discounted. She is known to have frequently used the alias Kelly, showing how widespread it was.

104 Kearley and Tonge, founded in 1878, has gone through a number of metamorphoses including the International Stores Group and is now the Somerfield chain of supermarkets.

105 *A new System of Anatomy*. Sir Solly Zuckerman. Oxford University Press. London 1961. p.299.

106 Peter Sutcliffe, the Yorkshire Ripper, lived at the extreme north-east edge of the area of West Yorkshire in which his victims were killed and the first three victims were the nearest ones to his home. After that, as his confidence grew, he moved further and further from what criminologists call his anchor point, but he never – as far as is known – killed anyone to the east or north of his base.

107 Testimony of DC Halse at the inquest on Catherine Eddowes. He said: 'There were three lines of writing in a good schoolboy's round hand. The size of the capital letters would be about ¾in, and the other letters were

in proportion. The writing was on the black bricks, which formed a kind of dado, the bricks above being white.' *The Daily Telegraph*, 12th October 1888.

108   Sir Charles Warren. Report to the Home Secretary, 6th November 1888.

109   Judith Flanders, *The Invention of Murder*. Harper Press. London, 2011.

CHAPTER TWELVE

110   The impetus for the Vigilance Committees was the worrying reduction in sales in shops, not just in the East End but in cities across the country. Many small shops stayed open late at night to cater for people who were at work during the day, but now there was a marked reluctance for people to be abroad after dark.

111   *The Daily Telegraph*, 3rd October 1888.

112   The *Morning Advertiser*, 1st October 1888, was one of many newspapers that reported Mrs Mortimer's account. They are so nearly identical that it is likely that a single reporter interviewed her and then sold the account to a press agency or to several newspapers.

113   Judith Flanders, *The Invention of Murder*. Harper Press. London, 2011.

CHAPTER THIRTEEN

114   *The Daily Telegraph*, 12th October 1888.

CHAPTER FOURTEEN

115   The old Truman's Black Eagle Brewery still stands in Brick Lane but today is used as a centre for the arts, shopping, meetings and events.

116 Report on the inquest of Francis Craig, The *Fulham Chronicle*, 13th March 1903.

117 *Queen Victoria in her Letters and Journals: A Selection.* Ed. Christopher Hibbert, Sutton Publishing Ltd, 2000.

118 Evans, Stewart P. and Keith Skinner. *Jack the Ripper: Letters from Hell.* Sutton Publishing, Stroud, 2001.

CHAPTER FIFTEEN

119 Other people have noticed and commented on the fact that all five of the canonical murders took place within four or five days either side of three successive new moons. Most notably was the eminent (or notorious depending on your point of view) psychiatrist Dr Lyttleton Forbes Winslow, who took an intense interest in the affair at the time and is one of the many hundreds of people named as a suspect in the years since. He ascribed the timing to fits of periodic mania connected with the phases of the moon – classic lunacy in fact. The most likely explanation is that Francis did not want to venture out on nights when the moon was anywhere near full and make the risk of recognition greater.

120 Although the procession took place within the bounds of the city, the authorities insisted that extra police were drafted in from the Metropolitan area. In Sir William Logsdail's magnificent painting showing the Lord Mayor's coach rounding the bend in front of the Royal Exchange an hour or so before the discovery of Mary Jane's body, the helmets of both the City Police with their distinctive crests and the Metropolitan Police with their central bosses can be made out.

121 *The Star*, 10th November 1888.

CHAPTER SIXTEEN

122   *The British Medical Journal*, 15th June 1901, p.1, 523.

123   Since the opening of London's first fish and chip shop in 1860, by 1888 fish and chips had become by far the most popular takeaway food in Britain.

CHAPTER SEVENTEEN

124   Elizabeth's elder brother George had died in 1871 of tuberculosis but it was so prevalent in 19th-century Britain as not to be significant.

125   In this he was quite right. As has been noted before, Francis was in the habit of wearing an Inverness coat that had capacious sleeves, a cape over the shoulders and large pockets. He would have had no difficulty in concealing a knife and carrying away organs such as a heart, a kidney or a uterus.

126   Most people have taken the mutilation of her face as being indicative of the depths to which the murderer had sunk and, no doubt to an extent, they were. However, the main purpose was probably to prevent her recognition in the event that photographs or artists' impressions were published later as had been the case with the other victims. The tentative mutilations to Catharine Eddowes's face may have been to provide a link with this one and to prepare himself psychologically for what he knew he had to do to Elizabeth.

127   Inquests were expensive and the cost fell upon the ratepayers of the district in which they were held.

128   The identity of Julia Venturney is another of the uncertainties that surround the Ripper story. The *East London Advertiser* reporting the inquest

on 17th November stated that she was German, although genealogi-
cal research recently published on the *Rootschat* website seems to have
established her identity beyond reasonable doubt. The confusion about
her name and her nationality springs from the fact that she was born
Julia Charlotte Cook in Fulham in 1841 and married an Italian by the
name of Antonio Venturini. The Italian pronunciation of the name as
'Ventooreenee' doubtless gave rise to the many variations that appear
in the census and other documents including Ventouni, Venteney and
Vanturney. At the time of the Ripper murders Julia was a widow and
living at 26 Miller's Court with a man by the name of Harry Owen. She
later adopted the name Lottie Owen and, extraordinarily, later moved
into the very room in which Mary Jane Kelly had been murdered. When
the Canadian woman journalist Katherine Blake Watkins visited Miller's
Court in 1892 she interviewed Lottie, not apparently realising that it
was Mary Jane's friend Julia, although Lottie had difficulty in speaking
due to a broken nose that she had incurred in a kick from her partner's
boot. Watkins wrote an account of the meeting in the *Toronto Daily Mail*
in February 1892 in which she described the blood stains still being visible on the wooden partition beside the bed on which Lottie now slept.

129 No trace of anything personal beyond her clothes was found in the
room. Mary Jane was known to have received letters whilst at Miller's
Court and surely she is likely to have kept some or to have had some
other mementos of her former life, but none were found.

CHAPTER EIGHTEEN

130 *East London Advertiser*, 24th November 1888.

131 See http://www.osffranciscans.com/ It is tempting to wonder whether
the authorities were hedging their bets with regards to Mary Jane's religion. Her funeral set off from a Church of England parish church and
she was buried in a Catholic cemetery by an Anglo-Catholic priest.

132 Unusually she also has two entries in the quarterly Indexes of Deaths under both Kelly and Davies.

133 Bodleian Law Library, Oxford.

CHAPTER NINETEEN

134 Notes accompanying the divorce petition and affidavit of Francis Spurzheim Craig.

135 Strictly speaking he should still have described himself as Married. If he knew his wife to be dead he should have described himself as a Widower. He could have applied to have her presumed dead after seven years but he did not do so. Only if he had successfully divorced his wife could he describe himself as Single.

136 On 16th August 1819, volunteer cavalry charged a peaceable crowd which had gathered in St. Peter's Fields, Manchester, to hear political speeches in favour of the Reform movement. Fifteen people, including some policemen, were killed and many more trampled underfoot. Coming so soon after Waterloo it became known as the Peterloo Massacre.

137 William Etty (1787–1849) was an English painter well known for his titillating depictions of the naked female form which managed to gain public acceptance through their classical and historical subject matter.

138 The use of the word den to mean an office or study is another interesting use by Francis of an Americanism not generally used in Britain at the time.

139 In fact Sir Charles Warren had returned to the army after resigning as Metropolitan Police Commissioner and at this time he was commanding Thames District although, understandably, he had kept a very low profile.

CHAPTER TWENTY

140   *Evening Telegraph*, 28th March 1901.

CHAPTER TWENTY TWO

141   Simpson, Keith. *Forensic Medicine*. Edward Arnold, London, 1958.

Index